Globalization and Social Movements

Edited by

Pierre Hamel
Professor
University of Montreal
Canada

Henri Lustiger-Thaler
Associate Professor of Sociology
Ramapo College
USA

Jan Nederveen Pieterse
Associate Professor in Sociology
Institute of Social Studies
The Hague
The Netherlands

and

Sasha Roseneil
Professor of Sociology and Gender Studies
University of Leeds
UK

Published by PALGRAVE MACMILLAN
Houndmills, Basingstoke, Hampshire RG21 6XS and
175 Fifth Avenue, New York, N. Y. 10010
Companies and representatives throughout the world

PALGRAVE MACMILLAN is the global academic imprint of the Palgrave
Macmillan division of St. Martin's Press, LLC and of Palgrave Macmillan Ltd.
Macmillan® is a registered trademark in the United States, United Kingdom
and other countries. Palgrave is a registered trademark in the European
Union and other countries.

Outside North America
ISBN 0-333-72535-2

In North America
ISBN 0-333-72535-2

This book is printed on paper suitable for recycling and
made from fully managed and sustained forest sources.

A catalogue record for this book is available from the British Library.

Library of Congress Catalog Card Number: 2001021876

Transferred to digital printing 2003

Printed and bound in Great Britain by
Antony Rowe Ltd, Chippenham and Eastbourne

Globalization and Social Movements

WITHDRAWN

Also by Pierre Hamel

ACTION COLLECTIVE ET DEMOCRATIE LOCALE

Also by Henri Lustiger-Thaler

ARTFUL PRACTICES: The Political Economy of Everyday Life (*editor with Daniel Sale*)

POLITICAL ARRANGEMENTS: Power and the City (*editor*)

URBAN LIVES: Fragmentation and Resistance (*editor with Vered Amit-Talal*)

Also by Jan Nederveen Pieterse

DEVELOPMENT THEORY – DECONSTRUCTION/RECONSTRUCTIONS

GLOBAL FUTURES: Shaping Globalization

WORLD ORDERS IN THE MAKING: Humanitarian Intervention and Beyond

THE DECOLONIZATION OF IMAGINATION (*co-editor*)

Also by Sasha Roseneil

COMMON WOMEN, UNCOMMON PRACTICES: The Queer Feminisms of Greenham

CONSUMING CULTURES: Power and Resistance (*co-editor*)

DISARMING PATRIARCHY: Feminism and Political Action at Greenham

PRACTISING IDENTITIES: Power and Resistance (*co-editor*)

STIRRING IT: Challenges for Feminism

Contents

Notes on Contributors

Barry D. Adam is University Professor of Sociology at the University of Windsor, and author of *The Survival of Domination* (1978), *The Rise of a Gay and Lesbian Movement* (1995), *Experiencing HIV* (*with Alan Sears* 1996), and co-editor of *The Global Emergence and Gay and Lesbian Politics* (1999). He has also published articles on new social movement theory, on gay and lesbian issues, and on social aspects of AIDS. Website: *http://www.cs.uwindsor.ca/users/a/adam*.

Ranjit Dwivedi is a Lecturer in Sociology in Delhi University and has a PhD in Development Studies from the Institute of Social Studies, The Hague. His thesis 'Resource Conflict and Collective Action: The Sardar Sarovar Project in India' earned him a distinction. His research interests include environmental conflicts, alternative development, peoples' movements and displacement and resettlement issues.

Catherine Eschle is a Lecturer in the Department of Government at the University of Strathclyde, Glasgow. She is the author of *Global Democracy, Social Movements and Feminism* (2001).

Antimo L. Farro is Professor of Sociology at the University of Rome 'La Sapienza'. He has recently published *Il conflitto dopo la lotta di classe* (2000) and *Les mouvements sociaux* (2000).

Pierre Hamel, PhD, is Professor of Urban Planning and Sociology at the Université de Montreal. He is also director of a PhD program at the same university and a member of the Interdisciplinary Research Centre on Social and Economic Regulations and Transformations. His research focuses on social movements, citizen involvement and urban governance. He is the author of *Action collective et démocratie locale* (1991) and co-editor of *Action Collective et Enjeux Institutionnels* (1999).

Henri Lustiger-Thaler is Associate Professor of Sociology at Ramapo College of New Jersey. He has been an active member and key organizer of Research Committee 47 of the International Sociological Association. He has published widely on social movements and collective action in French and English. His current research interest focuses on generational transformation and collective action. His most recent article is featured in Janet Abu-Lughod (ed.), *Sociology at the Millennium* (2000). His most recent book is *Urban Movements in a Globalizing World* (co-editor, 2000).

Louis Maheu, PhD, is Professor of Sociology and Dean of the Graduate School at the Université de Montréal. He is past president of the Research Committee on Social Movements and Social Classes of the International Sociological Association. Among his recent publications are the edited volume *Social Movements and Social Classes: the Future of Collective Action* (1995) and 'Social Movements in Quebec: Environmental Groups as a Cultural Challenge to the Neo-Corporatist order' in *Quebec Society: Critical Issues* (edited by M. Fournier *et al.*, 1997).

Angela Miles teaches in the 'Feminist Theory and Practice in Global Perspective' programme of the Ontario Institute for Studies in Education, University of Toronto. She is a member of Toronto Women for a Just and Healthy Planet and the author of *Integrative Feminist Perspectives: Building Global Visions, 1960s–1990s* (1996).

Valentine M. Moghadam is Director of Women's Studies and Associate Professor of Sociology at Illinois State University. Born in Iran and previously a senior researcher with the United Nations University, she has published extensively on gender and development issues and on women and social change in the Middle East and North Africa. Recent publications include 'Revolution, Religion and Gender Politics: Iran and Afghanistan Compared' (*Journal of Women's History*, Vol. 10, No. 4, 1999) and 'Gender and Globalization: Female Labor and Women's Mobilizations' (*Journal of World-Systems Research*, Vol. 5, No. 2, 1999).

Jan Nederveen Pieterse is Associate Professor in Sociology at the Institute of Social Studies, The Hague. He is well known for his work in the area or Third World studies and on social movements. His publications have included *White on Black: Images of Africa and Blacks in Western Popular Culture* (1992), *Racism and Stereotyping for Beginners* (1994) and *Global Futures: Shaping Globalization* (2000).

Aaron Pollack has spent many years of research and project work in Guatemala and Mexico. He holds an MA in Development Studies from the Institute of Social Studies in The Hague. He was born in the USA.

Sasha Roseneil is Professor of Sociology and Gender Studies and Director of the Centre for Interdisciplinary Gender Studies at the University of Leeds. She is also Secretary/Treasurer of Research Committee 47 of the International Sociological Association. She is the author of *Disarming Patriarchy: Feminism and Political Action at Greenham* (1995) and *Common Women, Uncommon Practices: the Queer Feminisms of Greenham* (2000), and co-editor of *Practising Identities* (1999) and *Consuming Cultures* (1999).

Jean-Guy Vaillancourt is Professor of Sociology at the University of Montreal, where he teaches environmental sociology, sociology of religion and sociological theory. He is the author, editor or co-editor of more than 20 books and special issues of journals, mostly in the areas of ecosociology and sociology of religion. Among these titles are *Papal Power* (1980), *Essais d'écosociologie* (1982), *Roots of Peace* (1986), *Environnement et développement* (1991), *Instituer le développement durable* (1994), *La recherche sociale en environnement* (1996), *L'énergie au Québec* (1998), *Les sciences sociales de l'environnement* (1999) and *La gestion écologique*.

Introduction: the Shifting Global Frames of Collective Action

Pierre Hamel, Henri Lustiger-Thaler, Jan Nederveen Pieterse and Sasha Roseneil

Globalization as metaphor for societies in flux and transformation

This collection of essays is about collective action and globalization. To even utter this juxtaposition belies a certain prejudice or acquiescence to a mindset of globalization problematics in their many similar and opposing voices. But, is globalization as a process, event or discourse conceivable without the deeply evocative nature of collective action? We doubt it is. Indeed, as is pointed out in many of the contributions to this collection, globalization and collective action are in deep dialogue, if not fused to one another's future practical and theoretical agenda. This integrality may be the only way to escape the discursive minefields which accompany the varying portraits of globalization in economics, political science, sociology and a litany of other social sciences. Hence, our starting point is that collective action can never be far from an analysis of global phenomena or a global focus on human organization and its complex arrangements. Nor should it, if globalization is to be viewed as a way to better understand this period of late modernities, and the spinning of human action beyond the local, or conversely deeply spun within the local, and the cross-border implications these entail for global democratic practices.

The contributions to this collection will contextualize, through case studies and theoretical reflection, the linkages between collective action theories, social movement practices and the phenomenon of globalization. All the perspectives contained herein force us to rethink what globalization has come to mean and the way in which we can use such insights to advance our understanding of basic transformations occurring in the diverse societies we live in at the beginning of this new

1

millennium. Yet, whatever our understanding of globalization, suffice to say that the simple truth of its constant evocation has taken on a resonance that only the meta notion of modernization could so readily boast – that is, as a spatially selective presaging of inevitability and progress in human affairs and conduct. But, as the song goes, maybe, . . . 'it ain't necessarily so'.

Is globalization as clear a term as we would like it to be? The more critical consensus captured in this collection is that it is not. Perhaps globalization, from a social movement perspective, is best understood as a metaphor for a specific body of actions, beyond territorial borders, and the manner in which they become institutionalized, seek institutionalization or strategically avoid it. Furthermore, once the North–South perspective enters into play, the paradigm of predictability and risk embedded in the globalization thesis shifts dramatically. And, as in many things, the singularity that defines the basic Western premises of modernization or globalization has shown itself, once more, to be chauvinistic and in need of more unpacking, as it tries to account for the 'outer-societies', or non-Western communities, at the interface of global collective actions and social movements.

Nowhere is this more evident than in the real space of global configurations, power and its unequal distribution. As Paul Hirst and Graham Thompson (1999) have pointed out, much of globalization can still be understood through the concentration of power and geography, not its unboundedness: 91.5% of foreign direct investment, and 80% of trade take place in parts of the world where only 28% of the population resides. Globalization in this strong spatial version reveals itself in terms of the geographies of power, or, more specifically, the local labour power that produces global wealth. Zygmunt Bauman (1998) offers this same spatial image, of the wealthy who travel the globe freely searching for adventure, whilst the poor and globally disadvantaged are chained to place, with echoes of Ulf Hannerz's (1996) reference to global cosmopolitans, the 'new travelling middle classes' who privilege an identity based on mobility, fluidity rather than territory.

What then of the local places and global spaces of disadvantage far removed from the North. Or, has at least some of what we have long identified with the South moved North in pockets of global ambivalences? And, through what collective actions do these hybrid-like global processes express themselves, for example, as in identity-based cultural attachments witnessed in the strong Dominican presence in the Washington Heights district of New York City, where English is seldom heard or culturally embedded? Do these actions still need social movements, or social movement theories for that matter, in order to express their sense of displaced collective selfhood? If so, can we still refer to their actions in the same way in which we have nominally understood what a social movement is or once was? Has collective action become more significant and important in the face of globalization than contemporary social movements seem to be? Indeed, has collective action left its social movement shell, throwing rational choice and identity-based paradigms into the ephemeral winds of change?

Globalization: North and South

An undisputed feature of the condition is the wide and glaring global hiatus between wealth and poverty. One would like to say it's a feature of global experience, but for how many of us is it a matter of experience? Worlds of experience are segmented and representations across the fence are coded. Global poverty is routinized – 'the poor will always be with you'. Aid fatigue is periodically interrupted by emergencies that prompt selective media attention and 'out-of-the-sky' relief campaigns. Refugees are objects of charity, asylum seekers objects of scrutiny, illegal immigrants are criminalized along with drug traffickers and crime syndicates. The steady succession of development fixes and failures is crowded out by global economic management; poverty alleviation and development are being outmanoeuvred by managing global growth, in the vague expectation that a rising tide will lift all boats.

While the buzzword is globalization, uneven development trails globalization like its shadow. Globalization is uneven among countries and regions, among regions within countries and among categories within regions. While globalization is often characterized as 'truncated globalization' or 'Triadization', concentrated in the triad of Western Europe, North America and Japan, its reach extends further. While the development gap between the advanced economies and newly industrialized economies has narrowed, the gap between these and most developing countries is widening. This reflects a partial reversal of an earlier trend of gradual integration of developing countries in the international division of labour. With regard to trade, international capital flows and foreign direct investment, there has been a marked downturn in the participation in the world economy by developing countries since the beginning of the 1980s. In this context what is at issue are differences at multiple levels: material differences and technology gaps, measured in the familiar statistics of GNP per capita and human development; transnational economic regimes; power differentials relating to geopolitics, security and prestige; and differences in perceptions and images.

Globalization or divided worlds

One of the features of collective reflection in media and social science today is the profound discrepancy between perspectives North and South. On either side, perceptions are schematic and together they make up a stylized exchange of stereotypes. Since global inequality is a major part of the contemporary collective condition, it also features in collective reflection, but how deeply? The buzzword is globalization, but we inhabit a divided world. We still inhabit a cardboard world of stereotypes and caricatures. In media and social science there is a wide discrepancy between experiences and perceptions North and South, between the worlds of experience of the world's majority who are poor and the world's minority in the North. In the North, social science is taken or takes itself to be at the forefront of collective understanding, while mostly it's too self-absorbed to take account of the experiences and perspectives of the world majority. Whether it concerns modernity, postmodernity or globalization, they tend to represent a narrow Western or Northern view. In the South the engagement with Northern perspectives is often out of context, out of touch with their historical context and cultural variation. In the North, New Age scientists are foraging mystical traditions in the South on the basis of schemas and stereotypes, without understanding the variations in philosophy and practice. In the South, seeking to negotiate modernity, the European Enlightenment is scrutinized – Kant, Hegel, Habermas – without understanding that the Enlightenment also had a dark side, that the Romantics were also part of the Enlightenment (Herder, Carlyle, Nietzsche). Lack of depth, lack of nuance, lack of experience and understanding exist on either side: the North–South chasm in experience and reflection still creates the impression of our living in a paper world, making gestures to cut-outs rather than real figures. In a word, schematic understandings are found North and South, of the Enlightenment, modernity, poverty, cultures. No wonder that the émigrés from the South in the North are so influential in literature and social science, for they and few others bridge the different worlds of experience.

North–South inequality runs deep, as does an inverse application of globalization through the 'de-territorialization of poverty' (that is, the rich in the South and the poor in the North). This relates profoundly to world images and perceptions of globalization that are held also among the middle class in the South (Gopal, 1998). Of course, the South is in the North and the North is in the South and privilege and poverty are no longer neatly geographically divided. Yet the overall distinction between North and South, crude as it is, still makes sense. In demographic terms they are the minority world and the majority world. They are 'worlds' because they offer complete life worlds. The division does not simply run between middle class and underclass – as if globally these share similar consumption patterns, lifestyles and values. In some respects they do, but obviously class is not the only variable. Thus the middle class in the South shares many of the majority's economic, political and geopolitical frustrations and to some extent identifies with the nation, the region. The poor majority and the middle class in the South share national and regional destinies, suffer superpower geopolitics and geo-economics, Western double standards, and domestic political incompetence.

Multiplying modernities

Here the focus is on North–South differences in representation and analyses of global conditions, on different conditions (different modernities, different capitalisms) and on the articulations across different conditions. Existing analytics – such as dependency, imperialism, exclusion, conspiracy theories – are not adequate in dealing with these new relations. Thus, the economics of dependency overlooks reverse dependency – that is, the dependency of deindustrializing regions in the North (Wales, Scotland, Brittany) on investors from Asia (South Korea, Taiwan). The analytic of boomerang effects – such as the 'debt boomerang' (the debt crisis in the South curtailing demand for products from the North) – is too blunt to monitor and capture the multiple links and their ramifications. Risk analysis and the globalization of risk can be a relevant instrument but needs greater fine-tuning to be effective.

Another account of contemporary globalization refers to the separateness of the majority of humanity – the majority in large parts of Africa, Asia and Latin America who are removed from life in the fast lane, from the 'interlinked economies' of the 'Triad zone'. Exclusion is too crude and blunt a term to describe the actual situation. The middle class in developing countries participates in the global circuits of advertising, brand name consumerism and high tech services, which, at another end of the circuitry, increasingly isolate the underclass in advanced economies. The term exclusion ignores the many ways in which developing countries are included in global processes: they are subject to global financial discipline (as in structural adjustment and interest payments, resulting in net capital outflows) and part of global markets (resource flows, distribution networks, Diaspora and niche markets), global ecology, international politics, global communications, science and technology, international development cooperation, transnational civil society, international migration, travel, and crime networks. For instance, the public health sector in many African countries is increasingly being internationalized. Thus, it would be more accurate to speak of a situation of *asymmetrical inclusion* or *hierarchical integration*.

A classic term for this situation used to be 'combined and uneven development', but now one of the differences is that the units are no longer nations. It is this new pattern of uneven inclusion that generates anxiety and frustration. The disjuncture between global dynamics and existing political infrastructures and intellectual frames generates malaise bordering on angst and, in the process, inspires resistance and protest that are seeking effective political forms (Nederveen Pieterse, 1997: 80). In the South if one is not participating in global market production or consumption one still partakes of ads, media and movies, developmental regimes (such as structural adjustment), and economic, financial and political instability. Exclusion is again too blunt a terminology if what is at issue is to examine the new uneven links that are developing in the framework of accelerated globalization.

Thus, people in the South are *within* the reach of global mass communications and advertising, within the reach of the message but not necessarily the action. This is how an Albanian émigré describes the impact of Italian TV on Albanians during the old days of seclusion:

Step by step the entire advertising message is extracted from its (pragmatic) context . . . The ultimate result is that ads are viewed as windows to an upper reality. This is the reality where people, and things, and behaviors, and actions are light, colorful, beautiful. People are almost always good looking, clean, and well dressed; they all smile and enjoy everything they do, and get extremely happy, even when confronted with a new toothbrush. . . . The repeated contact with mirages of a reality *beyond* the wall not only created a diffuse desire, but also kept it alive for a sufficiently long time, so that desire could lose its initial property of being a(n) . . . impulse for action, and become a *state of mind*, similar to profuse, disinterested love.

(Vebhiu, 1999)

At the other end of the TV set, viewers experience 'long distance suffering' and engage in schizophrenic behaviour – limited or vague gestures of solidarity, while finding shelter in the 'chauvinism of prosperity' that is being sustained by institutions and media. Electoral politics in the advanced countries tends to exclude terrorists and welfare recipients and now often this also extends to asylum seekers, refugees and 'illegal migrants'. Globalization therefore evokes anger and anxiety in the South and tends to be experienced as yet another round of Northern hegemony, another round of concentration of power and wealth. The common metaphor for globalization in the South, in the slipstream of two hundred years of weary experience, is imperialism, neocolonialism revisited. But, analytically, this is mistaken: imperialism was territorial, state-driven, centrally orchestrated and marked by a clear division between colonizer and colonized; none of these features apply to contemporary globalization. Contemporary accelerated globalization is multidimensional, non-territorial, polycentric, and the lines of inclusion/exclusion are blurred and run between the middle classes and the poor North and South.

Multiple modernities

While the concept of imperialism does not apply and generates misleading analytics and politics, nevertheless this feeling itself is a political reality. What *is* common to both is the sense of powerlessness and frustration; only this time the dynamics of deprivation are different. So are the current geopolitical circumstances. The world of the 1970s is no more. Then the momentum of decolonization was still in motion, the Nonaligned Movement was strong; the Eastern bloc provided a counterbalance, and global alternative scenarios such as the New International Economic Order seemed to make sense. At the start of the twenty-first century, none of these conditions prevail. During the last twenty years globalization has coincided with a new period of hegemony of finance capital, in the wake of the recycling of petrodollars and the ensuing debt crisis, in some respects like the turn of the century, the epoch of Hilferding's finance capital. Open space is shrinking. Delinking as an option was overtaken by the new international division of labour in the 1970s and localism or building alternative enclaves has little future in the modern world, making the 'new protectionism' a loser strategy. Countervailing power now is located in the diffuse realm of 'global civil society', of civic organizations and NGOs, local and international.

Oppression fosters conspiracy theories of history as a convenient short cut. Much of the Middle East lives by a conspiracy theory centred on Zionism in league with the United States. In parts of Africa, the Caribbean and among African Americans, the lead conspiracy is white racism and its machinations. This is not to mention regional anxieties, such as India's worries about regional powers in league with foreign powers (Pakistan and China supported by the US, the Tamil Tigers supported by foreign elements) or Southeast Asian concerns about the possible decomposition of Indonesia. These are mirrored by conspiracy theories in the West – Jihad against McWorld, the clash of civilizations, an Islamic–Confucian combine against 'the West', or the Islamic bomb. The Saudis are supporting a girdle of conservative Islamic states (Sudan, Afghanistan, Pakistan) and movements. The 'Afghanis' (trained by the CIA in the war in Afghanistan) are a destabilizing force in states in the Arab world. Conflicts in the South are trivialized as minor skirmishes in the periphery, or alternatively yield doomsday perspectives – either the end of history or the end of the world. The issue is not that these phenomena do not exist – where there's smoke there's fire. The issue is one of labelling, relative magnitudes and explanatory force – hence the local/global circulation of misinformation and paranoia.

Ours is not a world of simple modernity or simple capitalism that exists in varieties of more or less, further or earlier, differentiated along a single-track path. That was the old panorama of evolutionism, developmentalism, modernization, and Westernization. Part of the problem is that the language of social science and politics invites the use of the singular – modernity rather than modernities, capitalism rather than capitalisms, industrialization rather than different types of industrialization. This generalizing language applies across the political spectrum, right and left, and is inhospitable to nuanced political thinking.

It is tempting to conceive of modernity as a single historical sphere, to which there may be different roads, but which is ultimately a singular experience. What matters in that case is only a before and after: pre- and post-modernity. Of course, within modernity differences run between early and advanced, high, radical, neo modernity, and at the edges of modernity there are variations as well – peripheral, failed, truncated and hybrid modernities, but these all refer back to more or less of a single modernity. On the other hand, from here it would be a small step to spatio-temporal variations – such as European, American, Japanese, Asian modernities, and variations within each of them (such as Northwest, Southern, Eastern, Central European variants). Another argument is to distinguish among different *sequences* in modernization processes, as is common in Asian analyses. Gradually, there has been a move away from conceptualizing modernity in the singular (Nederveen Pieterse, 1998), a direction this present collection of essays fully endorses.

Multiple capitalisms

A similar case can be made with respect to different capitalisms. There is recognition of multiple 'cultures of capitalism' (Hampden-Turner and Trompenaars, 1993) even among advanced industrialized countries. There are also different modes of regulation among different forms of national capitalism varying according to historical antecedents and cultures of capitalism – statist on the European continent, Manchester liberalism in Britain, free enterprise in pioneer America, statist in Japan. With regard to industrialization, distinctions run not merely between first and latecomers but also between late late-comers and very late comers to industrialization, or different generations of industrialization along with different stages of industrialization. East Asia belongs then to the fourth generation of industrialization.

Thus multiple modernities and capitalisms are each conditioned and articulated by historic and geographical circumstances and each take on a different character on account of different modes of fusion and articulation. Acknowledging the geographical and historical differentiations of modernity, capitalism, industrialism is one concern, analysing the relationship is another. What is the relationship between difference and sameness, between the variations and the theme? This is not a world of different realms that are neatly separated – modern and premodern, North and South, and so on. Besides the different modernities in Asia, the Middle East, Africa, the Americas and Europe, there is also the interaction of modernities and capitalisms. Understanding this interplay is a major key to contemporary dynamics. 'We live in a world in which competition is not only a feature of inter-firm relations, but of the relations between different capitalist economic systems' (Applebaum and Henderson, 1995: 3).

Post-Fordism, for example, which brings together discussions on capitalism and industrialization, is usually discussed as if it only concerns dynamics in the advanced economies of the North. But the actual options available and directions taken are likely to be more influenced by the *interactions* among different modes of capitalism than is indicated by merely examining varieties in the North, as if these represent the front end of capitalism (which is not tenable in view of the rise of Pacific Asia) and as if the front end is not affected by the rear. Thus 'national variants of Fordism' include peripheral Fordism (Mexico, Brazil), hybrid Fordism (Japan) and 'primitive Taylorization' (Southeast Asia) (Peck and Tickell, 1994: 286–7) and the question is, how are they related?

While post-Fordism and postmodernity are important analytics for understanding dynamics in the North, for a complete understanding we should consider the relations *between* post-Fordist economies, newly emerging markets and developing countries. The ramifications of the 'East Asian Miracle' economies are a case in point. First, East Asian economies have been new investors in deindustrializing regions of the North and Eastern Europe, thus impacting on regional uneven development in the North. Second, labour standards in newly emerging markets (lower wages, longer working hours, less unionisation) are affecting labour standards in multinational corporations in their operations North and South. Third, the rhetoric or perception of less government intervention in the newly emerging markets (while in several ways bogus) is being used to reinforce structural reform globally and government rollback in the North. Fourth, the financial crises in the newly emerging markets – the Tequila crisis, the Asian crisis, the Latin American crisis – have reverberated on markets North and South. This has led to serious consideration of the architecture of the international financial system from Wall Street and the Treasury to the IMF. It has generated the notion of *contagion* as a successor to the Cold War domino theory. In other words, links *between* economies in the North and the newly emerging markets are affecting developments North and South. This is unfolding at the level of material exchanges and economic and financial regulation and simultaneously at the level of rhetoric, discourse and imaging.

These diverse spaces are not simply stray parts and add-ons in a random arrangement but part of a structured, dynamic and self-reflexive configuration. Thus, the relevant distinction now does not run between 'good' capitalism (social market, Rhineland) and 'bad' capitalism (wild, casino), according to Petrella (1996), but between national and global capitalism. The articulation of different capitalisms and modernities is being processed and channelled through global capitalism and global hegemony.

Imperial continuities – the British Empire succeeded by US hegemony – have informed the global career of capitalism. Nesting in the interstices of empire and hegemony, and carried on its waves, Anglo-American enterprises have become the leading and thus dominant form of global capitalism. Its economics, neoclassical economics, has become the norm of economic thought. Keynesianism was an interlude that was only partially implemented. The Bretton Woods institutions have become de facto global spearpoints of Anglo-American capitalism. The Washington consensus, or what is left of it, still rules – if only because of the absence of a coherent alternative. Because of the size and complexity of the United States as a large multinational state it is difficult for significant changes to pass through Congress. On issues of global significance – trade policy, financial regulation, environmental and labour standards – there is a stalemate so that by and large the conservative common denominator tends to prevail. The structural stalemate in US politics is reproduced in global affairs, transmitted via the decomposing (post) Washington consensus and international institutions.

As part of global hegemony, differences are acknowledged but they are being erased in the terms in which they are being acknowledged – as more or less of the same, early and late along the same course. Globalization has overtaken development or, more precisely, developmental globalism has become the successor to developmentalism; structural adjustment has become the successor to modernization. Both refer to alignment in the global ranks, the subsumption of differences under a single standard set by the centre. Since the 1980s development policy has increasingly come to mean world market integration: through improvements of infrastructure, human resource development, structural adjustment, deregulation. If development was traditionally premised on the principle of a special status and treatment of developing countries, globalization means the end of development.

The global erosion of communities and the local reinvention of belonging

Contemporary accelerated globalization refers to a new distribution of power and comes in a package together with other trends, of informalization, informatization, flexibilization and the difficulty of sustaining community. The ramifications of North–South articulations range from security, migration, media representation to regional conflict, labour unrest and the continuing advent of social movements, all part of the complex landscape of singular and multiple modernities.

Since globalization is central to the redefinition of North–South relations, global processes are more and more involved in the production of local modernities and the spatial surfaces these processes play themselves out on. Globalization has therefore revealed itself to be a condition of modernization inasmuch as it transforms the central features of modernity, beginning with the components of differentiation and specialization which used to be the main harbinger of social change during the nineteenth century. Beyond the divergent representations of globalization discussed thus far, and specifically in regards to the problem of modernity(ies), globalizing forces have without a doubt introduced dramatic changes in the meaning of community. They have been associated with the erosion of norms and trust (Kantor and Pittinsky, 1996) as well as with the emergence of new manufactured risks (Beck, 1992).

Globalization, one could say, is changing the very nature of the social. The distinction proposed by Ulrich Beck (1998) between 'unidimensional modernity' and 'reflexive modernity' is useful in understanding this phenomenal process. While unidimensional modernity is a rationalization of tradition, reflexive modernity introduces a new approach pointing to the rationalizing of rationalization itself. In this case, it is as if industrial production no longer produces an industrial society but something other that can be perceived through the individualization processes of institutions. Therefore, if globalization needs to be understood as acting through a variety of spatial categories (Crang, 1999: 168), as a main component of reflexive modernity, it has an impact as well on the lived experience of social actors. Globalization therefore converges with shifts in the pattern of consumption as well as the informational mode of production. It redefines the way individual actors cope with professional and interpersonal networks. It also contributes to a deep revision of the sense and experience of spatial belonging that social actors once underwent in industrial society.

Democracy or globalization?

These elements can be more easily perceived if we look at the way globalization changes the meaning of community or reshapes communities. Social actors, in whatever circumstances, have the capacity to revise or redefine models of social and cultural integration. This, of course, depends on the actors' capacity to cope with the new challenges and issues brought forward by the informational and global economy. In this sense, social actors are involved in new cultural fields where the very meaning of democracy is at stake. Is it possible for democratic renewal and representative forms of political accountability to survive within the new political culture characterized by decentralization, mixed with a profound revision of traditional politics? What are the capabilities of citizens to revise the traditional vision of democracy, once captured by the nation-states' extant obligation to guarantee the rights of citizens, in the face of new and rising global economic actors and institutions such as the World Bank or IMF?

This issue has been raised in a variety of different contexts over the last few years. It has been associated with what has been referred to as a paradox of democratization (Pateman, 1996: 8). This paradox unfolds in the following way: though democratization is proclaimed in universal terms, citizenship and its attendant rights have always been associated with specific states. From a global perspective, this begs the question of the aforementioned growing inequalities between North and South, as well as within each of these regions. Over the last 15 years, social movements all over the world have been seeking to improve political climates as well as living conditions, bringing new challenges to states, both democratic and undemocratic, whilst forwarding a progressive vision of global citizenship. Individual strategies are often reinforced or sustained by collective ones. It is here that we often see social movements, particularly amongst NGOs, aiming to transform or adapt a traditional vision of democracy to the reality of the new globalized world order.

In fact, social movements have had little choice but to adapt to the new global paradigm of collective action (Sklair, 1995). In this they have had to take note of recent social and economic transformations in terms of changing class structures, the reinforcement of cosmopolitanism and new global political opportunity structures. Additionally, it is not only the material conditions of mobilization that are transformed, but also people's definitions of selfhood and identity. From this perspective, we can see different strategies taken on by collective actors in their efforts to cope with the new and emerging issues of global modernities. While some movements are taking advantage of the new opportunities created by the transformation of living conditions in a global setting, others are combating its detrimental effects. And, whilst some actors and some movements are involved in creating international networks, others prefer to focus on locality with a more defensive attitude, protecting space that is being submerged in risk-filled and destabilizing processes, a miniaturization of global social processes (Lustiger-Thaler, 2000).

The essays

These collective actions emerge in the varied contributions to this collection on globalization. In the first section, called 'Globalization Discourses', Jan Nederveen Pieterse's chapter, 'Globalization and Collective Action', sets the analytical stage for many of the arguments presented here, by unpacking the options that the collective action of globalization currently has. Pieterse considers the shifting context of globalization and observes a pattern of collective actions emerging in the form of: 'anti-globalization' discourses, which tend to be defensive and shortsighted; 'alternative globalization', which depends largely on global institutional reform; 'shaping globalization' which includes NGOs, but is premised on a complex matrix of multilateral and unilateral national as well as international processes; and 'quiet encroachment', wherein global collective actions emerge in the spaces in between the major social structures and institutions. For the time being, none of these variations, in Pieterse's view, carry a secure prospect for global transformation in and of themselves.

Henri Lustiger-Thaler, Louis Maheu and Pierre Hamel's chapter, 'Institutions and Global Collective Action', examines the context within which movement actors make decisions about selfhood in a rapidly globalizing world. They look at existing theoretical suppositions in an effort to recast the global problem of collective action and globalization from the purview of institutions. Modern social movements, they argue, are premised on negotiating three critical processes within the complexity of institutional life. First, under what conditions do subjects, individual as well as collective, make choices? By examining choice, in a globalized/institutional context, we receive a better understanding of new global constraints and opportunities for social movements. Second, how do these same subjects negotiate diverse milieus of belonging in a globalizing world? This raises the issues of post-identities, and what they refer to as 'extra-localities' – new spatial constructs existing between the local and the global – as part and parcel of being a modern subject. This equally raises, for them, the challenge of tracking communities in processes of global transition, stretching from localities to extended global milieus. Third, what processes socially embed the need to be recognized and (re)create a history of the subject, in the new global sequencing of shifting localities?

In 'Globalizing Civil Society? Social Movements and the Challenge of Global Politics from Below', Catherine Eschle enters the discussion on globalization and collective action through a critique of reigning notions of global civil society prevalent within the discipline of International Relations (IR). Eschle makes a convincing argument that this literature wholly neglects the complexity of societies that currently exist under the rubric of modern globalization processes. She favours a sociological-culturalist approach that focuses on the particularity, difference and emancipatory possibilities of social movements within the new global hierarchy. Eschle points to activities on the World Wide Web, as an apt expression of how the state and an institutional-led 'netting' of the world, through online technologies, nevertheless contains unexpected resistances and fertile grounds for collective actions.

In the second section, 'Global Identities: Gender and Sexualities', Sasha Roseneil states in her chapter, 'The Global, the Local and the Personal: The Dynamics of Collective Action in Late Modernity', that it is not her intent simply to 'globalize' the study of social movements but to examine its real practices. What is the interest of movements to be global? How does it occur? Roseneil's emphasis is upon the local and personal components of collective action. Her focus is on the women's peace movement, in particular Greenham Common in the UK. She examines how local and personal actions move and reconfigure issues upwards toward the global, as a form of politics and concerted social movement strategies. The women's peace movement at Greenham Common emerges in Roseneil's study as an example of the intimate matrix of personal, familial and political commitments, as a basis for global collective actions.

Valentine Moghadam's chapter 'Transnational Feminist Networks: Collective Action in an Era of Globalization', is a contribution to feminist theorizing on globalization. She looks at four case studies of transnational feminist networks – in Fiji, Belgium, Pakistan and Cyprus. Moghadam asks how the feminist movement has fared in view of the transnationalization of local action frames. Are women's movements inevitably local, or can one speak of a global women's movement? Moghadam answers that such movements may have a global dimension. Indeed, she asserts that the transnational character of the women's movement has profound implications for the general study of social movements and social theory in the era of globalization.

Angela Miles' chapter 'Global Feminist Theorizing and Organizing: Life-Centred and Multi-Centred Alternatives to Neoliberal Globalization' gives a view of what she refers to as 'transformative' or 'integrative' feminisms. Miles examines these feminisms as they are shaped by and shape new forms of multi-centred theorizing and organizing among women. She shows how emerging forms of global practice which are neither single centred nor de-centred are enabling us to conceive and therefore to create new non-homogenizing universalisms. This is just one example of the ways apparently 'identity-based' politics are both responding to and creating the possibility of new levels of general struggle built through the recognition and celebration of diversity rather than its denial.

In 'Globalisation and the Mobilisation of Gay and Lesbian Communities', Barry Adam examines how sexual preference movements have, much like the women's movement, sought to immerse themselves proactively in global networks. Adam situates his general analysis of the gay and lesbian movement within a broader consideration of political economy and the manner in which sexuality is reproduced throughout the world. For Adam, international gay and lesbian cultures have been globalized through the circulation of ideas in cities and metropoles. Gay and lesbian social movements are therefore privy to transnational cultural dissemination, ranging from gay consumerism to social protest.

The third section, entitled 'The Multiplicities of Globalization', covers a range of topics traditionally kept outside the Western framing of globalization processes. In 'Cross-Border, Cross-Movement Alliances in the late 1990s', Aaron Pollack examines the relationship between social movements and national borders in the age of informationalization and globalization. Pollack argues that collective actions are increasingly going global in their response to neoliberal economics. Technologies such as the Internet have exploded the social movement constituency on any given local issue and rationalized contact on global issues. Pollack discusses case studies as diverse as the Zapatista Army of National Liberation (EZLN), development-related NGOs, environmental networks, and anti-WTO global actions. For Pollack the test of the new global collective actions will be if they can truly represent themselves as a collective spirit, whilst recognizing the strengths and specificities of each member.

Globalism and the environmental dimension is taken up by Antimo Farro and Jean-Guy Vaillancourt in their chapter, 'Collective Movements and Globalisation'. In this contribution, Farro and Vaillancourt address the differences and similarities between the growth of environmental movements in the developed and developing world. The affirmation of identity is a central theme in their work. The authors trace identity concerns from the Maghreb to the central cities of the North, through environmental protests, examining the various components of collective action which come into play at each critical step. For these authors, global environmental initiatives unfold, in both North and South contexts, in tandem with processes of economic and cultural domination and resistances to the authority of ruling actors.

Ranjit Dwivedi in 'Environmental Movements in the Global South: Outline of a Critique of the "Livelihood" Approach' looks at the phenomena of social movements in the South. He develops categorization of Third World movements in India, the Philippines, Brazil, Nigeria and Kenya. Dwivedi argues that these movements, rather than being solely concerned with traditional livelihood issues, which directly affect their communities, are extremely multi-dimensional and firmly entrenched in the local/global, power/knowledge nexus, aimed at global democratic renewal.

What all the above contributions point to, in their various empirical and theoretical arguments, is that globalization as a concept and process is firmly ensconced in the discourse of North and South relations, women's issues, sexualities, the fluidity of modern identity concerns, institutional transformation and environmental practices; in short, social movement dynamics are at the cutting edge of contemporary social change. While the term globalization has been used less precisely than many might like, it clearly points to a fundamental shift in the manner in which the collective actions of actors unfold and gravitate from a local expression to an intense global concern. This alone should force us to nuance and decentre the reified objects contained in our all too secure master frames, as we privilege a different kind of planetary thinking. Collective action, and its social movement expressions, may offer in the final analysis one of the few remaining ways to think about a 'global planet', one that is both critically sound and grounded in a twenty-first-century renewal of the social sciences.

References

Applebaum, R.P. and J. Henderson (1995) 'The hinge of history: turbulence and transformation in the world economy', *Competition and Change*, 1(1): 1–12.

Bauman, Z. (1998) *Globalization: European Perspectives*, New York: Columbia University Press.

Beck, U. (1992) *Risk Society (Towards a New Modernity)*, London: Sage.

Beck, U. (1998) 'Liens personnels et individualisme positif. Le conflit des deux modernités et la question de la disparition des solidarités', *Lien social et politiques – RIAC*, 39 (spring): 15–25.

Castells, M. (1996) *The Rise of the Network Society*, Oxford: Blackwell.

Castells, M. (1997) *The Power of Identity*, Oxford: Blackwell.

Crang, M. (1999) 'Globalisation has conceived, perceived and lived spaces', *Theory, Culture and Society*, 16(1): 167–77.

Gopal, S. (1998) 'Images of world society: a Third World view', *Social Science Information Journal*, 50(3): 375–80.

Hampdon-Turner, C. and F. Trompenaars (1993) *Seven Cultures of Capitalism*. New York: Doubleday.

Hannerz, U. (1996) *Transnational Culture: Culture, People, Places*, London: Routledge.

Hermet, G. (1997) 'The concept of community in political science', paper presented at the IPSA 17th World Congress, Seoul.

Hirst, P. and G. Thompson (1999) *Globalization in Question: the International Economy and Possibilities of Governance*, Cambridge: Cambridge University Press.

Kantor, R. Moss and T.L. Pittinsky (1995–96) 'Globalisation: new worlds for social inquiry', *Berkeley Journal of Sociology*, 40: 1–19.

Lustiger-Thaler, Henri (2000) 'The miniaturization of collective action: ghettoes and global space', in P. Hamel, H. Lustiger Thaler and M. Mayer (eds), *Urban Movements in a Globalizing World*. London: Routledge.

Nederveen Pieterse, J. (1997) 'Globalisation and emancipation: from local empowerment to global reform', *New Political Economy*, 2(1): 79–92.

Nederveen Pieterse, J. (1998) 'Hybrid modernities: mélange modernities in Asia', *Sociological Analysis*, 1(3): 75–86.

Pateman, C. (1996) 'Democracy and democratization', *International Political Science Review*, 17(1): 5–12.

Peck, J. and A. Tickell (1994) 'Searching for a new institutional fix: the *After*-Fordist crisis and the global–local disorder', in A. Amin (ed.), *Post-Fordism*, Oxford: Blackwell, pp. 280–315.

Petrella, R. (1996) 'Globalisation and internationalisation: the dynamics of the emerging world order', in R. Boyer and D. Drache (eds), *States against Markets: the limits of Globalisation*, London: Routledge.

Robertson, R. (1992) 'Glocalization: Time-Space and Homogeneity-Heterogeneity', in M. Featherstone, S. Lash and R. Robertson, *Global Modernities*, London: Sage, pp. 25–44.

Sklair, L. (1995) 'Social Movements and Global Capitalism', *Sociology*, 29(3): 495–512.

Vebhiu, A. (1999) 'Albanian migration and media', Amsterdam, unpublished paper.

Part I
Globalization Discourses

1
Globalization and Collective Action

Jan Nederveen Pieterse

There are many simplistic and schematic assessments of globalization
going around and also when it comes to social movements, polemics
easily prevails over analysis. So the first step in a reflection on globalization and collective action is to problematize globalization. Globalization may refer to a process, an awareness or a variety of projects.
Turning to collective action, the first concern is to address the globalization of collective action, or collective action as a globalizing force. A
second concern is the different strands in collective action in relation
to globalization. Here four main currents are distinguished: anti-
globalization, alternative globalism, shaping globalization or global
reform, and 'quiet encroachment' – or gradual collective adjustments to
and in globalization. In reality, of course, these currents overlap and
each sprawls broadly around a central theme. For each current this
chapter gives a profile of its claims and ideological or theoretical lineages, and a sketch of what it means in emotional and imaginary terms,
or in terms of political psychology. Finally it turns to their prospects –
that is, the likely or possible future options of each of these positions.

In an earlier paper on globalization and emancipation (Nederveen
Pieterse, 1997a) I argued for a political continuum from local empowerment to global reform, such that local empowerment connects with
efforts towards democratization and reform at wider levels of governance. If local action is a preference there is still a difference between
inward- and outward-looking localism. What is needed is not only local
empowerment but also global empowerment. Implementing such an
agenda would involve greater cooperation among civic organizations,
including labour organizations, and developing multilevel connections
from local organizations to international networks working on global
reform. This was a programmatic paper; the present chapter is wider in

ambit and seeks to scan and analyse the wide variety of collective action in relation to globalization.

Unpacking globalization

Unpacking globalization is necessary because the theme lends itself easily to rhetorical spill-over and ideological manipulation. Recourse to social science provides no remedy because each discipline has its own take on globalization. In effect at present we have widely dispersed globalization discourses based on profoundly different premises and regularly occasioning a dialogue of the deaf. This globalization reductionism feeds into popular perceptions and stereotyping, which in turn inform collective action. Without a separate analytics of globalization, a discussion of globalization and collective action might easily become tautological or a matter of circular reasoning: (perspectives on) collective action echoing the premises built-in in the first place. Since globalization is multidimensional and open-ended, at minimum what can be done is to provide insight in its multiple dimensions (Table 1.1).

These may also be termed dimensions of globalization. Globalization, thus, is shorthand for several major interwoven trends. A few brief points may further develop this perspective. (i) To distinguish contemporary globalization from long-term trends it may be appropriate to speak of *accelerated globalization*. (ii) Contemporary accelerated globalization comes in a package together with informatization (the role of information and communication technologies), flexibilization (that is, changes in production systems towards flexible production), and the reconfiguration of states and regionalization. (iii) Recent accelerated globalization coincides with the prominence of neoliberalism and the drive to free markets. What is usually presented as deregulation in effect implies re-regulation. Structural adjustment means the alignment of economic regimes and standards of accounting to Anglo-American standards. (iv) Arguably, accelerated globalization is driven or at any rate conditioned by technological changes, but technology needs unpacking as well. Current globalization may be characterized as, among others, a macroeconomic phenomenon driven by microeconomic changes – that is, at the level of firms. (v) Globalization is a process and not an outcome: it refers to the trend toward the growing interconnectedness of different parts of the world, not to their *being* interconnected.

Besides these dimensions and trends we can distinguish several

Table 1.1 Globalization according to social science disciplines

Disciplines	Time	Agency, domain	Keywords
Economics	1970s>	MNCs, banks, technologies	Global corporation, world product, global capitalism
Cultural studies	1970s>	Mass media, advertising, consumption, lifestyle, identity	Global village, McDonaldization, Jihad vs. McWorld, hybridization
Political science, international relations	1980s>	Civil society, social movements, INGOs	Internationalization of the state. Competitor states, postinternational politics, global civil society
Sociology	1800s>	Modernity	Capitalism, industrialization, urbanization, nation-states, etc.
Political economy	1500s>	Modern capitalism	World Market
History, anthropology	5000 BC>	Cross-cultural trade, migration, technologies. World religions	Global flows, global ecumene Widening scale of co-operation over time

further levels to globalization. First, globalization as a *process* – of which a matter-of-fact definition is the growing interconnectedness of different parts of the world, or globalization in itself (*an sich*). Secondly, globalization as *awareness* – that is, the awareness and recognition of growing interconnectedness; or globalization as subjectivity, for itself (*für sich*). And thirdly, globalization as *project* – the advocacy and pursuit of particular *forms* of globalization and attempts to manage and steer globalization in a particular direction, or globalism. Globalization projects are endeavours with a global horizon and scale; their objectives may be strategic, political, economic, social or cultural (Table 1.2).

These projects are concurrent, overlapping and interactive. Each represents different ways of following, appropriating, navigating and or negotiating new technologies and opportunities. Together they make up the field of really existing globalization politics, or the à la carte globalization menu. Collective action, then, is one slice of and

Table 1.2   Globalization projects

Globalization projects	Agents
Strategic globalism	Superpower politics, NATO
Corporate globalism	International banks, multinational corporations, transnational enterprises
Economic and financial global management	International financial institutions, WTO, G-7
Developmental globalism	World Bank, UN agencies (UNDP and so on)
Ecological globalism	UNCED, Global Environment Facility
Media globalism	'Media Ind.', CNN
Global humanism	UN Declaration of Human Rights, Amnesty International
Feminist globalisms	'Sisterhood is Global' (Nairobi, Beijing, Cairo meetings)
Labour globalism	ILO, trade union internationalism
Islamic globalisms	Umma politics
Catholic globalism	Vatican (for example, Lumen 2000)
Ecumenical globalism	Interreligious dialogue, as in World Council of Churches
Consumer globalism ('everyday globalism')	'McDonaldization'
Anti-globalism	Localism, new protectionism, delinking

stream in globalization politics, while other dimensions are politics and projects on the part of governments, international institutions, regional bodies and corporations. Summing up: *collective action in relation to globalization is shaped by globalization as process, reflects particular subjectivities in relation to globalization, positions itself in relation to ongoing globalization projects and, implicitly or explicitly, involves a project.* Before turning to collective action globalization projects, let us consider the globalization of collective action, or alternatively, collective action *as* globalization.

The globalization of collective action

Perhaps it is because it is so obvious that this phenomenon is often overlooked: much collective action itself is a globalizing force. It is carried by technological infrastructures and possibilities, propelled by political opportunities and driven by necessity. From the outset, then, globalization is not something that occurs *outside* collective action and vice versa: globalization is rather a spatial expression or domain, a condition and medium of collective action.

Of course, globalization is often associated with hegemonic and corporate forces (as in corporate globalism and 'Americanization'), but it should not be overlooked that globalization is also an everyday popular experience and activity, as in consumer behaviour and lifestyle choices. The salience of 'corporate globalism' (Gurtov, 1988) and its impact in everyday experience is due not least to advertising. Spending on advertising has risen exponentially since the 1950s:

> Total global advertising expenditures multiplied nearly sevenfold from 1950 to 1990 . . . They grew one third faster than the world economy and three times faster than world population. In real terms, spending rose from $39 billion in 1950 to $256 billion in 1990 – more than the gross national product of India or than all Third World governments spent on health and education. . . . In 1950, advertisers spent $15 for each person on the planet, while in 1970 they spent $27, and in 1990, $48.
>
> (Durning, 1993: 80)

The structural trend underlying this trend is the corporate drive to establish global brand names, so that the globalization of demand would match the globalization of supply (Ohmae, 1992). This is prompted by the rising costs of research and development and technology, in combination with the shorter shelf life of products. The writing is on the wall and advertising images are omnipresent. However, to take corporate globalism at face value is, by the same token, to mistake the package for the product – that is, to overestimate advertising and to mistake the corporate aspiration to globalize demand with the outcome.

In a broad and deep historical sense the antecedents of the globalization of collective action go back to, among others, cross-cultural trade and migration, transnational religious networks, Renaissance humanism and various transnational political alliances (diplomatic and military) and affinities. Over time it has found expression in sentiments that accompanied the eighteenth-century Enlightenment and the internationalisms of the nineteenth century. Examples are the wide gesture of Beethoven's 'Alle Menschen werden Brüder', Kant's cosmopolitanism, the Quakers' anti-slavery position, the abolition movement and the pathos of the Romantics. It took shape in Jacobinism, in the working-class internationalisms and women's movements (Billington, 1980). At the turn of the century, anti-imperialist and anti-colonial movements came to the fore (Nederveen Pieterse, 1989). Examples of transnational collective action at the time are 'Ethiopianism' in Africa and beyond, the Nahda in the Middle East, and the reactions to Japan's victory over Russia in 1905 that rippled through Asia. Anti-imperialism was in many ways an international struggle that evoked transnational networks and solidarities. This experienced an upsurge at the time of decolonization. Cultural internationalism developed rapidly after the First World War (Iriye, 1997).

The peace movement of the 1950s was transnational. A high tide of transnational social movement connections was '1968' and the multiple cross-linkages between decolonization struggles, the American civil rights movement, anti-war and student movements and labour struggles. Out of this period came the justice and peace, liberation theology, solidarity and human rights movements, the global anti-Apartheid movement, the peace movement, indigenous peoples networks, the growth of NGOs and their transnational networks, and environmental movements. By the 1980s the idea of 'planetary' social movements was an established theme (Hegedus, 1989). Civil society activism in Eastern Europe that contributed to the 'velvet revolution' and the demise of the Soviet bloc (Keane, 1988) contributed to the prominence of 'civil society'. In the 1990s, several UN conferences that were designated 'global' also served as a rendezvous for transnational social action.

In the 1990s, transnational collective action has been re-thematized, with the emphasis on information and communication technologies. In Castells' 'network society' this is an overarching motif (1996). The Zapatistas using the Internet for transnational mobilization receives model status in this kind of treatment. While 'connectivity' has become a strategic theme in management and business, in social thinking present times are baptised as 'the age of connexity' (Mulgan, 1998: 19f).

In all these expressions, collective action is not just being globalized but also *globalizing* – that is, it is an active translocal and transnational networking force – deploying and appropriating networks, vocabularies and information and communication technologies. Several contemporary social forces have an interest and stake in globalization and as such act as *promoters* of globalization – of the *kind* of globalization that they want to be a part of. This applies to NGOs, especially international NGOs and transnational advocacy NGOs such as Greenpeace, Friends of the Earth, Amnesty International, along with indigenous peoples' networks and women's movements.

This process may be interpreted as a *democratization of cosmopolitanism* – a *relative* democratization, relative to the elite transnationalism of dynastic and aristocratic alliances and clerical and scholarly networks, from the Church to humanism and Freemasonry. Relative also in the sense that not every movement or individual is, of course, globally mobile to the same degree (Massey, 1993). Even so it may be argued that on the whole these are times of growing social empowerment – although some would argue the reverse (Berger, 1998). For instance, in development policy, participatory development has become the conventional wisdom (Oommen, 1998). Even in diplomacy, the traditional preserve of elites, people-to-people relations play a growing part and give rise to 'multi-track diplomacy' (Rupesinghe, 1996). James Mittelman (1996: 10) rightly notes that 'New social movements – women's groups, environmentalists, human rights organisations, etc. – are themselves global phenomena', but then he adds: 'a worldwide response to the deleterious effects of economic globalisation'. This is a surface interpretation that too easily absorbs transnational collective action within a single one-dimensional logic.

Transnational social networks go way back – arguably, all the way to long-distance trade, cross-cultural linkages and the 'world religions'. Collective actions have defined epochs and shaped history. Looking back it is also clear that every age has sought to label and capitalize on the *form* of such networks, claiming that this particular shape was novel in its reach and historic in its significance. So did the Jacobins and their republican networks (the 'age of democracy'), the nineteenth-century national movements (the age of nationalism), the working-class movements, the socialists of the Second and Third International (the era of socialism), the decolonization movements (the era of anti-imperialism), and so forth. Considered against the historical backdrop of the changing forms of transnational social solidarities over time, the present emphasis on the role of information and communication technologies may be put in perspective. It may be easily exaggerated and overblown, misreading form for content and mistaking tides and currents for long-term trends. Calls for transnational action long precede the use of the Internet, and the momentum of transnational solidarity should not be mixed up with the role of contemporary technologies. Besides, the Internet is also a site of conflict and contestation. At any rate, collective action, past and present, is structurally implicated in globalization. Against this backdrop we turn to the specific positions taken by social movements in relation to globalization.

Anti-globalization

Rapidly, in the span of a few years, globalization has become a focal point of social criticism, a gathering point of collective discontent – due to financial instability, economic crisis, global inequality, deepening poverty and social exclusion, job loss, Americanization, and environmental deterioration. Among the culprits feature the IMF, WTO and MNCs. Globalization has become a medley of miseries and in the process 'the "problem of globalisation" has taken hold as a common integrating force and foe for contemporary social movements' (Lynch, 1998: 155).

An example of collective action along these lines is the *International Forum on Globalisation*, campaigning, organizing teach-ins and publishing: 'the IFG attempts to delegitimise the current order by emphasising the loss of control over economies and social welfare, on the part of governments (local, state, regional), peoples and communities. It highlights the inequities resulting from globalisation through frequent use of the term "global apartheid"' (Lynch, 1998: 157). The term *global apartheid* usually refers to a scenario among others (Falk, 1994; Group of Lisbon, 1995), but on the part of the IFG it is presented as destiny (Mander and Goldsmith, 1996). A fundamental move on the part of the IFG and other movements is to 'Introduce a new concept: *economic globalization* as the central factor affecting people's jobs, communities, and the environment' (Mander quoted in Lynch, 155).

Because of accelerated globalization, localities are exposed to unfamiliar global forces of an unpredictable character that affect people's livelihoods and produce insecurity. In addition people's nervous system must assimilate new signals, information inputs and pressures, so that people feel emotionally highly-strung. Anti-globalization, then, is like the reaction of a porcupine under stress, putting up its spikes. In anti-globalization discourse globalization is portrayed as an alien juggernaut, a hostile, uncontrolled force – a kind of King Kong globalization. Fed by a deep undercurrent of paranoia, it involves a conspiracy theory of globalization – as the highest stage of capitalism, the latest form of imperialism and neocolonialism revisited (Sivanandan, 1998). This kind of globalization talk, of course, reworks well-worn ideological and theoretical themes. The lineages of anti-globalization include anti-capitalism (reading capitalism as 'colonization of the life world'), dependency theory (especially delinking), ecological concerns, anti-Americanism, identity politics and political localism.

A key question to ask is whether anti-globalization is an effective politics to further emancipatory agendas, for instance the agenda of 'just development' (Banuri et al., 1997). The political function of anti-globalization talk may be to serve as a counterweight to the global babble of liberalisation zealots and management gurus, and thus contribute to the mobilization of political will in support of national controls on capital markets and economic policies. But, analytically and, ultimately, politically, there are several problems with this position. (i) It narrows globalization to economic globalization, so that the target of criticism is taken as the definition of the field, in effect echoing the economistic perspective of corporate globalism. (ii) It reduces economic globalization to free market capitalism and liberalization. The issue is quite simple: if neoliberalism is the target, then why attack globalization? (Nederveen Pieterse, 1997b) (iii) It conflates economics with capitalism and capitalism with free enterprise capitalism, thus erasing from the picture precisely those elements that might offer a way out of the institutional fix – such as social market capitalism, social liberalism and various options for controlling free market capitalism. (iv) If a serious debate on regulating capitalism (Soros, 1998), the 'Third Way' (Giddens, 1998) or the 'Neue Mitte' is called for, this position rules it out in the first place. (v) In the process, it leaves oneself, one's own actions and agency out of the picture, creating an 'us and them' dichotomy – globalization is 'them', cast as an alien hostile juggernaut, while 'we' stand apart untainted and morally superior. This disavows the question and the possibility of shared engagement and responsibility. (vi) Further, the major weakness of anti-globalization is its failure to offer an alternative politics – that is, a politics beyond localism. (vii) In view of its lineage in anti-colonial discourse, the island politics of anti-globalization is more a political project than an economic agenda. It is reminiscent of the 'liberated zone' approach in anti-colonial struggles and revolutionary politics. It represents an 'island politics' of establishing enclaves of autonomy. The politics of splendid isolationism may not be entirely free of provincial pathos: that life in the province is more virtuous than in the (rich but decadent and self-seeking) metropolis. Interpreted in emotional terms, anti-globalization is a form of protest politics. It combines politics of resistance with a culture of complaint.

In governmental circles a hard-nosed matter-of-fact, no-nonsense approach to globalization has become commonplace. For instance, according to American political scientists, by any account 'globalisation is a reality, not a choice. "You can run but you can't hide" might serve as the mantra for the age . . . The real choice for governments is not how best to fight globalisation but, how to manage it, which will require creative policies both at home and abroad' (Haass and Litan, 1998: 6). Governments often act as conduits of globalization but, as argued above, the same applies to social movements. It is not clear by virtue of what analysis, or politics, social movements could afford to ignore what governments and international institutions cannot. What does matter is to discriminate *which kind* of globalization governments, international institutions and social movements accept or promote; however, the wholesale rhetorical position taken in anti-globalization precisely rules out such fine-tuning.

A related question is what scope for social action and alternative policies this position offers. According to Cecelia Lynch, 'the anti-globalisation movement at base provides an example of what social movements are able to do most effectively in world politics, that is, delegitimise particular discourses and paths of action in order to legitimise alternatives' (159). Yet there are several problems along the way.

> One major issue involved is the problem of articulating a positive nomenclature to provide an alternative to market capitalism. Earlier in the century, antiwar groups consciously took on the appellation of "peace movement"; but it is unclear what the anti-globalisation movement has in common to provide a positive normative foundation. Possibilities are "sustainable development", "local control", and so forth, but local control has normative difficulties, while sustainable development connotes little, explicitly, in the way of connection with "human" rights. More importantly, however, the normative content of relocalisation programs such as the "new protectionism" is problematic (160).

The heading 'anti-globalization' is not promising. In effect anti-globalization is a politically disabling, not an enabling discourse. In the words of Lynch (1998: 149), the outcome is 'the discursive demobilisation of movements on questions of economic praxis'. 'Social movements' discursive demobilisation vis-à-vis globalisation is compounded by the lack of knowledge, or common articulation, of against whom or what any challenge to globalisation is targeted' (163).

Of course, it is possible to criticize (particular forms of) globalization without adopting an anti-globalization position. Anti-globalization rhetoric stands in contrast to more effectively targeted positions – such as the French 'Observatoire de Mondialisation'. The Zapatista project and their international encounters is at times presented as aimed 'against neoliberalism' (de Angelis, 1998), which is a more intelligent and politically enabling target than 'globalization'. In its more recent positions the International Forum on Globalization has also moved closer to globalization, rather than anti-globalization. This brings us to two different options for collective action – alternative globalism and global reform.

Alternative globalism

Each of the globalism projects listed above (Table 1.2) could be termed an alternative globalism, but they are not all associated with collective action in the sense of popular social movements of some kind. Of those that are associated with collective action, several tend to be single-issue oriented (such as women's, ecological and labour movements). What might be considered an alternative globalism is political Islam. Unlike other movements this represents a holistic alternative, it encompasses a worldview, a way of life, a historical formation as well as a geographical space, stretching from Morocco to Southeast Asia. Its scope includes Islamic politics and law (sharia), Islamic geopolitics, Islamic economics and social policy, Islamic science, and Islamic identity and culture. To a varying extent these owe their present salience not to collective action per se, but to government-sponsored initiatives, which in turn are made possible by rentier oil economies. Nevertheless, although perceptions and realities are difficult to disentangle here, Islam is a significant movement, which is at times presented as the most significant challenge to the hegemony of the 'Triad' globalization of North America, Europe and Japan. It is a challenge that cannot be captured under the usual headings of neo-Marxism, Maoism, Guevarism, Fanonism, or Gandhian influence.

The lineages of Islam as alternative globalization include civilizational legacies, anti-colonialism, anger and frustration about Western double standards and cultural disaffection. Ever since the Nahda (the Arab awakening of the late-nineteenth century), Islam has been repeatedly held up as a challenge and alternative to Western hegemony, at times under the heading of Arab unity. Benjamin Barber captured this under the rhetorical heading of *Jihad vs. McWorld* (1996). It forms part of Samuel Huntington's *Clash of Civilisations* (1996). But from hereon the story unravels. Islam is fractured; the umma is a delta of many streams – Sunni and Shiite, clerical Islam, Sufism and folk Islam. The different forms of Islam in the Arab world, Iran and Turkey, South and Southeast Asia, Africa and Europe are each historically and culturally articulated. 'Like other religions, Islam is not a generic essence, but a nominal entity that conjoins, by means of a name, a variety of societies, cultures, histories and polities' (Al-Azmeh, 1993: 60). In addition, the distinctive character of Islamic institutions may be more a claim than a reality: for example, it may be argued that what is 'Islamic' in Islamic science may be a matter of packaging rather than content. The actual dependency of Islamic modernization on Western technologies and examples tends to be downplayed (just as Europe downplayed its dependence on Islamic and Arabic influences in earlier times).

The worlds of Islam are alternative, bricolage modernities – appropriating technologies and institutions, borrowing from outside while revisiting historical and cultural resources. By the same token they are not stand-alone alternatives. Thus, Islamic globalism is a sprawling cluster of cultural affinities and its reality is that of a political aspiration, which nevertheless exercises regional influence and an uneven hegemony (Beeley, 1992). If Islamic Jacobinism intensifies under the sway of accelerated globalization (Ahmed and Donnan, 1994; Ray, 1993), the actual dependency – technological, economic, political and cultural – of Islamic societies precludes its becoming much more than a political fiction.

The psychological profile of Islamic globalism is a negative unity – united without, divided within. Without a common opposition to the West there might not be any umma politics, and what is there is largely political fiction. Part of political Islam is a critique of capitalism, which it shares with Roman Catholicism. Both Islam and Catholicism reflect the ethos of an older, medieval political economy, in which 'community' values prevail over merely commercial and economic interests.

Shaping globalization

This concerns forms of collective action that seek to shape or influence globalization. A premise of this approach is a distinction between the *form* and the *trend* of globalization. In the 1970s international reformism found expression in proposals for a New International Economic Order. The NIEO is now being rearticulated under different geopolitical and economic conditions. It takes a broad variety of expressions, from modest, technical adjustments in international institutions to wide-ranging and radical proposals for global economic and financial regulation. This includes a variety of global taxes, global social contracts, 'greening' the international political economy (Lipietz, 1995), global Keynesianism, democratizing international financial institutions, UN reform, and democratizing global governance (Falk, 1994) and social development proposals (Ekins, 1992; Deacon et al., 1997). The central thrust is to achieve social justice on a world scale. The challenge is to merge contemporary technologies with the general objective of social justice. Following Gurtov (1988), Greider (1997: 469) uses the term 'global humanism': 'If this new consciousness does gather force, it will start from a shared understanding that the market cannot deliver certain values to people and must be governed by them'. Greider's programme includes 'Restore national controls over global capital. Tax wealth more, labour less. Stimulate global growth by boosting consumer demand from the bottom up' (472). Together these add up to a budding global reform movement (Nederveen Pieterse, 1999).

The lineages of this kind of approach are several. 'New World Order' thinking goes back to the French Revolution and the 1920s initiatives that led to the League of Nations and to present concerns with strengthening the international legal order and international human rights advocacy. Other strands include the tradition of labour internationalism, global Keynesianism, notions of global civil society, and aspirations towards a universal planetary ethics, from Kant to Habermas and Hans Küng (1997).

Accordingly several different emotional profiles underpin shaping globalization. Firstly, a matter-of-fact appraisal of globalization, of the inequities of globalization as well as its complexity. A different strand is 'If you can't beat them, join them'. Generally global reform is based on an outward- and forward-looking approach. It is a propositional politics, not merely a protest politics. Its psychological profile is optimistic, either as in 'apocalypse postponed' or in utopian versions, as in the high-minded outlook of planetary ethics.

Quiet encroachment

Anti-globalization, shaping globalization and alternative globalism are loud, overt politics; they are deliberate, ideological and propagandistic, and involve a degree of posturing and deliberate simplification. By and large this also applies to Islamic globalism. Quiet encroachment belongs to a different dimension altogether. The premise for understanding this category of collective action is that social change does not necessarily take place underneath a large banner or neon-lit sign proclaiming SOCIAL TRANSFORMATION IN PROGRESS. Social changes more often take place gradually, imperceptibly, coming from unexpected quarters and in unanticipated ways. Asef Bayat's (1998) analysis of street politics in Tehran and Cairo, from which this terminology and perspective is derived, draws attention to the many ways in which urban street hawkers and other poor folk slyly make use of opportunities and niches to advance their interests. Low visibility is a strategic condition of action of this type. It would not be appropriate, as Bayat insists, to categorize this under the heading of everyday resistance politics à la James Scott, because it adds up to more than merely sabotage or politics of resentment; its net effect is transformative. Its collective character is occasional. Its mode of organization is circumstantial. Michael Mann's (1986) observation that social change often emerges from the 'interstices', the spaces *in between* the major social structures and institutions, in the nooks and crannies of structural change, points in the same direction. What belong in this category, for instance, are the vast transnational networks of informal trade by migrants and diasporas (Portes, 1995, 1996; Kotkin, 1992). What also belong are gradual changes in public opinion, media representations and political discourse, quietly encroaching upon fixed positions.

Quiet encroachment is not a 'loud' politics. Its theoretical lineages are negligible because by its character this is not an ideological position; it is rather a matter of collective pragmatism and opportunism in which the weak defend their interests if need be against the grain of major institutions and official policies. Even so its net effect over time may be one of gradual collective emancipation, though with two provisos. First, because quiet encroachment is informal it lacks an ethical dimension. Its informality also puts a limit on the potential institutionalization of the changes achieved. Secondly, it is not clear where the line runs between state weakness on the one hand and quiet encroachment as popular empowerment on the other. Clearly the rich practice quiet encroachment much more effectively than do the poor. Furthermore, crime networks are constantly on the look out for loopholes in institutions and regulations.

The emotional profile of quiet encroachment is blurred. The basic attitude is pragmatic, commonsensical, low profile. It is chameleon politics and politics by improvisation. It may be a matter of *wu-wei*, or 'doing by not-doing'; or Taoism in action, fluid like water that seeps and goes wherever it can, as a gradual and subtle corrosion of power politics. It may be casual but is not necessarily unconscious.

Prospects

The future of *anti-globalization* politics is probably durable and lasting: as durable as globalization anxiety. Its fundamental appeal stems from conditions of social exclusion and feelings of angst and alienation. Its appeal is as lasting as the politics of protest and disaffection. Its appeal may gradually recede as globalization becomes normalized and domesticated. The political effect of anti-globalization is likely to remain limited and indirect. It is likely to take the form of localism, for instance in the form of new protectionism. This will have limited impact inasmuch as nowadays delinking is a politics of alienation rather than a viable political option (Nederveen Pieterse, 1994). Its impact is limited because it is critique rather than construction, protest rather than proposition, resistance rather than transformation. Limited because in essence it lacks an alternative agenda, at least a practical agenda, except possibly for local enclaves, so its effect is likely to remain local. And indirect in that by comparison to the strident rhetoric of anti-globalization, global reform proposals may appear reasonable and gain acceptance (not unlike the way in which, in the past, social democracy seemed acceptable compared to the threat of communism). In other words, much of the net political impact of anti-globalization is likely to accrue to global reform.

The future of *alternative globalism* is elusive. As to political Islam, Islamic societies may be alternative modernities but not a world-scale alternative. Historically, the Islamic world achieved its peak due to its intercontinental middleman status. Furthermore, in the future there is no 'go-it-alone' status for Islam. Islam is much too fractured, technologically dependent and economically wired to the Triad economies to produce and achieve an alternative scenario. Islam as a global alternative is a political fiction that is being held up for propagandistic reasons on both sides of the fence, in a game of mirrors, a game of mutual stereotyping. This game may be as durable as the geopolitics of cultural difference, but its appeal is gradually being weakened by the quiet encroachment of globalization. There is presently no option but to recognize and negotiate contemporary globalization as the latest form of 'global patrimony' (Al-Azmeh, 1993: 35), which means that the actual future of alternative globalism lies in global reform.

With regard to *shaping globalization*, the significance of global reform is likely to grow over time proportionate to the degree that globalization is accepted as a condition, routinized as a process and normalized as a domain and object of political engagement. This involves the twin processes of the domestication of globalization and the democratization of global politics. By its nature global reform is a long-term politics. Two kinds of theories and futures – with regard to collective action and globalization – interact in this context. Prominent scenarios of globalization are (i) global apartheid; (ii) G-7 world management; (iii) regional blocs; (iv) asymmetric multilateralism; (v) symmetric multilateralism; (vi) global democratization ('cosmopolitan democracy'). If the most likely scenario is asymmetric multilateralism, the main challenge is to what extent this can be transformed in the direction of symmetric multilateralism. At issue is countervailing power at the global level. To what extent are international institutions such as the WTO, IMF and World Bank conducive to collective actions that seek to steer them toward a more symmetric direction? Dialogues between the World Bank and NGOs are well established and, increasingly, dialogues between civic organizations and the WTO and IMF have been coming on stream (Scholte, 1998).

While NGOs play a growing role they are also subject to questioning – as to their legitimacy, internal organization and accountability. They are viewed alternatively as the great hope for the future and as a form of subpolitics, the institutionalization of which might lead to a re-feudalization of politics. Their role varies according to their membership, issues (environment, development, human rights, peace, security, women's rights), mode of organization, methods of intervention (media, lobbying), the need or willingness of GOs and international institutions to cooperate, and North–South relations. Other relevant social forces are professional organizations (epistemic communities) and media.

With regard to the political impact of global reform, its future to a large extent depends on the degree of overlap or friction between the action spectrum of social movements and NGOs and the policy spectrum of governments and international and intergovernmental institutions. This degree of overlap is affected in turn by changes in public opinion, media representations, and economic and geopolitical conditions. The UN-sponsored 'global summits' have been occasions for the fractious alignment of the discourses and agendas of civic organizations, governments and international institutions. The follow-up conferences, 'five years after' (and next, 'ten years after') point to an ongoing dialogue.

The politics of global reform depends on the degree of overlap between:

- the action and strategy spectrums of civic organizations;
- the policy spectrum of governments and international institutions;
- trends in international politics across the spectrum of multilateralism and unilateralism; and
- media representations.

With regard to governmental policy spectrums, Haass and Litan (1998) distinguish three approaches in US politics to addressing the problems of the global economy. One is a hands-off approach which 'embraces the free market and would abandon IMF-like rescue packages'. The second approach, 'governing globalisation', involves 'the creation of new institutions to lend structure and direction to the global market-place', complementing the IMF, such as an International Credit Insurance Corporation. (Here we find George Soros, Felix Rohatyn, Henry Kaufman, along with UN circles, Richard Falk, Hazel Henderson and others.) The third approach is more modest and lies *in between* these two positions: a managed approach – for example, involving an earnings insurance for American workers.

At a general level the scope for global reform may be considered as a function of three variables: shifts and divisions within dominant power blocs and interest coalitions, crises, and collective action. The feasibility of alternatives also depends on rifts and divisions among the powers that be. Crisis is an important teacher in history for it is when the status quo cannot be reproduced that alternatives become not merely possible but necessary. This line of thinking is part of the dialectics of disaster (Aronson, 1983). A case in point is the 'Asian crisis' and its spill-over effects, which in the region is perceived as both a threat and an opportunity for democratization.

The new politics involves a paradoxical task. The programme of 'global humanism' is of such momentum and scale that what comes to mind is a grand coalition politics as virtually the only thinkable way in which such global reform could be accomplished. 'Globalization from below' (Falk, 1994) involves the same limitation. The juxtaposition of 'globalization from below' with 'globalization from above' suggests that these are somehow distinct and separate tracks, which creates a false opposition. It is the *combined* impact of all these processes and forms of collective action that, in time, may yield significant change. Collective actions may delegitimize the status quo and introduce alternatives into public discourse, gradually making them part of common sense. Over time the combined effect of divisions within hegemonic coalitions, crises and collective actions may result in a 'new common sense' – in other words, a different hegemony.

The prospects of *quiet encroachment* are, by its nature, subtle, of low visibility also into the future and unpredictable. Quiet encroachment is likely to be a significant factor over time. Politics cannot all be programmatic, controlled or controllable. However, to define the emancipatory character of quiet encroachment, conceptual fine-tuning is necessary as a condition for political finesse.

In conclusion let us consider these collective angles on globalization and ask, which is best capable of delivering collective emancipation or 'just development'? In my view anti-globalization is both analytically wrong and politically counterproductive. The future of alternative globalism lies in global reform. Shaping globalization is a minimum requirement and a necessary, though not a sufficient condition for just development. Quiet encroachment is not to be discounted, but not to be counted on either, for by its nature it is elusive and not programmatic.

References

Ahmed, A.S. and H. Donnan (1994) *Islam, Globalisation and Postmodernity*, London: Routledge.
Al-Azmeh, A. (1993) *Islams and Modernities*, London: Verso.
Angelis, M. de (1998) '2nd Encounter for Humanity and Against Neoliberalism, Spain 1997', *Capital and Class*, 65: 135–57.
Aronson, R. (1983) *The Dialectics of Disaster*, London: Verso.
Banuri, T., Shahruck, R.K. and M. Mahmood (eds) (1997) *Just Development: Beyond Adjustment with a Human Face*, Karachi: Oxford University Press.
Barber, B.J. (1996) *Jihad vs. McWorld*, New York: Ballantine Books.
Bayat, A. (1998) *Street Politics: Poor People's Movements in Iran*, Cairo: American University in Cairo Press.
Beeley, B. (1992) 'Islam as a global political force', in A.G. McGrew and P.G. Lewis et al., *Global Politics*, Cambridge: Polity Press, pp. 293–311.
Berger, J. (1998) 'Against the defeat of the world', *Race and Class*, 40(2/3): 1–4.
Billington, J.H. (1980) *Fire in the Minds of Men: the Origins of the Revolutionary Faith*, New York: Basic Books.
Chin, C.B.N. and J.H. Mittelman (1997) 'Conceptualising resistance to globalisation', *New Political Economy*, 2(1): 25–39.
Castells, M. (1996) *The Information Age: the Rise of the Network Society*, Oxford: Blackwell.
Deacon, B., Hulse, M. and P. Stubbs (1998) *Global Social Policy*, London: Sage.
Durning, A.T. (1993) 'World spending on ads skyrockets', in L.R. Brown, H. Kane and E. Ayres, *Vital Signs 1993–1994*, London: Earthscan/Worldwatch Institute, pp. 80–1.
Ekins, P. (1992) *A New World Order: Grassroots Movements for Global Change*, London: Routledge.
Falk, R. (1994) *On Humane Governance: Towards a New Global Politics*, Cambridge: Polity.
Giddens, A. (1998) *The Third Way: the Renewal of Social Democracy*, Cambridge: Polity Press.
Greider, W. (1997) *One World, Ready or Not: the Manic Logic of Global Capitalism*, New York: Simon & Schuster.
Group of Lisbon (1995) *Limits to Competition*, Cambridge, MA: MIT Press.
Gurtov, M. (1988) *Global Politics in the Human Interest*, Boulder, CO: Lynne Rienner.

Haass, R.N. and R.E. Litan (1998) 'Globalisation and its discontents', *Foreign Affairs*, 77(3): 2–6.

Hegedus, Z. (1989) 'Social movements and social change in self-creative society: new civil initiatives in the international arena', *International Sociology*, 4(1): 19–36.

Huntington, S.P. (1996) *The Clash of Civilizations and the Remaking of World Order.* New York: Simon & Schuster.

Iriye, A. (1997) *Cultural Internationalism and World Order*, Baltimore: Johns Hopkins University Press.

Keane, J. (ed.) (1988) *Civil Society and the State: New European Perspectives*, London: Verso.

Kotkin, J. (1992) *Tribes: How Race, Religion, and Identity Determine Success in the New Global Economy*, New York: Random House.

Küng, H. (1997) *Global Ethics for Global Politics and Economics*, Oxford: Oxford University Press.

Lipietz, A. (1995) *Green Hopes: the Future of Political Ecology*, Cambridge: Polity Press.

Lynch, C. (1998) 'Social movements and the problem of globalisation', *Alternatives*, 23(2): 149–74.

Mander, J. and E. Goldsmith (eds) (1996) *The Case Against the Global Economy and for a Turn Toward the Local*, San Francisco: Sierra Club.

Mann, M. (1986) *The Sources of Social Power*, Cambridge: Cambridge University Press.

Massey, D. (1993) 'Power-geometry and a progressive sense of place', in J. Bird, B. Curtis, T. Putnam, G. Robertson and L. Tichner (eds), *Mapping the Futures: Local Cultures, Global Change*, London: Routledge, pp. 59–69.

Mittelman, J.H. (1996) 'The dynamics of globalisation', in idem (ed.), *Globalisation: Critical Reflections*, Boulder, CO: Lynne Rienner, pp. 1–20.

Mulgan, G. (1998) *Connexity*, rev. edn, London: Vintage.

Nederveen Pieterse, J. (1989) *Empire and Emancipation*, New York: Praeger.

Nederveen Pieterse, J. (1994) 'Delinking or globalisation?', *Economic and Political Weekly*, 29(5): 239–42.

Nederveen Pieterse, J. (1995) 'Globalisation as hybridization', in M. Featherstone, S. Lash and R. Robertson (eds), *Global Modernities*. London: Sage, pp. 45–68.

Nederveen Pieterse, J. (1997a) 'Globalisation and emancipation: from local empowerment to global reform', *New Political Economy*, 2(1): 79–92.

Nederveen Pieterse, J. (1997b) 'Going global: futures of capitalism', *Development and Change*, 28(2): 367–82.

Nederveen Pieterse, J. (1999) 'Future studies and global futures', in Z. Sardar (ed.), *Rescuing All Our Futures: the Future of Future Studies*, Twickenham/Westport, CT: Adamantine Press/Praeger, pp. 146–62.

Ohmae, K. (1992) *The Borderless World*, London: Collins.

Oommen, T.K. (1998) 'Changing paradigms of development: the evolving participatory society', *Journal of Social and Economic Development*, 1: 35–45.

Portes, A. (1996) 'Transnational communities: their emergence and significance in the contemporary world-system', in R.P. Korzeniewicz and W.C. Smith (eds), *Latin America in the World Economy*, Westport, CT: Greenwood Press, pp. 151–68.

Portes, A. (ed.) (1995) *The Economic Sociology of Immigration*, New York: Russel Sage Foundation.

Ray, L.J. (1993) *Rethinking Social Theory: Emancipation in the Age of Global Social Movements*, London: Sage.

Rupesinghe, K. (1996) *From Civil War to Civil Peace: Multi-track Solutions to Armed Conflict*, London: International Alert.

Sivanandan, A. (1998) 'Globalism and the left', *Race and Class*, 40(2/3): 5–18.

Scholte, J.A. (1998) *The International Monetary Fund and Civil Society: an Underdeveloped Dialogue*, The Hague, Institute of Social Studies, Working Paper no. 272.

Soros, G. (1998) *The Crisis of Global Capitalism*, New York: Public Affairs.

2
Towards a Theory of Global Collective Action and Institutions

Henri Lustiger-Thaler, Louis Maheu and Pierre Hamel

Our intent here is to begin a rethinking of the institution as a global phenomenon for the sociology of social movements. That which we have long understood to be the main function of institutions, for example, normative regulation associated with the spatiality of the city or nation-state, is being re-routed through a growing awareness of the ambivalences contained in systems of human action more and more configured through complex processes of globalization. One result has been a move away from the study of structural features of institutions to a focus on the way institutional actors and new collectivities recognize and acknowledge each other as players in a diversity of social/ cultural practices which are more and more institutionally defined in global terms. Institutionalization, as an agonistic, conflict-laden process, constrains and enables the experience of cultural practices. Hence, it is infinitely more inscribed with meaning than that captured in approaches which point to the routinization of the emergent norm, or in Weber's term, the unfolding of instrumental rationality as the basis for a social relationship. Indeed, with the advent of globalization the institution has become a concept that requires re-theorization. The present chapter is a modest contribution to this overall task.

Historically, the institution as a 'milieu' for collective action was overwhelmingly evident in the movements of the 1960s and in the earlier conflicts which structured the dense period of capitalist industrialization at the turn of the twentieth century. These conflicts were mediated in institutions which prided themselves on their ability to absorb generational, class and national conflicts. After the experience of the 1960s it is understandable that social movement theorists would be drawn towards theorizing the 'extra-institutional', where conflict appears to be less mediated (Offe, 1987). More recently, from a different purview, but still in the general realm of the 'extra-institutional', attention has been focused on the spectral world of fundamentalist and right-wing militia movements (Castells, 1996). In both cases, these actions can be said to bypass the regulations of the nation-state, indeed affronting it through posing issues of social and political control, as was demonstrated in the events of Seattle 1999.

But, how do movements, such as were present in Seattle, fare when addressing contentious issues, particularly concerning labour, from a global perspective? Can they represent, for our times, at least a semblance of what the working classes represented for an earlier modernity (Eder, 1993; Pakulski, 1995; Roth, 1996)? There are some features of contemporary collective action that could positively substantiate this – such as the feminist, ecological, anti-war, gay and lesbian movements, amongst others. But these movements are awash in ambivalences which fracture their overall global effect. This fragmentation has opened the door to important questions about how we have come to frame the symbolic, cultural and social experience of the West, and the kinds of historical subjectivities that are included and excluded, exposing globalization itself to the pitfalls of a modernist/postmodernist Western discourse. However, in spite of this, new social movements do suggest for at least the 'global West' a different social epoch in terms of the centrality of new conflicts in the constitution of late-modern societies. Social movements are indications of the stratificational layering of modern forms of collective action in relation to new and emerging arenas of conflict (Maheu, 1995).

From the institutional traditions of the nation-state to global non-correspondence

What is striking in the traditional approach to institutionalization is the immediacy with which actors develop relations of correspondence to systems of collective action. From the perspective of the institution, negotiating these relations is clearly a valued good, to the extent that struggles and claims are addressed through a variety of politico-institutional arrangements. Historical class settlements and their compromises have been the extant result of this process. It has also produced the epistemological framework for the neocorporatist debates of the 1970s. While these enframings have largely structured our understanding of the central conflict between capital and labour, the traditional paradigm has not been absent from more recent social movement approaches.

Its residual has been alive and well in analyses of popular movements of the 1960s. The traditional approach to institutionalization has also reappeared in analyses of the new social movements, in the form of the extra-institutional framing of action as a way to explain resistances against imposed identities. These have been attempts to explain cultural identities – their insider and outsider statuses – through a self-defining, self-limiting politics poised against traditional identities, particularly class/national/ethnic forms of identification.

The traditional thesis is premised upon three deeply ingrained epistemological elements of institutionalization, all couched within an expansive discourse of the nation-state:

1. There is an always ongoing adjustment between a precarious state of social relations and the regulation of ongoing social conflicts. This unfolds in a context where social relations develop through a filtering-down process which stresses normalization. This understanding of institutionalization presages the naming of a site, in the time/space relations of actors, harbouring important implications for social settlements that take the form of social and political institutions. Social institutions, in this regard, weave into the fabric of a national civil society its norms, authorities and hierarchies. They thus have an inherently conservative character, as they lay the groundwork for national culture.

2. According to the traditional thesis, institutions are in continuous if liminal processes of transcription in so far as they are basically routinized conflict-laden social relations. The traditional paradigm, in this perspective, harbours within its bosom an exchange of social relations that are then inscribed within an ensemble of politico-institutional systems. These 'pick up' the residue of conflict *post de facto*. This has pointed to the conventionalization of social action. It also aligns actors with systems of action, creating yet another basis for social correspondence from city to region to nation-state. This correspondence is by nature imperfect since challenges to stability are channelled through constant efforts to return to homeostatic relations of equilibrium, the backbone of the nation.

3. The 'emancipatory' promise, or emphasis placed on extra-institutional dimensions of collective action, do not escape this master-framework. On the contrary. The traditional paradigm represents a binary explanation of social processes. What is mediated by definition engenders a logic of resistance contained in the non-mediated, as an object of reification, in this case the nation. The non-mediated is there-

fore a never-ending source of chaotic processes which emerge as a basis for restructuring the realm of the mediated, *ergo* defining the boundaries of the interior/exterior borders of regions, sites, locales.

This perspective of institutionalization informs a wide range of studies devoted to social movement analyses and the process of institutionalization. It is inspired by the Weberian residual of rationalization and its attendant bureaucratic forms of rationality which are largely national. It puts into action a process of political regulation undergirding the relations of social movements to the state. But, there is a stirring in the current literature on globalization which tells us that the traditional paradigm may have exhausted itself as an explanation for collective action as well as providing an adequate basis for a theory of the state. The clearest indication of this is what we call a 'partial institutionalization' explanation, one that is very popular in the current literature.

The partial institutionalization approach differs from the paradigm just described above. It defines a field of action that takes into account the problem of social correspondence between actors and systems of action in late-modernity and problematizes it within certain limits. Social movements, from this view, are actors that challenge the symbolic order as a cultural practice. They are only partially institutionalized, as opposed to a 'traditional' explanation of entry prerequisites into a social relationship. This thesis, we argue, is well documented by studies that track the way in which movements deal with political opportunity structures, often national, as they channel their protest actions through varying forms of contentious politics. Yet, though it is describing the flux of social relations in the face of institutions, the partial institutionalization thesis offers no theoretical insight towards explaining this process. This perspective, and one only has to think about political opportunity perspectives, has not produced a convincing analysis of the relational process that exists between movements and institutions, except to posit various degrees of sociopolitical absorption and resistance.

Therefore the partial institutionalization approach sees areas of social correspondence between actors and institutions, and these become the basis for strategic relations with institutional norms, authorities, and so on. But does this approach capture the full complexity of relations between actors and systems of action outside the construct of national boundaries? What of the problem of non-correspondence in contemporary social relations, that the process of globalization so readily brings to the fore? In our view, the partial institutionalization thesis is but an indicator, though a powerful one, of the decline of the traditional paradigm as an explanation of late-modern transformations. How, then, do we intervene in the impasse of theory, wherein collective action and institutionalization are still seen through the prism of sequential phases or cumulative linkages, rather than as embedded phenomena that are more and more premised on informational flows and the global fragmentation of collective action?

Collective action is situated today at the junction of rupture and transformation, processes that are not at all typical of pre-modern or what we have come to associate with modern forms of transformation. Institutionalization within this junction is determined by social forces that are more and more relational and global. For these reasons, we can no longer conceive of institutions as instituted micro-sociological phenomena (*institué*), or even an established order of things (Foucault, 1976). Nor can we look at the institution as an instituting (*instituant*), interactionist, performative feature of the actor (Lourau, 1970), if the latter is theoretically set adrift from the more relational/structural characteristics of action and its situational embeddedness in a global context.

It is important to maintain a differentiation between interactionist and institutional conceptions of social change in this regard. The institution is not the product of a pure unilateral voluntarism of a collective actor. It harbours more than intersubjective relations. Nor is the instituted social order a closed entity, regimented to the point where all renewal, rupture and transformation are located on the outside in the extra-institutional (Maheu and Toulouse, 1993). Bourdieu's insight on relational phenomena is of some importance here. The milieus of institutions and institutionalization are captured by his insistence on the deeply sociological character of relations: 'what exists in the world are relations – not interactions between agents or the inter subjective ties between individuals' (Bourdieu, 1993: 59). Nowhere is this more true than in a consideration of global processes of collective action.

In multiple ways, and propelled forward by massive transformations in global/local time and corresponding informational systems, actors and institutions remain in conflict and submerged in tensions not caught by the traditional paradigm, the partial institutionalization or the interactionist perspectives. All are part and parcel of the discourse of the nation. Institutions contain multiple layering of social ambivalences which suggest several problems for theory.

Firstly, institutions in late-modernity are deconstructing – that is, they are more fragile and fragmented than we have recognized them to be, suggesting increasing levels of non-correspondence and more and more subject to global tensions. Secondly, this devolving character scatters their legitimacy into a cultural field that is itself under enormous pressures for social and political accountability. And thirdly, the oppositional collective actions that emerge from this are ultimately struggling less with alliances, or 'sets of tactical coherences', than with combating the hegemony of the social, cultural and/or politically reconstituted norm, supported by an institutional process of social containment. It is for this reason that institutionalization in late-modernity is concomitant with the recurring weakness in the norm rather than its stabilization as in the old paradigm. It is this weakness, or rather the sense of global chaos (Jessop, 2000) that operates around it, which informs our discussion of social exclusion later in this chapter.

How can we think about the institution as a phenomenon that enframes structural relations of power, indeed the state, while also emerging as a playing field for identity and social experiences around the sense of a global consciousness, again summoning the recent collective action which took place in the protests which occurred in Seattle 1999? The latter demonstrated that institutions contain collective action, but do not capture it. In a global context, the container function of institutions exemplified by the nation-state no longer holds the explanatory power it once did for collective action theories.

In the pages that follow we argue that it is necessary to move beyond the container function. We will also be taking a critical distance to approaches that portray institutional actors engaged in a self-production process. Analyses of the social containment function of institutions must be supplemented with the problematization of the institution as an experiential/relational field *in the first instance* and one that marks globalization, and its incurring consciousness as a starting point for new theories in collective action. One of the features of institutions in late-modernity is that they are flexible post-Fordist-like constructs. Institutionalization signifies a process through which social movements traverse milieus ridden with ambivalences, agonistic and conflictual relations as experiential entry points in the construction of a conflict.

Globalization, reflexivity and authenticity: an institutional double movement

The notion of institutionalization that we are suggesting must be rethought in light of multiple Western modernities (Nederveen Pieterse, 1992), and the certainty of uncertain futures in global patterns of interactions (Adams, 1994). These processes have become so complex that chaos theory has been invoked to explain them (Buell, 1994). From this view, new forms of institutionalization, both locally and globally, must be seen as part of the problem of transforming social relations, developed in contexts largely stripped of traditional mechanisms of support (Beck, 1992; Giddens, 1991). Ulrich Beck has framed this dilemma in a provocative way. He has argued that we are in need of 'ideas and theories that will allow us to conceive the new, which is rolling over us in a new way, and allow us to live and act within it' (1992: 12).

Our point of departure is that institutions are increasingly at the forefront of the 'new' in the sense that they are implicated in the very construction of action rather than what the old paradigm understood as its mediational input/output zones. Institutions are points of entry for the construction of personal and social experiences. They have emerged, from a long history of actional interfaces, as meaningful human activities at the very foundations of late-modern collective action. Their internal activity requires a new language of explanation. The internal characteristics of the institution can be explained by the following three critical factors of structuration. These represent the pillars of our argument about the transformed nature of late-modernity:

- the overt globalization of social action frames;
- reflexive forms of action embedded within informational networks;
- how actors relationally construct authenticity as part of the subjective experience of late-modernity.

Each of these factors of structuration contains an institutional double movement. This expresses itself through the relationship between the containment of action (social correspondence) on the one side (locally/nationally embedded actions), and the 'non-correspondence' between actors and systems on the other (global consciousness and actions). Non-correspondence suggests a disenfranchisement between the composite personal, political and cultural experiences of the actor and the ability of the institution to fully contain conflictual relations that emerge from these phenomena. *As such, non-correspondence is at the basis of institutional crises and transformations as well as being at the very basis from which institutions serve as experiential entry points for collective action.* It engenders a mode of conflict where institutions offer a milieu for re-embodying social entities, indeed creating fields, through relational experiences more and more premised upon global modes of thought and action.

Globalization

Globalization is central to the relational form of the late-modern institution. This is heightened by the premise that nowadays collective action occurs more systematically than ever at a distance, and at a greater speed, fed by an acceleration of history. Digital modes of communication and rapid transport all entail the 'act of acting' from a distance. These are cultural reconfigurations that have a massive transformative effect on ongoing institutional mechanisms. Along with dramatically altered global and informational flows, capital flows and class relations, these processes short-circuit nations, localities and regional frontiers. New global conditions of action, and the accompanying construction of personal and social experiences they entail, disrupt traditional institutional arrangements. Indeed, we might argue that from a local perspective, the containment function of institutions regarding the construction of action is under severe duress. The lag between action and structure plays itself out here as a developmental lag in the political economy of local and global institutions. This is occurring not only in the collapse of political regulation within nation-states as regards trans-nationalised collective action (Tarrow, 1994), but also in mixed results of NGOs as well as in the demise of formal global institutions such as the UN.

Here, too, institutions and institutional frames of action are constructed as a double movement: the containment function of institutions, or the lack of, as exemplified by a non-correspondence between actors and systems, is dialectically embedded with institutional entry points reconfiguring global moments and their local spaces. As Roland Robertson (1992) has pointed out, the phenomenon of globalization is not just about 'the objectiveness of increasing connectedness' but is also about 'subjective and cultural matters'. Robertson (1995) furthers his analysis by suggesting that the dichotomy of the local and the global is largely a false one. Locality can be seen as an aspect of globalization. Robertson offers the term 'glocalization' to refer to the subjectivity of global discourse. As John Eade (1996) suggests in reference to Robertson's work, 'glocalisation refers, in the subjective and personal sphere, to the construction and invention of diverse localities through global flows of ideas and information' (1996: 4). The global effect on the modern institution is clearly of such a countenance. Institutions both embed and disembed action through the creation of global and local spaces, of extended milieus and significant cultural/personal spaces (Durrschmidt, 1997).

The containment function as well as experiential entry point role of institutional arrangements are an important and strategic issue. Because of this double movement, late modern institutions are facing problems of coherence and legitimacy. It should therefore be no surprise if the traditional institutionalization paradigm would point to unmediated social processes, the 'extra-institutional', rather than focus on the relational conflictual terrain where actors and institutions transform the construction of experience and collectivities. As Barbara Adams (1994) has argued, in a context of globalization the construction of experience proceeds through global culture. This takes the form of a personal experience of 'global-izing culture'. The personal experience of global-izing culture involves the networking of citizens, the stretching of agency – the creation of new functional roles that are developed in interaction – to wider social processes that provide direct access to politics.

Adams's point is that the difference between the globalization of social processes, as an historical trend, and the more personal globalizing culture of experiencing, constitutes the current ambivalent framework of global institutional forces. Global-izing culture involves relationships to, and absorption within, locally based institutions. It also points to how institutions are embedded in local spaces and stretched in real time to global relationships operated from a distance.

Institutions regulate the personal experience of global culture as well as serving as entry points for experiencing the stretch (from the local to the global) through the creation of subject positions and new social relations. The coupling of local forces with larger trans-nationalized social issues and political spaces through informationalization pry open yet new structural opportunities for collective action and experience building. One could certainly argue that within the European community, local, regional and national institutions were at times strengthened by legal and political opportunities in the new European politico-institutional setting (Gaspard, 1995). The dynamic of social struggles concerning ecological issues, as well as women's issues, has been strengthened by the global/local axis.

Reflexivity and informational networks

Anthony Giddens (1991) makes a convincing argument when he suggests that action thrives on knowledge spinoffs. Actors exist in complex systems that consume, produce and stock diverse forms of knowledge. These agents cannot inscribe themselves in an action without interpreting and utilizing diverse forms of knowledge in their interactions with abstract systems. This assumes a certain contextualizing of 'knowledge as action'. But, this is also a form of knowledge that repeats and modifies itself as it constructs social reality. Actors utilize more and more complex knowledge and action systems in late-modernity. In fact, they operate as symbolic analysts (Reich, 1991). This, of course, is a theme in the recursivity of knowledge, an action that folds back on itself in the refurbishing of the symbolic and social order. What distinguishes reflexivity in late-modernity is the tempo, accessibility and acceleration of action. This trend, steered as well by the informational collapse of time and space, cultural globalization, has opened us up to multiple modernities within the West and their multicultural histories, through the interpenetration of the First, Second and Third Worlds.

Yet, the process of reflexivity remains empty without a consideration of the informationalization of action frames themselves. This latter perspective owes much to the work of David Lyon (1988) and Manuel Castells (1989; 1996). Castells has argued that informationalization and economic globalization are at the basis of a new societal form where never before have such 'fundamental macro-structural forces operated independently from society's values and conflicts' (1996: 1). We would extend this insight by pointing to the problem of institutionalization as a part of the global abstraction of relations of domination, another indication of the non-correspondence between actors and systems of action. Informational networking injects new forms of relational mediations between actors and institutions, creating a temporal impasse, an ambivalence, a lag between problems of structure and action. In sum, institutions are confronted by the reflexivity of actors, their own internal reflexivity and expanded informational networks, the former and latter structured by a double movement between the containment of action and experiential reflexivity.

If we were to extend this line of reasoning, institutions in late-modernity are confronted with their own internal reflexivity as a result of new knowledge bases. These systems of knowledge fix and mediate conditions and resources of action by their own recursiveness. Part of the double movement is therefore an enabling of reflexive symbolic systems of knowledge to expand and further transform internal structures, hence the social reality that influences and frames collective action.

On the one hand, institutions reflexively contain action and actors, complex symbols and norms, as well as sophisticated role sets and organizations through their container function as symbolic and normative markers for social relations. But, on the other hand, the subject is structured through, and around, an encoded 'relationality' that is experiential to its very core. So much so that subject-positions themselves are little more than experientially-coded institutional roles. Institutions are now more than ever dependent on the absorption of the external reflexivity and diversity of agents that frequent, and in their myriad ways, influence, subvert and contest them. At this level of analysis, institutions in late-modernity are ambivalent milieus, sites that actors have no choice but to engage with and actively modify as points of social entry.

Authenticity and the subject

Personal and social experiences are at the centre of a storm moving through institutions. The way they 'roll over' the authority of convention and tradition is however an open question, in view of tradition-maintenance, tradition-construction and tradition-reordering (Heelas, Lash and Morris, 1996). Late-modernity is largely about the encoding of experiences that problematize the local and the regional as shifting moments within the global. Western, eastern, northern and southern cultural divisions, so long ensconced in their separate narrative histories, have returned to us as global. The spatio-cultural movement of experiences has thus become one of the structural hallmarks of a critical late-modern agency. Experiencing, as a structural trait, cannot be disassociated from the stakes of late-modernity around issues of reflexivity and global/informationalization processes. Here, the problem of late-modernity presents itself as a confrontation between rationalization and subjectivation, creating yet another basis for speculating on the authenticity of the subject.

Experiencing, as a structural trait, has much in common with Alain Touraine's recent inquiries in *The Critique of Modernity*. For Touraine (1992b), modernity is a conflictual movement of historicity supported through, but never completely mastered by, the difficult articulation of subjectivation and rationality. But it is also about passion, creativity and rupture based upon an affirmation of subjectivity that produces its identity, and finally a historicity that socially reproduces itself. Charles Taylor (1989) places emphasis upon this very element of late-modernity. To position oneself, in the world, from the standpoint of the social production of self and receive knowledge of one's difference through social conflict, is part of the construction of a culture of authenticity, a culture of the late-modern subject.

Through the encoding of experience, institutions demonstrate yet another moment of their immanence or double movement. Institutions hinder the act of experiencing and in the same instance facilitate the encoding of experience. In one sense, through the availability of resources, in their many forms of communications and information, and the ensemble of social roles, institutions are markers and containers for experiential practices. *What is significant is their capacity to normatively and politically regulate the production of experience.* Our argument is that personal and social experiences cannot but traverse systems of action and their constitutive institutions. From this point of view, social, political, cultural or global institutions are a product, an outcome, filled with experiences that eventually become channelled and conventionalized.

But at the same time, the institution is a field, a social space, an ensemble of systems of action, through which conventions and traditions are contested by the encoding of experience which recursively structure the milieu of the institution. In this regard, institutions and experiencing are not only socially engaged, but entangled: the institution is the point of social entry into a network of social relations through the construction of agency and collective action in search of an identity. Politics, the recognition of human rights, the sociocultural horizon of democracy and the dialectical tension between subjectivation and rationality cannot be conceived of without having institutions as points of entry into social relations. These together produce a culture of authenticity and its vast quarters of experiential knowledge.

We are therefore interested in thinking about experience as a social and institutional construction, a global practice, an intersecting flow of subject-centred entities as opposed to its encasement in an identity, result of conflict or affirmation within a given institution. To examine experience is therefore to look at the conditions of its relational production, that which makes it visible within the institution. The philosopher Joan Scott has been instructive here: 'it is not individuals who have experiences, but subjects who are constituted through experience' (Scott, 1994). Experience in this sense becomes not the origin of our explanations, about late-modern institutions, but rather that which we seek to explain; that which we understand to be immanent to the process of institutionalization.

In a summation of this section, we would argue that the three critical dimensions of reflexivity/informationalization, globalization and authenticity are battlefields in the life of the institution, from a collective action perspective. They are equally components for rethinking state theory, as they are part and parcel of the global configuration of agency and its effects upon the state. Indeed, the state is present throughout these three processes as it itself is reconfigured in regional, national and local institutional milieus.

These transformations represent what we believe Ulrich Beck refers to as the new 'that is rolling over us in a new way' (1992: 12). Personal and social experiences traverse and transform, in one and the same instance, systems of action and their constitutive institutions. The institution is hence a relational field of informational flows, subjectivities and local–global entangled spaces, a complex system of action. These, paradoxically, emerge from a system that both hinders and is transformed by its own agency so well captured by the relational critique (Emirbayer and Goodwin, 1994; Bourdieu, 1993; Abbott, 1988; Elias, 1978). Hence, the world of collective action is not necessarily premised on coherent entities, but rather on a sequencing of the attributes of entities that are only rendered actionable in the context of other entities (Abbott, 1988). The primary unit of analysis is the changing roles that emerge in a transaction rather than the constituent element themselves (Emirbayer and Goodwin, 1994), hence the importance of the social containment function of the institution and the non-correspondence of actors and systems. These act less in the classical Hegelian dialectical understanding than as a frictional conflict-laden field of relational phases sustaining institutional entry points for the construction of experience and society. The starting point for theory must therefore be an analysis of the experience of changing subject-positions which emerge from a shift in collective action frames within the institution. These are premised on reflexive/informational, global and subject-centred frames of reference. Institutions have not become less rigid, but more flexible in the relational possibilities they offer actors.

Contestation in this new paradigm occurs when institutions serve as entry points for the conflictual construction of identities and collectivities, where a contradiction emerges between a space of flows within the informational society and a space of meaning (Castells, 1996), or the experience of meaning construction related to identity- and community-building issues in a localized frame of reference. Contradictions that express themselves in experiential terms become functional when entities are influenced by the context of other entities. This takes place in terms of collective conflictual refusals and new forms of regulation: the relational effects of the institutional double movement structuring the reflexive, global and subjective moment. Collective action is therefore always confronted by a rapid modification of its own epistemological content and scale of interaction.

Social exclusion: global non-correspondence and global consciousness

It is important to restate that the view of institutionalization put forward in this chapter does not rest on the idea of the institution as a marker at the end of a cyclical social movement process, but rather as a relational combination of contexts or fields of action that are taking on global proportions from the perspective of consciousness. The institution, therefore, is not solely the point of a conventionalization of social action, as in the life-cycle approach, but rather a constitutive set of social circumstances which produce themselves through the effects of knowledge and action. It is therefore critical to theorize the way institutions relate to forces of domination and exploitation, in particular the problem of relative deprivation as an exclusionary mode of production. How does the institution reflect the state as a series of authorities?

Relative deprivation as a model of interaction connotes a system of societal stratification that forms the basis for social exclusion. Social exclusion in civil society was thus defined as the furthest horizon of exploitation stemming from class conflict and compromise. Relative deprivation has also referred to the realm of the political. We have indeed moved from a theory of relative deprivation based on a poverty of resources, to a political theory of society where the relationship between opportunity, contention and democracy becomes a defining feature of modernity. There is another way, however, that can help us reframe the issue of relative deprivation and stratification, one that focuses on an in-depth dimension of experiencing and community-building.

In late-modern societies there is a dimension of stratification that cannot be disassociated from the self, the conflictual construction of community (Lustiger-Thaler, 1994) and global issues of subjectivity. The modern role of the institution is central to this. Institutionalization is a set of relations that provoke both personalized and generalized features of subjectivity. Here, the more familiar terminologies of relative deprivation, in their neo-marxist and post-marxist frames of reference, are of little help. In a late-modern model of relative deprivation, institutional stratification functions as a basis for exclusion around the problem of embodied/disembodied subjectivity and embeddedness within meaningful spaces and global informational flows of action. This embodiment–disembodiment takes place through the construction of subjects and collectivities.

Three institutional dimensions of subjectivity can be considered here. Each in turn is the basis for a form of exclusion as they also connote non-correspondences between actors and systems. In other words they, too, contain a double movement. These are essentially global/ reflexive/informational conditions, political questions for a late-modern theory of state and society.

1. Under what conditions do subjects, individual as well as collective, make choices?
2. How do these subjects negotiate milieus of belonging? This raises the problem of communities in transition, stretching from localities to extended global milieus.
3. What processes socially embed the need to be recognized as subjects and create a history of the subject, or community of subjects, through culturally shared global consciousness?

The problem of choosing, as a society or community, is central to the transformed status of late-modern institutional arrangements. There has been a retreat from collective actions rooted in the traditional division of labour and its identity-based features to a late-modern version where groups based on factors such as region, age, sex or health status are present throughout the many rationales of institutions. Increased attention to the social limits of growth – environmental devastation – has further pushed the moral envelope under which we make choices and the attendant institutional structures from which they function. The problem of choice has therefore placed the individual in a framework of deliberation that personalizes as well as collectivizes the act of choosing. Institutionalization is thus a process in which choice is deliberated in the first instance – that is, as an entry point about the experience of being able to choose. The problem of choice cannot be disassociated from the context of reflexive/informational networks, globalization as extended milieus and authenticity as an individual-collective subject's relation to history.

Belonging refers to the ability of an individual or collective to state one's preferences as a citizen and act upon it. The act of belonging, from an institutional perspective, collapses the separate logics of individuality and collectivity through problematizing community, rendering one's place in the associative society an ongoing struggle between personal and collective deliberations – that is, what is personal space, collective space, in the construction of a social conflict (Roseneil, 1996). And finally, recognition underlines that embodied subjectivity, both personal and collective, is only possible within institutional arrangements that operate on the principle of reciprocity. This would mean that institutionalization is necessarily embedded in local civil societies, configured around personal and collective experiences and embedded within global informational networks, which in their own course ignite conflict and relational non-correspondence between actors and systems. Nowadays, relative deprivation points to the matrix of an exclusionary process which denies reflexivity, access to the informationalization of action frames and subjective-collective authenticity through the non-correspondence between actors and systems of action.

Part of our definition of social exclusion can be understood as the stratificational counterpart of what Marc Augé (1996) has called *les non-lieux*, or non-places, that is, social locations that constrain the experiential conditions for choosing, belonging and recognition. These are social locations that are constructed from and for the experience of social transit. For Augé, the anthropological notion of *lieu* or place is where one produces identity, social relationships and history/memory. The non-place is a transitional moment where the experiential conditions of individual and collective subjectivity are weak, disembodied, scattered.

For our purposes, the non-place gains expression within the institution as the residue of non-correspondences between actors and systems. And, this is not only a question of identity constraints, as in the problem of authenticity, but of limited access to reflexive/informational and global knowledge and action networks as a form of relative deprivation. The ontological framing of social exclusion that we are offering is therefore dependent on the social status of experiencing. This leads us some way from a traditional ontology of conflictual social relations, to one of institutionally based exclusion that incorporates the personal and collective. Exclusion is more than ever part of the institutional universe, of its hierarchical structure, individually and collectively experienced in the anonymity of a non-place.

In the final analysis, institutions are interpolated structures. They can disengage the symbolic, ideological as well as political basis for an experience by siting it in limbo-like locations of action, temporary non-places. In a more general sense, institutions in late-modernity can keep actors at a distance from the social conditions necessary in the construction of an experience, about a subject-position. If experience is a social construct, and not a naturalized condition, it has an intense relationship to action, and social change. Welfare-dependent individuals struggling to define their subject-position, as a way to construct the autonomy of a sociopolitical experience, are an example of this deeply ambivalent and paradoxical situation, where experience has been deeply inscribed by what has already been rejected by the norm. The non-place strategically lacks a grounding from which to build anything other than the experience of transit or unstable identities, solidary contractuality, or social incoherence.

Social exclusion is part of a strategy of the denial of the subject. This offers a very different notion of how resistance takes place. Institutionalization, as a relational process, brings to the foreground issues of choosing, belonging and recognition. All are central to institutional life. All collective actors are involved in their pursuit. The institution therefore faces challenges to its stratificational hierarchy through its changing structure of exclusions and the relational conflicts that emerge from them. But social exclusion also has another effect. Instead of empowerment through protest and resistance, instead of the organic solidarity of civil society, we have the creation of the 'excluded society' as a functional entity. Here, contentious acts, rather than contentious politics, occur through practices of resistance in everyday life, making for a scattered, segmented and ambivalent relation to a more fully coherent model of collective action and theory of the state. The excluded society emerges in the 'hidden transcripts' of actors and 'the weapons of the weak', to which observers such as James C. Scott (1990) and Bill Jordan (1994) have drawn our attention.

What conclusions can be drawn from this still early reading of the nature of the late-modern institution and its exclusionary processes and milieus in a process of globalization? The first is that an understanding of modern processes of institutionalization is unavoidably central to the study of contemporary social movements. It should also be clear that relative deprivation, the foundation for exclusionary practices, is itself relative to the societal type and institutional form in which it exists and the level of knowledge and power it seeks to explain. Reconceptualizing relative deprivation allows us to think differently about the social structures of institutions, their stakes and probable futures. In a context of late-modernity, relative deprivation must also refer to those deprived of the experiential possibilities of action, as they are socially secluded in non-places.

The strategic organization against social exclusion in a late-modern context must therefore comprise a recognition of the institution as a place of transformation, infinitely wrapped in a web of human possibilities and destinies. To accord the institution any less of a presence in our theoretical thought, and our thinking about social movements, is to ignore one of the critical challenges in contemporary deliberations about the future of global collective action.

References

Abbott, A. (1988) 'Transcending general linear reality', *Sociological Theory*, 6, pp. 169–86.

Adams, B. (1994) 'Running out of time', in M. Redclift and T. Kenton (eds), *Social Theory and the Global Environment*, London: Routledge, pp. 92–112.

Augé, M. (1996) *Non-places: Towards an Anthropology of Super-modernity*, London: Verso.

Beck, U. (1992) *Risk Society: Towards a New Modernity*, London: Sage.

Bhabha, H. (1994) *The Location of Culture*, London: Routledge.

Boggs, C. (1986) *Social Movements and Political Power*, Philadelphia: Temple University Press.

Bourdieu, P. (1984) *Distinction: a Social Critique of the Judgement of Taste*, Cambridge, Mass.: Harvard University Press.

Bourdieu, P. et al. (1993) *La misère du monde*, Paris: Seuil.

Buell, F. (1994) *National Culture and the Global System*, Baltimore: The Johns Hopkins University Press.

Castells, M. (1996) 'Insurgency Movements: the Zapatistas and American Militias', paper presentation, *Globalization and Collective Action Conference*, University of California at Santa Cruz, 17 May.

Castells, M. (1989) *The Informational City*, London: Blackwell.

Cohen, J. and A. Arato (1992) *Political Theory and Civil Society*, Boston, MA: MIT Press.

Cohen, J. (1985) 'Strategy or identity: new theoretical paradigms and contemporary social movements', *Social Research*, 52(4): 663–716.

Dalton, R. and K. Manfred (eds) (1990) *Challenging the Political Order*, New York: Oxford University Press.

Durrschmidt, J. (1997) 'The delinking of locale and milieux: on the situatedness of extended milieux in a global environment', in J. Eade (ed.), *Living the Global City*, London: Routledge, pp. 32–47.

Eade, J. (1997) 'Reconstructing places', in J. Eade (ed.), *Living the Global City*, London: Routledge, pp. 94–104.

Eder, K. (1993) *The New Politics of Class: Social Movements and Cultural Dynamics in Advanced Societies*, London: Sage.

Elias, N. (1978) *The Civilizing Process*, New York: Urizen Books.

Emirbayer, M. and J. Goodwin (1994) 'Network analysis, culture and the problem of agency', *American Journal of Sociology*, 99, pp. 1411–53.

Foucault, M. (1976) 'Two lectures', in C. Gorder (ed.), *Power/Knowledge: Selected Interviews and Other Writings by Michel Foucault, 1972–1977*, New York: Pantheon Books.

Gaspard, F. (1995) *La question de l'égalité des chances hommes-femmes clans la contexte de l'Union Européenne*, Montréal: Université de Montréal.

Giddens, A. (1991) *Modernity and Self-Identity*, London: Polity Press.

Gouldner, A. (1979) *The Future of Intellectuals and the Rise of the New Class*, New York: Continuum.

Heelas, P., Lash, S. and P. Morris (eds) (1996) *Detraditionalization*, London: Blackwell.

Jessop, B. (2000) 'Globalization and entrepreneurial cities and the social economy', in P. Hamel, H. Lustiger-Thaler and M. Mayer (eds), *Urban Movements in a Globalising World*, London: Routledge, pp. 81–100.

Lourau, R. (1970) *L'Analyse institutionnelle*, Paris: Éditions de Minuit.

Lustiger-Thaler, H. (1994) 'Community and the contingencies of everyday life', in H. Lustiger-Thaler and V. Talai, *Urban Lives*, Toronto: Oxford University Press of Canada, pp. 20–44.

Lyon, D. (1988) *The Information Society: Issues and Illusions*, Cambridge: Polity Press.

Maheu, L. (1995) 'Introduction', in Louis Maheu (ed.), *Social Class and Social Movements: the Future of Collective Action*, London: Sage, pp. 1–17.

Maheu, L. and J.-M. Toulouse (1993) 'Gestion du social et social en gestation: perspectives d'analyse et principaux enjeux', *Sociologie et sociétés*, 25(1): 7–23.

McAdam, D., Tarrow, S. and C. Tilly, 'To map contentious politics', *Mobilization*, 1(1): 17–34.

Melucci, A. (1980) 'The new social movements', *Social Science Information*, 19(2): 199–226.

Melucci, A. (1985) 'The symbolic challenge of social movements', *Social Research*, 52(4): 789–816.

Neidhardt, F. and D. Rucht (1991) 'The analysis of social movements: the state of the art and some perspectives for further research', in D. Rucht (ed.), *Research on Social Movements: the State of the Art*, Frankfurt/Boulder: Campus/Westview Press, pp. 421–64.

Offe, C. (1984) *Contradictions of the Welfare State*, Cambridge, MA: MIT Press.

Offe, C. (1987) 'Challenging the boundaries of institutional politics: social movements in the sixties', in C. Maier (ed.), *Changing Boundaries of the Political*, Cambridge: Cambridge University Press, pp. 63–105.

Pakulski, J. (1995) 'Social movements and class: the decline of the Marxist paradigm', in L. Maheu (ed.), *Social Class and Social Movements: the Future of Collective Action*, London: Sage, pp. 55–86.

Pieterse Nederveen, J. (1992) *White on Black: Images of Africa and Blacks in Western Popular Culture*, New Haven, CT and London: Yale University Press.

Reich, R. (1991) *The Work of Nations: Preparing Ourselves for 21st Century Capitalism*, New York: A.A. Knapf.

Roberston, R. (1992) *Globalization*, London: Sage.

Roberston, R. (1995) 'Globalization: time – space and homogeneity – heterogeneity', in M. Featherstone, S. Lash and R. Robertson (eds), *Global Modernities*, London: Sage, pp. 62–79.

Roseneil, S. (1996) 'The Personal and the Global', paper presented at the Globalization and Collective Action Conference, University of California at Santa Cruz.

Roth, R. (1996) 'Social Movements and Institutionalization', paper presentation, Cornell University, March.

Rucht, D. (1988) 'Themes, logics and arenas of social movements: structural approaches', in B. Klandermans et al. (ed.), *International Social Movement Research*, vol. 1, *From Structure to Action*, Greenwich, CT: JAI Press, pp. 305–28.

Scott, J.C. (1985) *Domination and the Arts of Resistance*, New Haven: Yale University Press.

Scott, J.W. (1992) 'Experience', in J. Butler and J.W. Scott (eds), *Feminists Theorize the Political*, New York and London: Routledge, pp. 22–40.

Tarrow, S.G. (1994) *Power in Movement*, Cambridge: Cambridge University Press.

Taylor, C. (1989) *Sources of the Self*, Cambridge: Cambridge University Press.

Touraine, A. (1992a) 'Beyond Social Movements?', in M. Featherstone (ed.), *Cultural Theory and Cultural Change*, London: Sage, pp. 125–45.

Touraine, A. (1992b) *Critique de la modernité*, Paris: Fayard.

3
Globalizing Civil Society? Social Movements and the Challenge of Global Politics from Below

*Catherine Eschle**

In recent years, considerable academic attention and diverse political aspirations have focused upon the role of social movements in 'civil society'. Confronted with the collapse of state-led socialism in Eastern Europe and the social democratic consensus in the West, many on the Left have seized upon long-standing traditions of civil society theory and the burgeoning activities of contemporary movements as sources of emancipatory possibilities which are not centred on the state. Liberals have also turned to the concept of civil society as a potential reservoir of richer moral justifications for the new hegemony of the market. Furthermore, as awareness grows of the role of transnational interconnections in shaping current realities, an argument is emerging that civil society is global in scope, or that social movements should strive to make it so. Indeed, the last few years have seen a proliferation of literature on 'global civil society', particularly within the discipline of International Relations (IR).

Although they diverge significantly on the details, IR theorists writing about global civil society (such as Martin Shaw, Ronnie Lipschutz, Richard Falk and Laura Macdonald) are concerned with several broadly similar themes.[1] They share an analytical concern to move beyond approaches in IR which emphasize the overwhelming and unchanging power and dominance of states in global politics. Drawing on theories of globalization, advocates of global civil society argue that states are increasingly circumscribed by transnational economic forces and that new forms of social intervention and popular mobilization are emerging. They also share a belief in the urgent need to develop modes of governance and/or forms of participation in global politics which are not channelled through states, may supplement states, or even challenge their hegemony. Finally, their work focuses particularly on the actual and potential role in global politics of non-state actors, including non-governmental organizations (NGOs) and social movements.

There is little doubt that the notion of a global civil society represents a significant innovation within IR and that it carries inspirational appeal for theorists, practitioners and movement activists. However, in this chapter I will argue that it has serious limitations as a description of and strategy for social movement activism. It will become clear that the concept has been used in contradictory ways and is somewhat poorly grounded in existing theoretical traditions. However, this is not the central reason why we should treat it with scepticism. More significantly, there are deep-seated problems with the notion of civil society itself and with the possibility of stretching it to encompass global politics. The chapter engages particularly with 'postmarxist' theories of civil society and global civil society, which present a mode of analysis and describe a sphere of social movement politics that purports to be both anti-statist and anti-capitalist. Although I am broadly in sympathy with postmarxist analytical and normative goals, it seems to me that the vision of civil society as a sphere of oppositional emancipatory movement politics significantly misrepresents social movement activity and offers an unrealistic, even counterproductive, political project – particularly on a global scale.

The chapter is divided into four parts. I begin with a brief discussion of the divergent traditions of thought on civil society before pointing to the distinctive aspects of contemporary revivals, including the emergence of a postmarxist perspective and an emphasis upon the role of social movements. In the second part, I examine globalized versions of the concept, attempting to clarify the ways in which they reflect and depart from the themes in the civil society literature more generally, and delineating a postmarxist version which foregrounds global social movement activity. In the third part, I put forward the argument that the notion of global civil society is an analytical and political millstone around postmarxist necks: firstly, in its analysis of globalization; secondly, because of the reification of boundaries and spheres which is a general characteristic of civil society theory; and thirdly, because of a failure to acknowledge and theorize the political implications of the differences which exist globally between movements. The chapter then offers some suggestions for tackling these three issues in ways that move us beyond global civil society whilst retaining the postmarxist commitment to emancipatory social movement politics which are global in scope.

Retrieving civil society

The concept of global civil society is confusing and contested. It can imply very different political projects and very different interpretations of social movement activity. This is partly because the notion of civil society itself is 'rich in historical resonances . . . [and] many levels and layers of meaning, deposited by successive generations of thinkers', often from starkly different normative traditions.[2] The briefest trawl of these traditions reveals, at minimum, hegelian, liberal, marxist, and gramscian variants of civil society. Hegel initiated the sharp analytical distinction between state and civil society, describing the latter as a realm of economic association and civil institutions which constituted a stage in man's ethical trajectory toward the potential moral universalism of the state. In contrast, liberal thinkers insisted that the sphere of economic and civic association should not be subordinated to the state but, rather, regarded as the source of state sovereignty. The accumulation and exchange of property became the normative foundation of civil society, in need of protection from the power of the state and, paradoxically, also in need of its limited mediation. Marx responded that the liberal ideology of civil society functioned to disguise the class interests of the bourgeoisie and the state which acted in its interests. He stripped civil society of its 'epiphenomenal' ethical and institutional aspects to reveal its 'anatomy' as a realm of antagonistic economic struggle. Finally, in an influential modification of Marx's analysis, Gramsci retrieved the ethical and institutional dimensions and characterized civil society as the site of the consensual production of the cultural hegemony of the bourgeoisie – and as the appropriate realm for socialist struggle.[3]

The picture is further complicated by the fact that contemporary theorists have adopted a somewhat 'pick-and-mix' approach to these traditions. What is more, the current revival of the notion of civil society has at least three distinctive characteristics. Firstly, the primary concern of contemporary theorists across the political spectrum has been to strengthen the distinction between civil society and the state. The relevance of liberal teachings about the dangers of state oppression and the need for autonomous societal organization has been strongly reasserted, with more radical advocates of civil society urging the need to develop a 'post-statist politics'.[4]

Secondly, a distinctive 'postmarxist' approach to civil society has emerged. Postmarxists are so-called because they accept the veracity of aspects of Marx's critique of capitalism and his belief in the necessity of collective emancipation from capitalist exploitation, but reject those elements of historical materialist analysis which reduce oppression to economic oppression, social struggle to class struggle, radical change to the transformation of the mode of production, and civil society to market relations.[5] Influenced by New Social Movement theory and the writings of Eastern European dissidents, postmarxists argue for the necessity of a plurality of emancipatory struggles and strategies, the radical democratization of relations throughout society and, often, the revitalization of civil society. Jean Cohen and Andrew Arato's development of the notion of civil society has been particularly influential, differing from other leftist and liberal versions by excluding economic actors and structures. Civil society is envisaged as a sphere of association distinct from the state *and* from capitalist economic life, and as a potential site of challenge to both.[6]

Thirdly, contemporary discussions of civil society are distinguished by their focus upon the role of social movements. Cohen and Arato in particular have argued that: '. . . social movements constitute the dynamic element in processes that might realize the positive potentials of modern civil societies. We also hold that our reconstructed theory of civil society is indispensable to an understanding of the logics, stakes, and potentials of contemporary social movements.'[7]

Cohen and Arato claim that contemporary social movements are characterized by a 'dual logic', concerned both with reshaping cultural norms through everyday life practices and with pressuring and containing the 'big structures' of state and economy. These strategies are 'self-limiting' in that they do not aim at the seizure of centres of power but at the defence, expansion and modernization of civil society, the gateway into both everyday life and political society and the locus of the democratization of both. Civil society is thus both target and terrain of social movement activity.

There is one important continuity between versions of the civil society ideal, old and new. Civil society and the social movements or other actors which inhabit it are assumed to be located within national boundaries. While it is incontrovertible that civil society developed historically in close relationship, with the nation-state, this relationship, or the possibility that it might be changing, is rarely explored. Rather, the state lurks unacknowledged as the container of civil society, reflecting what Jan Aart Scholte describes as the pervasive 'methodological nationalism' within the social sciences: 'This common sense conception holds that all social relations come packaged in national/state/country units that divide the world into neatly distinguishable "societies"'.[8]

Clearly, recent events such as the collapse of communist regimes in Eastern Europe, so central to the revival of interest in civil society, cannot be explained satisfactorily in terms of purely endogenous dynamics. However, while some reference to this fact and to other transnational dynamics can be found in contemporary civil society literature, analysis is usually limited to the comparison of movement activities and to concepts of civil society that remain fundamentally inscribed within national boundaries. Furthermore, although there is some reference in contemporary civil society literature to the notion of globalization, this is not invoked in order to make empirical claims about the scope of civil society or social movement activity but, rather, in order to justify a cosmopolitan ethical stance that posits the existence of a single moral community transcending state boundaries.[9] We are left with a vision of a plurality of civil societies, inhabited by social movements and other civic associations, contained within states but morally and practically connected, empirically comparable, and cosmopolitan in outlook.

Globalizing civil society

The major claim of theories of civil society in IR is that globalization has produced a situation whereby civil society should be seen as actually or potentially *global in scope*. Before I examine the ways in which notions of global civil society relate to the themes explored above, it would be helpful to clarify the way in which globalization, 'a term as ambiguous as it is popular', is being deployed here.[10] It seems to me that debates within IR have been dominated by what could be called a 'political-economic' approach to globalization. This emphasizes that economic, technological and ecological developments have moved beyond the control of individual states, undermining their capacity to provide materially for their citizens, uphold their autonomy and sustain internal political legitimacy. The resulting failures of social provision and protection are likely to give rise to increasing disillusionment and unrest amongst the citizenry, encouraging their mobilization in new and technologically advanced ways which could undermine the state still further.[11] This account of globalization surfaces in some form throughout the global civil society literature, supplemented by the claim that such political-economic processes will require or give rise to a shift in values and cultural forms within global civil society. Although there is general agreement that the development of global civil society is or would be a good thing, opinions vary as to whether the processes of political-economic change that give rise to it should be seen as progressive or problematic. A relatively optimistic liberal assessment can be found in the report of the Commission on Global Governance, *Our Global Neighbourhood*, which welcomes economic liberalization and political interdependence whilst recognizing the need for institutional reform with the co-operation of global civil society.[12] A more critical view is put forward by Falk, who argues that 'functional failures in security, environmental and economic structures' create conditions of crisis and make it a political imperative to bring a nascent global civil society to fruition.[13]

The literature on global civil society also reflects, at least in part, the three key themes of the civil society revival outlined above. The central focus remains the distinction between civil society and the state – or, rather, the distinction between *global* civil society and the state *system*. It is important to recognize, however, that this focus has not been generated directly by the debates within the civil society literature. Rather, it should be understood in the context of the ongoing dispute in IR over the disciplinary hegemony of 'realist' state-centric theory. Realism is predicated on the view that the primary global political reality, and thus the central focus of IR, is the necessarily conflictual nature of interactions between autonomous states in an 'anarchical' system. Normatively, realists have been charged by critical theorists with taking the status quo as a given and with actively working to reproduce its oppressive and violent relationships. Empirically, they have been accused by interdependence theorists of failing to acknowledge the growth of non-state actors and of the co-operative and complex relationships which bind states together.[14] However, while interdependence theorists offer an empirical analysis of what are essentially residual interactions of 'non-state' actors understood in terms of their impact upon states, the notion of global civil society appears to escape state-centrism, to offer a richer contextual analysis of the historic and normative relationship between states and other social institutions, and to hold up the possibility of changing that relationship.

While proponents of global civil society share a common analytical opposition to state-centrism, their political views about the desirable relationship of global civil society to the state system vary widely. It seems to me that two basic political positions can be discerned on this issue. The first is statist in orientation, as exemplified in Martin Shaw's account of global civil society. Primarily concerned with the changing nature of violent conflict in a globalized world, Shaw is not optimistic that new norms of responsibility and intervention can be formulated by civil society actors. He ends up looking to the development of a global state, 'a messy aggregation of increasingly interdependent but still largely autonomous state apparatuses', to be the carrier of a cosmopolitan ethic and to civilise global society.[15] Although the ideal of a *global* state of any description is not one that is widely shared, a similarly statist normative orientation characterizes the liberal UN report *Our Global Neighbourhood* which urges civil society actors to cooperate with states in order to overcome the adjustment difficulties of globalization. From a very different, neo-gramscian, political perspective, Laura Macdonald arrives at a not dissimilar conclusion, arguing that civil society energies should be 'directed at strengthening the abilities of nation states to resist the totalising impact of globalisation'.[16] The opposing post-statist, or even anti-statist, argument can be seen in the work of Richard Falk and Ronnie Lipschutz. These authors claim that global civil society actors should work to undermine rather than strengthen the 'cast-iron grid [of the state system] that exercises a transcendent despotism over reality'.[17] 'It is not 'realistic' or 'sufficient' to invest our energies in the outworn hopes of earlier decades . . . The essence of a political agenda at this historical time is the transformation of the state by non-violent means'.[18]

Both Falk and Lipschutz offer what I would term a postmarxist vision of global civil society. Admittedly, this categorisation of their work is in some ways problematic. Falk, for example, is more usually seen as a radical or cosmopolitan liberal.[19] However, his version of civil society is not conventionally liberal in that it does not include market relations. Furthermore, the postmarxist view which I described above is not restricted to *ex*-marxists; rather, it combines aspects of a marxist-informed critique of capitalism with fundamentally liberal concerns. Lipschutz, on the other hand, draws on a neo-gramscian framework. However, particular confusion surrounds the claim to a gramscian heritage in the literature on global civil society, as in civil society revivalism more generally. For example, Shaw, Macdonald and Lipschutz all claim to be influenced by gramscian ideas yet Shaw does not articulate an anti-capitalist politics in contrast to the other two; Macdonald and Shaw include corporate actors, or their representative organizations within civil society, but Lipschutz excludes them – while still granting a role to individual consumers.[20] It seems to me that a distinction between liberal, gramscian and postmarxist versions of civil society is helpful here, and that the ideas of Lipschutz and Falk constitute a global version of the latter. Both writers are critical of the oppressive aspects of capitalism and describe a realm of global civil society that excludes corporate actors. They understand global civil society to be distinct from both the state system *and* the capitalist economy and to constitute a potential site of challenge to both. Thus Falk urges 'civil society forces' to redouble their efforts to 'expose the abuses arising from the regulatory vacuum' of the global market 'and to resist globalising initiatives (NAFTA, GATT) that neglect the well-being of the most vulnerable social sectors'. Lipschutz stresses that 'it is simultaneous individual resistance to the consumer culture of global capitalism and collective resistance to its short- and long-term effects that give life and power to global civil society'.[21]

Furthermore, these postmarxist theorists of global civil society foreground the role of social movements. Their belief that movements have a significant global dimension is not uncontroversial. As I argued earlier, the foundational assumption of methodological nationalism has encouraged sociologists and political theorists to assume that movements are contained within sharply distinct national units. Conversely, IR theorists have tended to focus on interactions between those units. If we also take into account the influence of realism and empiricism in IR, it should not surprise us that social movements have been dismissed as ineffectual or misguided in the face of *realpolitik* – as in E.H. Carr's famous characterization of the inter-war peace movement as dangerous 'utopianism'[22] – or simply ignored as irrelevant to the discipline. However, empirical evidence of a global dimension to social movement identity, organization and strategy is now well-documented and increasingly incontrovertible. In the most general terms, there has been an astonishing proliferation of groups since the Second World War, organizing around a growing number of issues seen as actually or potentially global in scope. Many movement organizations now routinely tap into and target intergovernmental institutions, conferences and law, and are embedded within a proliferating number of transnational organizational frameworks. Movement membership is drawn from increasingly dispersed geographical locations, encouraging the extensive use of new forms of communications technology which enable simultaneous action in diverse places.[23]

The postmarxist account of global civil society emphasizes the quantity and political significance of this global activism and the causal role of globalization processes. We should note, however, that the term 'social movement' is not used consistently. For example, Lipschutz prefers to talk about 'networks of economic, social and cultural relations ... occupied by the conscious association of actors in physically separated locations, who link themselves together in networks for political and social purposes'. Falk, on the other hand, moves from a focus on social movements to an analysis of 'transnational social forces [that] provide the only vehicle for the law of humanity'.[24] These are rather opaque conceptual shifts which are not grounded thoroughly in existing debates on collective action or social movements. Consequently, Lipschutz and Falk offer a less nuanced and more polemical analysis of social movements (or networks, or social forces) in civil society than that developed in the postmarxist civil society literature outlined in the first part of this chapter. Lipschutz and Falk do, however, echo similar ideas about the emancipatory potential of social movements, agreeing that movements contest values and cultural practices as well as lobbying political and economic institutions, and that they aim to defend and expand global civil society rather than to seize economic and state power. Thus Falk argues that movements 'connect practices in everyday life with the most general aspirations of politics including global restructuring' and manifest a 'liberatory orientation' which 'renounces violence as means and subordinates the control of state power to other goals'. He characterizes movements as 'citizen-pilgrims', striving to develop alternative values that challenge the most exploitative aspects of capitalism and that, in particular, undermine the technocratic, militaristic, anti-democratic ethos of the state system.[25]

More problems than solutions

Notwithstanding the inconsistent and underdeveloped aspects of the postmarxist vision of global civil society, it undoubtedly represents an innovative contribution to a post-statist, anti-capitalist emancipatory theory and politics. However, I believe that it has significant drawbacks as both an analysis of social movement activity and as an emancipatory ideal. Indeed, all versions of global civil society theory are problematic. They share a limited understanding of globalization; they are based, like all theories of civil society, on the analytical construction of a bounded sphere which misrepresents and misdirects activism; and they fail to grapple with the implications of differences between actors within such a sphere. I shall deal with each of these points in turn.

The limitations of globalization theory?

Perhaps the most obvious weakness in notions of global civil society is that they are underpinned by a solely political-economic variant of globalization theory. To reiterate, this approach to globalization emphasizes the development of economic, technological and ecological regulatory issues that cannot be solved by individual states and that under-mine state power and legitimacy, encouraging popular mobilization. Irrespective of whether these processes are interpreted in a liberal light as progressive or in critical terms as precipitating crisis, this amounts to a unidimensional and linear model of global change. Yet as Anthony Giddens has convincingly argued, processes of globalization actually manifest themselves across diverse social institutions and most areas of life and they unfold in complex, contradictory and unpredictable ways. Their impact has been highly uneven, disrupting oppressive relation-ships of power and constituting new ones, and engendering diverse responses.[26] The political-economic variant of globalization and the global civil society literature that draws upon it thus do not capture the fact that social movement activists are likely to be affected and to react in context-specific and often conflictual ways. Nor do they capture the robustness of many state and institutional responses. As several theo-rists have pointed out, the state system is historically adaptable and several states may be extending their powers in new ways under con-temporary conditions.[27] Shaw's argument that a global state could be developing thus deserves more than passing attention. Furthermore, the underlying assumption that states are 'in decline' can encourage an over-optimistic picture of the significance and ability of social move-ments. Of course, none of these criticisms are intended to deny the pos-sibility that a more detailed and nuanced form of globalization theory could offer fruitful insights into social movement activity, as will be dis-cussed below. It is even possible that such an investigation could enrich the concept of global civil society – were it not for other, more serious problems with this concept.

Boundaries and spheres

A fundamental problem with all forms of the civil society ideal, global or not, is the conceptualization of social and political life in terms of distinct, bounded spaces or realms. Now, the notion of a 'realm' may be useful to the extent that it gives some indication that individual actors do not operate within a vacuum but are embedded within more extensive social structures and institutions. It also gives an idea of the physical extent to which certain structures and institutions extend. However, the state, civil society and the economy do not actu-ally exist as distinct physical and spatial entities in this way. State power, for example, is much more ideological and diffuse than its physical representations, with tentacles extending far into social life. Further-more, as critical and feminist theorists have long argued, the analytical construction of boundaries between separated spheres may function to disguise those tentacles of power, misrepresenting what are, in fact, mutually constitutive aspects of social life and reproducing oppressive relationships within society.[28] Finally, the conceptualization of politics in terms of bounded spheres may especially misrepresent and reify social *movements*. As R.B.J. Walker argues, a 'politics of movement cannot be grasped through categories of containment . . . through a metaphysics of inclusions and exclusion, whether of insides and out-sides or aboves and belows'.[29] Although movement activists are physically located, the politics of movement escapes territorial and spatial categories and disrupts the neat state/economy/civil society categorization of social life. The implications of all of this are twofold.

Firstly, the analytical construction of bounded spheres encourages the empirical misrepresentation of much social movement activity. For example, the substantial accreditation of NGOs to bodies such as the United Nations Environmental Programme, and the involvement of these groups in official government delegations to UN-organized interstate conferences like the 'Earth Summit' held at Rio in 1992, indi-cates that movements are systematically and actively penetrating the boundaries which theorists set up between state/economy/civil society. Such activity is at least as significant in terms of strategy as the parallel NGO forums which accompany UN conferences, or the cultural inno-vation and lifestyle politics of movements. It should be noted that boundary-crossing activities are recognized in non-global versions of civil society theory to a limited extent, as in Cohen and Arato's argu-ment that the lobbying of institutions and the more latent cultural activity of movements are both aspects of a 'dual strategy', directed into and out from civil society. However, even this analysis is limited. It fails to recognize that state and economic power has also thoroughly per-meated the activity of and relationships between social movements, as illustrated by the funding of Southern women's community groups by Northern feminist groups acting as channels for monies from the World Bank and Northern state governments.[30] The systematic nature of this two-way interpenetration indicates that civil society, as a sphere of social movement association located outside of structures of power, simply does not exist.

Secondly, the development of such a sphere does not appear to be a viable, emancipatory political aspiration, capable of presenting a chal-lenge to structures of power on a global scale. This claim does not mean that I am opposed to the postmarxist goal of creating forms of social interaction resistant to marketization and government intervention nor,

I hope, that I am insensitive to the achievements of the civil society strategy as adopted in the particular context of Eastern Europe in the 1980s. However, it seems to me that a global political strategy based on a denial or failure to recognize the systematic nature of the interpenetration of social movements, states and economic institutions will function to mask or reify these interpenetrations. What is more, a strategy aimed at expanding civil society and delimiting or democratizing the spheres of state and economic power is predicated on the belief that these spheres are ultimately beyond the influence of human agency and cannot be radically transformed. Perhaps most curiously, it appears blind to the hierarchical and oppressive relations that exist *within* civil society. One might have expected the power-structured relations of gender, race and culture, for example, to be brought to the fore by the non-economistic intent of postmarxist theory. However, the postmarxist versions of the civil society ideal examined here appear to reduce all sources of power and conflict to the state and market, and presume some kind of power-free interaction between movements if these twin structures can be 'pushed back' and democratized.

Universalism, difference and conflict

This brings me on to my third point of criticism: the failure of civil society theorists to take account of the multiple differences in power, form, strategy and ideology that exist between and within social movements. In particular, the postmarxist version of civil society has failed to grapple with the political implications of these differences and the conflicts that arise from them. This problem is not simply about misrecognition or neglect, but is also about the construction of categories of analysis and political projects that universalize the particular and located experience of the theorist. This would seem a significant shortcoming in theories with global explanatory and emancipatory ambitions.

The universalist aspirations of global civil society theory are hampered, in the first place, by prior Eurocentric assumptions. These assumptions are made explicit in Shaw's argument that, '[w]hat is at stake are the values of civil society as they have developed in the Western world ... these values [must be] strengthened, renewed and expanded in their area of influence on a global scale'.[31] Such values could include, for example, the belief that the individual is innately rational with strategic, negotiable interests and that this capacity for reason is universal. Western values also inform the notion that a civic public can be constructed on the basis of a liberal-pluralist agreement to disagree, or because of a belief in a higher, liberal-progressive telos (as in Shaw's aspiration toward a global ethic of responsibility), or on the back of the objective 'force of the better argument' (as in Falk's assertion of the imperative of global crises). However, as Walker has shown in his discussion of the Hindu revivalist social movement 'Swadhyaya', such foundational values are often not shared by non-Western groups:

> ... the notion of self that informs the entire movement ... is not separable from notions of the divine ... Given the centrality of the spiritual impulse here, public life ... must be infused with spiritual idealism in order to generate any kind of civic order ... the Vedic premises that inform this movement are rooted in claims about an immanent divinity. These premises do not always travel well ... [Nonetheless,] this movement is not shy about professing a certain universality.[32]

Walker's example indicates that non-Western, non-secular activism is either misrepresented under the rubric of global civil society, at least as it has been developed thus far, or must be excluded from it. My argument here is not necessarily that the values of the Swadhyaya movement are to be condoned, nor that all attempts to create universalizable categories or political projects should be rejected, nor that secular rationality is an invalid framework for the construction of such categories and projects. Rather, I am arguing against the prior assumption of the superiority and inclusivity of Eurocentric values and frameworks and the deductive imposition of such frameworks.

The Eurocentrism of notions of global civil society is exacerbated by the fact that theorists often attribute common aims and practices to all members of civil society, including social movements. This tendency to presuppose a unified perspective may occur because civil society is represented as a single actor rather than as a sphere containing a multiplicity of actors. More often, it occurs because theorists posit a common sociopolitical context to the mobilization of civil society members (given that globalization is seen, wrongly, as a uniform process) and then spuriously assume that a common context leads to common aims. Furthermore, some theorists have universalized a particular political project with which they have strong sympathies or affiliations. This has revived the spectre of vanguard politics in which a counterhegemonic political project can effectively be led by an enlightened few. Several of these problematic assumptions can be found in Falk's work, which presupposes that there is a need for a common response to a series of objectively verifiable global crises and also that the particular strategies of European and American peace movements are of universal applicability. Furthermore, Falk argues that such movements 'provide the vehicle for the law of humanity' that could allow us to overcome the failures of the present global order. In contrast, Shaw asserts that actors within civil society have failed to achieve the coherent cosmopolitan political consensus which he sees as desirable in order to control distant violence; a unified perspective (around values that have developed in the Western world) thus remains a political *aspiration.*

The assumption of a unified perspective amongst movements, or the aspiration to create such unity, encourages what Joe Foweraker in a different context has called a 'definitional fiat' whereby movements that do not share the perspective of the particular group taken as an exemplar by the theorist are simply defined out of existence.[33] Groups like Swadhyaya are thus not only conceptually excluded from global civil society; they are not recognized as social movements. Quite what these are or what they represent in global politics is entirely neglected; their non-existence confines them to a surplus, invisible realm of reactionary politics. This is more than an analytical problem, for history has shown that such reactionary politics have a habit of making a sudden and very nasty appearance. Oppression and conflict within civil society and between social movement actors cannot simply be wished away or ignored, and the neglect of this issue represents a central failing of postmarxist versions of civil society. It plays into the hands of those critics who argue that a civil society strategy is dangerously utopian and that we need to recognize the inevitable role of the state in civilizing society.[34] However, if we accept any version of the globalization thesis, a return to the historically dominant, sovereign nation-state appears to be a dream of the past and those theorists emphasizing statist politics have little option but to follow Shaw in his search for a global state. The prospect of such singular power and its potentially universalizing reach is, to say the least, unappealing. If Shaw is even half right and a global state is in the process of developing, it seems doubly important to preserve the commitment to the emancipatory social movement politics that we find in the postmarxist variant of the concept of global civil society. It is also doubly important to recognize the limitations of the concept of global civil society – and to move beyond it.

Beyond global civil society

This final section contains some suggestions for moving beyond global civil society in order to gain a richer understanding of the global context and impact of social movement activity, and to identify and further postmarxist, emancipatory, global political possibilities. Firstly, I argue that we need to construct modes of theorizing and political imagining that are not tied to physical spaces and reified boundaries. Secondly, I suggest that a fresh look at globalization could facilitate an understanding of the macro-context of social movements. Thirdly, I argue that an emancipatory politics aspiring to be global in scope could begin to tackle issues of difference, inclusion and exclusion by acknowledging the specificity of movements and working towards a politics of coalition-building.

Breaking through boundaries

If the theoretically constructed boundaries around the sphere of global civil society are dismantled, social movements can no longer be understood as operating from and within a single spatial location (other than the world as a whole). This does not mean, however, that no boundaries should be constructed in social and political thought, with theorists are left grappling with the global as an undifferentiated political space, or reduced to looking only at the particular. It is clearly necessary in some way to analytically compartmentalize social relations in order to grasp the nature of the parts and the relationship of parts to the whole. I would suggest that the 'critical realist' approach, as developed in the work of Andrew Sayer and others, or the 'structuration' theory of Giddens, could be useful in the analysis of global social movements. While actors (such as social movements), and structures (such as the global economy) are analytically distinguishable according to these approaches, they are nevertheless understood in terms of their dialectical, mutually constitutive relationship to each other, rather than as static and spatially separated.[35] Also, because critical realism examines parts in relationship to each other and to a dynamic social totality, it also offers an alternative to Shaw's argument that we need to contextualize social movements within global civil society in order to avoid studying them in a vacuum, and to the postmodernist urging that we can and should only study particular social movements and their subjective self-understandings.

But the question remains: how do we even begin to conceptualize or 'imagine' the global totality of, or macro-context for, social movement activity if not in terms of the spatial separation of the state system, global economy or global civil society? One way forward is suggested by the more holistic concept of *global society*. Society has traditionally been understood in methodologically nationalist terms as the aggregation of local social relations into relatively discrete national units. In IR there has been a narrow concern with *international* society, defined as 'a group of states . . . [that] have established by dialogue and consent common rules and institutions for the conduct of their relations'.[36] In contrast, Shaw argues that the arrangements between and within states are subsets of a larger field of human interaction called 'global society':

> . . . a diverse social universe in which the unifying forces of modern production, markets, communication and cultural and local political modernisation interact with many global, regional, national and local segmentations and differentiations . . . [It] should be understood not as a social system but as a field of social relations in which many specific systems have formed.[37]

While Shaw sees global society as a recent, progressive development, Fredrik Barth argues that society should never have been imagined as a nationally-bounded entity. The view of society as an aggregate of social relations or institutions, 'a shared set of ideas enacted by a population', or 'a bounded and ordered entity', represents for Barth a failed attempt to impose order and closure on a disorderly world, functioning to reify the hegemony of the nation-state and distort social research.[38] Barth and Ulf Hannerz urge us to focus instead on dynamic 'chains' or 'networks' of human actions and events. While Barth appears to deny any stasis or structure to human interaction, Hannerz acknowledges that networks are ordered asymmetrically and hierarchically. He also argues that networks cut across institutional spheres, link diverse groups and connect the local to the global.[39] I would suggest that these ideas offer an alternative to the imagery of separate spheres and Shaw's language of 'systems' and 'differentiations'. This is global society 'imagined' as a kind of web which is both the context for and cumulative result of networks of human activity – a mesh of dense and tangled power-structured interactions around and into which the activities of social movements are woven.[40]

Getting more from globalization

Despite my earlier criticisms of globalization as invoked in the literature on global civil society, it seems to me that there is an alternative 'sociological-culturalist' approach to globalization which can illuminate the ambiguous and dialectical relationship between global society and social movements. This approach focuses on the 'disembedding' of social activity from localized context and the stretching and deepening of social relations due to time–space compression, precipitating what Scholte describes as a 'supraterritorial' dimension to social relations.[41] It posits a mutually constitutive relationship between the local and the global whereby the local is seen as shaping and shaped by global dynamics, an analysis which reflects a general postmarxist methodological adherence to structural interpenetration and multi-causality. Furthermore, globalization is not understood in purely structuralist terms; the conscious interaction of people with these structures is both an outcome of and an input into processes of change. Globalization undermines and denaturalizes social norms and moribund political institutions, encouraging the rise both of fundamentalism and of reflexive radical activism, and of what Roland Robertson characterizes as 'the intensification of consciousness of the world as a whole'.[42]

The sociological-culturalist approach to globalization offers a more nuanced analysis of the global dimension of social movement activity than can be found in the global civil society literature. This is chiefly because it emphasizes the multidimensional, complex character of global change and thus the fact that movements may be affected, and may react in, highly different ways. It also usefully undermines the binary oppositions of local and global, structure and agency, progressive and reactionary. Social movements, it is suggested, are not pitted against global forces but are bound up within them; grassroots activism can be informed by global consciousness; supraterritorial organizational frameworks can be composed of particularist, reactionary groups. This helps us to understand the ambiguities of movements like that of the Zapatistas in Mexico, who reassert a localized, traditional identity against the imposition of highly disruptive and threatening globalized political and economic forces but who also strive to create organizational and communicative linkages which stretch across the globe. Furthermore, the sociological-culturalist approach to globalization reinforces the need to think about emancipatory politics on a global scale. While it problematizes the privileging of Western, cosmopolitan modes of thought and activism in notions of global civil society, it also fundamentally undermines the common leftist and ecologist response that truly oppositional struggle must re-assert the local against the global. As feminist activist Charlotte Bunch has written, '[a]ny struggle for change in the late-twentieth century must have a global consciousness since the world operates and controls our lives internationally already'. The strength of movements like feminism lies in their grassroots structure, 'but for that strength to be effective, we must base our local and national actions on a world view that incorporates the global context of our lives. This is the challenge of bringing the global home'.[43]

Acknowledging differences and building bridges

The recognition that movements operate in the context of globalized relations of power and social change would also seem to encourage the view that particularist movement struggles must find ways of connecting across the globe in order to forge any kind of meaningful oppositional politics. My earlier criticisms of the ways in which global civil society theorists have imposed Eurocentric standards and a unified perspective upon diverse social movements was not meant to condone a retreat to particularism. As Arturo Escobar and Sonia Alvarez argue:

> While respecting differences (and precisely as a way to strengthen them and learn from them), the time has come for greater communication and coalition building transnationally and transculturally, as a necessary strategy to oppose the consolidation of a 'new world order', according to the dictates of capital and of the global cultural, economic and military powers. Only people's *collective* resistance and creativity can fulfil this role.[44]

How movements can forge such collective resistance transnationally and transculturally without replicating imperialist relationships, and how this can be theorized without lapsing into the fallacy of the unified perspective, remains a central question for emancipatory theory and politics. Answers offered in the past are clearly inadequate. As Walker has argued, 'it is not a matter of imposing a common vision; nor of forging a united front capable of storming existing citadels of power; nor of identifying a clear common denominator upon which the interests of all critical social movements can converge'.[45] An increasing number of theorists and activists recognize the need to develop more humble, reflexive and 'self-limiting' analyses and practices which acknowledge the specificity of movements and grapple with the concrete differences in power and ideology between and within them. For example, work is being done on developing criteria to distinguish critical movements or radical currents within movements whilst allowing for the imperatives of culture and context.[46] Within feminism, there is a growing literature that seeks to mediate the particular and the general, striving to acknowledge and learn from diversity between individuals and also movements whilst still articulating common ground between them.[47] Also within feminism, there appears to be a convergence of thought around the possibilities of a 'politics of alliance', with alliances theorized as fluid, strategic, consciously created and recreated in the face of differences and exclusions.[48] Without offering any final solutions, these strategies confirm Walker's point that 'the forging of connections is crucial. Critical social movements begin in diversity but they are compelled to recognise that they act in the same world'.[49]

Conclusions

The literature on global civil society is in many ways innovative and radical. It has added to the critique of realist state-centrism in IR by importing rich philosophical debates into the discipline, foregrounding normative questions about the relationship of the state and state-system to other actors, and insisting on the possibility of changing that relationship. Significantly, it has drawn attention to the neglect of social movements in IR and charted their actual and potential role in global politics. Nonetheless, I have argued in this chapter that the notion of global civil society has significant limitations in terms of constructing an analysis of and programme for social movement activism. This is not simply because of the complexities within the literature and the fact that much of it is rather poorly grounded in existing traditions of thought on social movements and civil society. More seriously, the notion of a global civil society is limited by its reliance on simplistic interpretations of globalization theory, the neglect of differences between movements, and the reification of boundaries and spheres which is characteristic of all civil society theory. In particular, the postmarxist ideal of a global sphere of social movement activity that is separated from, and can challenge, economic and state power is not sustainable. It aspires to or assumes a common perspective and strategy shared by all movements and attempts to contain their socially embedded and politically diverse activities within a distinct realm, thus neglecting the differences between movements and reifying the structures of power which exist supposedly outside civil society.

This chapter has offered several suggestions for ways in which we can move beyond global civil society in order to gain a new analytical rigour in our analysis of social movements and a more genuinely radical postmarxist political agenda for a global politics from below. I have argued that it would be helpful to draw on critical realist epistemology, ideas about global society and a more nuanced sociological-culturalist analysis of globalization. Furthermore, it is imperative to grapple with the differences between movements and the possibilities of constructing coalitions between them. I have ended up with a tentative sketch of global emancipatory politics as the ongoing construction of coalitions between critical movements. This approach retains several postmarxist assumptions: that there is not one single cause or form of domination and inequality in the world; that privileging resistance against one form of oppression is partial and exclusive; and that there are multiple sites of conflict in a globalizing world necessitating multiple projects of emancipation. However, this approach also necessitates the rejection of the spatial metaphor and unifying assumptions of the postmarxist vision of global civil society. The emancipatory possibilities of social movement activism are perhaps best visualized in terms of the image of the web described above, in which the state system, global economy and other relations of power form a near-suffocating mesh over almost all of global society, filtering and constraining social movement activity. Nonetheless, movements can flourish in the most unexpected interstices, squeezing through and enlarging numerous gaps and developing parallel or cross-cutting networks which have the potential to weaken the stranglehold of intertwined structures of oppression on global social life.

Notes

*　I would like to thank Neil Stammers for his unstinting support and for his enthusiastic engagement with the issues discussed in this chapter. Thanks also to Martin Shaw and Fiona Robinson for their challenging and illuminating comments on earlier drafts.

1.　The accounts of global civil society which will be examined in this chapter are Ronnie D. Lipschutz, 'Reconstructing world politics: the emergence of global civil society', *Millennium*, 1992, vol. 21, no. 3, pp. 389–420; Richard Falk, 'The global promise of social movements: explorations at the end of time', *Alternatives*, 1987, vol. XII, pp. 173–96; Falk, 'The world order between inter-state law and the law of humanity: the role of civil society institutions', in Daniele Archibugi and David Held (eds), *Cosmopolitan Democracy: an Agenda for a New World Order* (Cambridge: Polity Press, 1995) pp. 163–79 and Falk, 'The states-system and contemporary social movements', in Saul H. Mendlovitz and R.B.J. Walker (eds), *Towards a Just World Peace: Perspectives from Social Movements* (London: Butterworths, 1987); Martin Shaw, 'Civil society and global politics: beyond a social movement approach', *Millennium*, 1994, vol. 23, no. 3, pp. 647–67; Laura Macdonald, 'Globalising civil society: interpreting international NGOs in Central America', *Millennium*, 1994, vol. 23, no. 2, pp. 267–85; and also the Report of the Commission on Global Governance, *Our Global Neighbourhood* (Oxford: Oxford University Press, 1995).

2. Krishan Kumar, 'Civil society: an inquiry into the usefulness of an historical term', *British Journal of Sociology*, 1993, vol. 44, no. 3, p. 376.

3. This brief discussion of traditions of thought on the idea of civil society and recent revivals has been drawn mainly from Kumar, 'Civil society'; Ellen Meiksins Wood, 'The uses and abuses of civil society', in R. Miliband, L. Panitch et al. (eds), *The Socialist Register* (London: Merlin Press, 1990) pp. 60–84; Jean L. Cohen and Andrew Arato, *Civil Society and Political Theory* (Cambridge, MA: MIT Press, 1995); John Keane (ed.), *Civil Society and the State: New European Perspectives* (London: Verso, 1988); Quentin Hoare and Geoffrey Nowell Smith (eds), *Selections of the Prison Notebooks of Antonio Gramsci* (London: Lawrence & Wishart, 1971), pp. 210–76.

4. Cohen and Arato, *Civil Society and Political Theory*, pp. 71–2; see also Keane, *Civil Society and the State*, pp. 1–28; Wood, 'The uses and abuses of civil society', pp. 63–4.

5. Cohen and Arato, *Civil Society and Political Theory*, pp. 2, 70–1; David Held, 'Liberalism, Marxism and democracy', in Stuart Hall, David Held and Tony McGrew (eds), *Modernity and its Futures* (Cambridge: Polity Press in association with the Open University, 1992), pp. 25–32; Keane, *Democracy and Civil Society: On the Predicaments of European Socialism, the Prospects for Democracy and the Problem of Controlling Social and Political Power* (London: Verso, 1988), pp. 56–64.

6. Cohen and Arato, *Civil Society and Political Theory*, especially pp. 2, 74–7. A very similar argument was put forward by Jeffrey Alexander in 'Rethinking "capitalism" in the context of the revival of civil society', paper presented at 'The Direction of Contemporary Capitalism: An International Interdisciplinary Conference' University of Sussex, 26–28 April 1996. It should be noted that other postmarxists invoke the concept of civil society in a different way – Keane, for example, includes commercial actors and emphasizes the role of the state in civilizing society. Others have rejected the concept altogether – see, for example, Ernesto Laclau and Chantal Mouffe, *Hegemony and Socialist Strategy: Towards a Radical Democracy* (London: Verso, 1985), pp. 179–81. The notion of civil society as a sphere of social movement activity distinct from both state and economy is clearly just one of a range of postmarxist ideas and strategies.

7. Cohen and Arato, *Civil Society and Political Theory*, p. 492.

8. Jan Aart Scholte, 'Beyond the buzzword: toward a critical theory of globalisation', in Eleonore Kofman and Gillian Youngs (eds), *Globalisation: Theory and Practice* (London: Pinter, 1996), p. 48.

9. Cohen and Arato, *Civil Society and Political Theory*, pp. 31–69; R.B.J. Walker, 'Social movements/world politics', *Millennium*, 1994, vol. 23, no. 3, pp. 682–3. The latter point was made by Jeffrey Alexander in discussion during a colloquium on 'Social Theory After 1989', part of The Direction of Contemporary Capitalism conference, University of Sussex.

10. Scholte, 'Beyond the buzzword', p. 45.
11. The notion of a political-economic version of globalization theory is, of course, rather crude and cannot do justice to the full range of literature on globalization which exists within IR. Nonetheless, it serves as an adequate description of a major portion of this literature. See, for example, several of the essays in Yoshikazu Sakamoto (ed.), *Global Transformation: Challenges to the State System* (Tokyo: United Nations University Press, 1994); J.A. Camilleri and J. Falk, *The End of Sovereignty: the Politics of a Shrinking and Fragmented World* (Aldershot: Edward Elgar, 1992); John MacMillan and Andrew Linklater (eds), *Boundaries in Question: New Directions in International Relations* (London: Pinter, 1995); James N. Rosenau and Ernst-Otto Czempiel (eds), *Governance without Government: Order and Change in World Politics* (Cambridge: Cambridge University Press, 1992); James H. Mittelman (ed.), *Globalization: Critical Reflections* (Boulder, CO: Lynne Rienner, 1996).
12. *Our Global Neighbourhood*, especially pp. 10–11; see also Scholte, 'Beyond the buzzword', pp. 50–1 and Andrew Hurrell and Ngaire Woods, 'Globalisation and inequality', *Millennium*, 1995, vol. 24, no. 3, pp. 448–54.
13. Falk, 'The states-system and contemporary social movements', pp. 15–17.
14. Seminal realist texts include E.H. Carr, *The Twenty Years Crisis 1919–1939* (London: Macmillan, 1939); Hans J. Morgenthau, *Politics Among Nations: the Struggle for Power and Peace* (New York: Alfred A. Knopf, 1948); Kenneth Waltz, *Theory of International Politics* (Reading, MA: Addison-Wesley, 1979). For a critical response, see Robert Cox, 'Social forces, states and world orders: beyond international relations theory', in Robert O. Keohane (ed.), *Neorealism and its Critics* (New York: Columbia University Press, 1986), pp. 207–10. J.C. Garnett effectively summarizes the response of interdependence theory to realism in 'States, state-centric perspectives and interdependence theory', in John Baylis and N.J. Rengger (eds), *Dilemmas of World Politics: International Issues in a Changing World* (Oxford: Oxford University Press, 1992).
15. Shaw, 'The global state and the politics of intervention', discussion paper published by the Centre for Studies in Global Governance at the LSE, p. 5. See also Shaw, *Global Society and International Relations: Sociological Concepts and Political Perspectives* (Cambridge: Polity Press, 1994), pp. 168–89. Shaw attempts to distance himself from a purely statist solution with the argument that 'much depends on the development of civil society at a global level'. However, '[c]ivil society can only develop in constructive relation with the state, in order to represent communities in relation to state power' ('The global state and the politics of intervention', p. 11). Thus civil society cannot, by definition, oppose the state or question its power.
16. *Our Global Neighbourhood*, pp. 253–62; Macdonald, 'Globalising civil society', p. 285.
17. Crawford Young quoted in Lipschutz, 'Reconstructing world politics', p. 391.
18. Falk, 'The states-system and contemporary social movements', p. 23.
19. See, for example, Ian Clark, *The Hierarchy of States: Reform and Resistance in the International Order* (Cambridge: Cambridge University Press, 1989), pp. 57–66.
20. Although Lipschutz retains a gramscian insistence on the influence of 'economic relations' on civil society, he emphasizes the ways in which these

are socially reproduced and contested, and is critical of what he sees as the economic reductionism of gramscian approaches to international relations. Lipschutz, 'Reconstructing world politics', pp. 399, 414–18; Shaw, 'Civil society and global politics', pp. 648–9; Macdonald, 'Globalising civil society', pp. 275–7.

21. Falk, 'The world order between inter-state law and the law of humanity', p. 177; Lipschutz, 'Reconstructing world politics', p. 418.

22. Cecelia Lynch, 'E.H. Carr, international relations theory, and the societal origins of international legal norms', *Millennium*, 1994, vol. 23, no. 3, p. 592.

23. Details of the global dimension of social movement activism can be found in Bice Maiguashca, 'The transnational indigenous movement in a changing world order', in Sakamoto (ed.), *Global Transformation*, pp. 359–79; Zsuzsa Hegedus, 'Social movements and social change in self-creative society: new civil initiatives in the international arena', *International Sociology*, 1989, vol. 4, no. 1, pp. 19–36; Jan Aart Scholte, 'Governance and democracy in a globalised world', paper for *The ACUNS/ASIL Summer Workshop on International Organisation Studies*, July 1995, pp. 36–47; Leslie Paul Thiele, 'Making democracy safe for the world: social movements and global politics', *Alternatives*, 1993, vol. 8, no. 3, pp. 280–2; Falk, 'The global promise of social movements', pp. 181–8.

24. Lipschutz, 'Reconstructing world politics', p. 393; Falk, 'The world order between inter-state law and the law of humanity', p. 170.

25. Falk, 'The global promise of social movements', pp. 173–4, 189–94.

26. Anthony Giddens, *The Consequences of Modernity* (Cambridge: Polity Press, 1990), pp. 55–63 and *Beyond Left and Right* (Cambridge: Polity Press, 1994), pp. 1–21.

27. Scholte, 'Governance and democracy', pp. 4–15; Ronnie Lipschutz and Ken Conca (eds), *The State and Social Power in Global Environmental Politics* (New York: Columbia University Press, 1993), p. 276.

28. See, for example, Carole Pateman, 'Feminist critiques of the public/private dichotomy' in her collection of essays, *The Disorder of Women: Democracy, Feminism and Political Theory* (Cambridge: Polity Press, 1989) pp. 118–40; Nancy Fraser, 'What's critical about critical theory? The case of Habermas and gender', in Seyla Benhabib and Drucilla Cornell (eds), *Feminism as Critique: Essays on the Politics of Gender in Late-Capitalist Societies* (Cambridge: Polity Press, 1987) pp. 31–56.

29. Walker, 'Social movements/world politics', *Millennium*, 1994, vol. 23, no. 3, p. 700.

30. Point made by Ann Marie Goetz in 'The women's movement and global NGOs: problems of accountability', paper presented at colloquium on 'Social Movements and Social Change: Local and Global', part of *The Direction of Contemporary Capitalism* conference, University of Sussex.

31. Shaw, *Global Society and International Relations*, p. 172.

32. Walker, 'Social movements/world politics', pp. 688–9.

33. Joe Foweraker, *Theorizing Social Movements* (London: Pluto Press, 1995), p. 34.

34. Kumar, 'Civil society', pp. 389–91; see also the critique advanced by Neil Stammers, 'Shadows from the East: the end of "new social movements"? the

limits of a civil society strategy', paper presented at the *Second European Conference on Social Movements*, 2–5 October 1996, Vitoria-Gasteiz, Spain, pp. 26–7.

35. Andrew Sayer, *Method in Social Science: a Realist Approach* (London: Routledge, 1992); Giddens, *The Constitution of Society: Outline of the Theory of Structuration* (Cambridge: Polity Press, 1984).

36. Hedley Bull and Adam Watson (eds), *The Expansion of International Society* (Oxford: Oxford University Press, 1984), p. 1; for a sustained theoretical development of the international society argument, see Hedley Bull, *The Anarchical Society: a Study of Order in World Politics* (New York: Columbia University Press, 1977). Laura Macdonald argues that the IR literature on international society represents an important intellectual precursor to the development of notions of global civil society in 'Globalising civil society', footnote 6, p. 269.

37. Shaw, *Global Society and International Relations*, p. 19.

38. Fredrik Barth, 'Toward greater naturalism in conceptualizing societies', in Adam Kuper (ed.), *Conceptualizing Society* (London: Routledge, 1992), pp. 17–23, 31.

39. Ulf Hannerz, 'The global ecumene: a network of networks' in Kuper (ed.), *Conceptualizing Society*, pp. 38–42.

40. The cobweb image was popularized in IR by John Burton in *World Society* (Cambridge: Cambridge University Press, 1972). Burton was attempting to develop an empirically testable model of a system of trans-societal communications linkages; his elaboration was liberal in orientation, rather mechanistic and lacked a concern with the reproduction of power or the possibility of resistance (pp. 23–51). However, as an analogy or tool to aid conceptualization, the image of the web remains potent (see the discussion by Anthony McGrew in 'Conceptualizing global politics', pp. 10–14 and 'Global politics in a transitional era', p. 313, both in McGrew and Paul G. Lewis (eds), *Global Politics: Globalization and the Nation-State* (Cambridge: Polity Press, 1992).

41. Scholte, 'Beyond the buzzword', pp. 45–6.

42. Robertson, *Globalisation: Social Theory and Global Culture* (London: Sage, 1992), p. 8 and also Giddens, *Beyond Left and Right*, pp. 5–7. I am also drawing on Robertson, 'Glocalization: time–space and homogeneity–heterogeneity' pp. 25–44 and Jan Nederveen Pieterse, 'Globalisation as hybridization' pp. 45–68, both in Mike Featherstone, Scott Lash and Roland Robertson (eds), *Global Modernities* (London: Sage, 1995); and, of course, Giddens, *The Consequences of Modernity*, Part I.

43. Charlotte Bunch, *Passionate Politics: Feminist Theory in Action* (New York: St Martin's Press, 1987), pp. 328–9.

44. Arturo Escobar and Sonia Alvarez, 'Introduction: theory and protest in Latin America today', in Escobar and Alvarez (eds), *The Making of Social Movements in Latin America* (Boulder, CO: Westview Press, 1992), pp. 13–14.

45. R.B.J. Walker, *One World, Many Worlds* (Boulder, CO: Lynne Rienner, 1988, p. 158.

46. Ibid., pp. 26–32; Stammers, 'Social movements, power, rights: toward a reconstruction of global society from below?', paper presented at the *First Regional Conference on Social Movements*, Tel Aviv, Israel, 8–10 September 1997, pp. 9–13.

47. See, for example, Laurel Richardson, 'Speakers whose voices matter: toward a feminist postmodernist sociological praxis', *Studies in Symbolic Interaction*, 1991, vol. 12, pp. 29–38; Iris Marion Young, 'Gender as seriality: thinking about women as a social collective', *Signs*, 1994, vol. 19, no. 3, pp. 713–38; Pratibha Parmar, 'Other kinds of dreams', *Feminist Review*, 1989, vol. 31, pp. 55–65.
48. See, for example, Lisa Albrecht and Rose M. Brewer (eds), *Bridges of Power: Women's Multicultural Alliances* (Philadelphia, PA: New Society Publishers, 1990); Chéla Sandoval, 'Feminist forms of agency and oppositional consciousness: US third world feminist criticism' in Judith Kegan Gardiner (ed.), *Provoking Agents: Gender and Agency in Theory and Practice* (Urbana and Chicago: University of Illinois Press, 1995), pp. 217–19; Chandra Talpade Mohanty, 'Cartographies of struggle: Third World women and the politics of feminism' in Mohanty, Ann Russo and Lourdes Torres (eds), *Third World Women and the Politics of Feminism* (Bloomington: Indiana University Press, 1991), pp. 4–5.
49. Walker, *One World, Many Worlds*, p. 158.

Part II
Global Identities:
Gender and Sexualities

4

The Global, the Local and the Personal: The Dynamics of a Social Movement in Postmodernity

Sasha Roseneil

> *'Think Global, Act Local'*
> *'Sisterhood is Global'*
> *'Workers of the World Unite'*
> Slogans of the environmental, women's and labour
> movements

Introduction

For over a century key social movements have operated on a world stage, with internationalist ethics and a global political imaginary. Labour movements, women's movements, peace movements, and, more recently, environmental movements have actively engaged in the construction of global identities and global political projects. As processes of cultural, economic and political globalization have intensified in the postmodern era, the global scope of social movement activity has also increased, both responding to globalization and producing it. Many of the leading theorists who have drawn attention to the salience of globalization in the understanding of the contemporary social condition have also pointed to the significance of social movements as forces for social transformation (Beck, 1998; Castells, 1997; Giddens, 1991; Melucci, 1989, 1996). In this context, then, it is surprising that empirical research on social movements has been so slow to attend to the 'planetary dimension' (Melucci, 1989) of contemporary collective action. Research has tended to conceptualize movements as bounded by the nation-states in which they appear to operate, and individual movements have largely been studied either within the context of national societies, or through cross-national comparisons. The extent and salience of transnational connections, border-crossings and global flows of people, ideas, information and resources within and between movements have been all but ignored.

But it is my argument that it is not enough just to 'globalize' the study of social movements; the global aspects of social movements cannot be studied in isolation from their local and personal dimensions. The contemporary world should be understood as produced through the dialectical relationship of the global and the local (Giddens, 1990, 1991; Friedman, 1994; Lash and Urry, 1994), and the global, the local and the personal (Giddens, 1991; Friedman, 1994; Robertson, 1992, Melucci, 1996). This chapter takes the case of one social movement, the women's peace movement, in its particular instantiation at Greenham Common, to explore the interplay of the global, the local and the personal in contemporary collective action. It is concerned with the dialectical dynamics whereby local and personal actions impact upon the global, as well as vice versa. Greenham was enmeshed in the globalizing processes of the late twentieth century, yet it was also firmly located within its specific locality and within a particular national tradition of political protest. Its global potency as a symbol of protest against nuclear weapons was derived, in part, from its very location, outside a Cruise missile base, and in the heart of pro-nuclear, pro-NATO Tory England, and from the way in which the actions performed by women at Greenham rendered global-level fears for the fate of the earth meaningful in terms of individual lives.

The global–local–personal context of Greenham

Back in the first half of the 1980s, with the new Cold War at its height and relations between the superpowers at an all-time low, the eyes of the world focused for a time on a small piece of ancient common land in the county of Berkshire, in England. The Women's Peace Camp outside the United States Airforce Base at Greenham Common came to symbolize the intense contestation which was being played out in many hundreds of places and numerous different ways, between the forces of global militarization and movements for peace and nuclear disarmament. Greenham, although located physically and in the public mind in this particular place, was more than its physical manifestation as an encampment of women, and its impact spread far beyond the immediate environment in which it was situated. But the camp was also just the most visible manifestation of a global women's peace movement, which stretched across several continents and mobilized many hundreds of thousands of women during this period of geopolitical crisis.[1]

The women's peace movement in Britain, and more specifically the Women's Peace Camp at Greenham Common, can be seen as having emerged in the early 1980s at the nexus of the global–local–personal dynamic of nuclear militarism. The movement coalesced and the camp was formed at the point at which geopolitics touched the consciousness of hundreds of individual women, and when these women each made personal decisions to get involved. This happened within global, national, local and personal contexts.

The long-term global context of Greenham was the globalization of military power in the twentieth century, particularly from the Second World War onwards (Giddens, 1990). The division of almost the whole world into two spheres of political influence and military alliance, dominated by the United States and the Soviet Union, and the development of a 'baroque arsenal' (Kaldor, 1982) of nuclear weapons, with their potential for global destruction, formed the backdrop to the specific developments of the late 1970s and early 1980s. The immediate global context of Greenham was the collapse of détente between the superpowers and the beginning of a new Cold War.[2] Although Carter's presidency had begun in 1977 with the stated aim of eliminating nuclear weapons, during his term of office the Arms Race intensified greatly. His exertion of pressure on NATO to deploy the neutron bomb, and the stalling and eventual non-ratification of the Strategic Arms Limitation Treaty (SALT II) signalled the deterioration of relations between West and East. Meanwhile, the Soviet Union began to deploy SS-20s and the backfire bomber in Eastern Europe, and then, on 12 December 1979 Carter persuaded NATO to take the 'twin track' decision. This constituted an offer to enter into negotiations with the Warsaw Pact about reductions in intermediate nuclear forces (INF) in Europe, whilst as the same time 'modernizing' NATO's intermediate nuclear forces by introducing ground launched Cruise missiles and Pershing II missiles. The plan was to deploy 464 cruise missiles in Britain, Belgium, the Netherlands and Italy, and 108 Pershing II launchers in West Germany, beginning in 1983.[3]

These missiles were part of a new 'generation' of 'theatre', or tactical nuclear weapons. Unlike earlier intercontinental 'strategic' nuclear weapons which could travel between the US and the USSR, 'theatre' nuclear weapons were designed for use on a nuclear battlefield within Europe. So whilst Cruise, Pershing and SS-20s were weapons of the global superpowers, their range and possible use was spatially bound: they were, in effect, regional weapons, 'euromissiles'. Moreover, the NATO decision constituted the formal enactment of a change in US nuclear doctrine. Schlesinger's new 'counterforce doctrine' said that US nuclear forces were henceforth to be aimed primarily at military targets – particularly command, control, communications and intelligence centres and nuclear storage facilities – rather than at centres of population. The implication of this was that NATO had moved from a strategy of deterrence to one which aimed to fight and win a nuclear war in Europe by means of a pre-emptive first strike. The vehemently anti-Communist rhetoric of the new Reagan administration and the US boycott of the 1980 Moscow Olympics underlined the deterioration of US/Soviet relations, and made it seem all the more likely that Europe would be their nuclear battleground.

Within this context the announcement that Cruise missiles were to be sited in Britain was the spark for the re-emergence of the anti-nuclear/peace movement, largely dormant since the mid-1960s. The identification of the United States Airforce (USAF) Base at Greenham Common as the first site for Cruise made tangible and highly specific the intensification of the global arms race and the otherwise diffuse and generalized global risk pertaining to the 'overkill' potential of the world's nuclear weaponry. Suddenly first strike nuclear weapons were to be based in Berkshire, less than seventy miles from London, and close to many of the largest towns and cities in Britain, bringing the probable site of any pre-emptive Soviet nuclear strike, or of a nuclear accident, within range of much of the population of England and Wales. The women's peace movement of the 1980s opposed all nuclear weapons and was not solely concerned with Cruise missiles, but the plan to install Cruise at Greenham provided a clear focus for campaigning and a specific target and place at which to direct attention.

The global context of Greenham had a gendered dimension, which contributed to the creation of Greenham as a women's peace movement. The state elites and transnational blocs which make foreign and defence policy, and the defence intellectuals and nuclear scientists who have developed nuclear strategy and weaponry are not only largely outside democratic control (Elworthy, 1989; Kaplan, 1984; Mann, 1987), they are also overwhelmingly male. As political decision-making moves from the local, through the national, to the transnational level, women are more and more excluded, and power is ever more exercised by men only. After a century of struggle by feminists for access for women to these political and scientific elites, decisions of far greater potential significance to the fate of the whole planet than had ever before been taken were still almost exclusively the preserve of men. The NATO/US decision to site Cruise at Greenham seemed to many of the women who formed Greenham, and to those who later got involved, to represent the power of distant, unaccountable military men over the lives and deaths of themselves, their friends and families. The 'nuclear fear' which characterizes the 'risk society' of the late twentieth century (Beck, 1992) was experienced by many women in a highly personal way, for instance in nightmares of nuclear war in which they or their children suffered terrible injuries.[4]

That this nuclear fear was translated into collective action, rather than just existing as individualized despair and depression, is to be explained by reference to the collective histories and traditions of protest, both transnational and specifically British, from within which these women came. There was a long history of anti-militarism amongst women in Britain (Liddington, 1989) and the feminist internationalism and anti-militarism of the Women's International League for Peace and Freedom (Vellacott, 1993) and of writers such as Virginia Woolf (1938), bequeathed an important, yet submerged, legacy of ideas on which the activists of the 1980s were able to draw in order to frame their critique of the nuclear politics of the superpowers.

More overtly, the intellectual resources with which Greenham and the women's peace movement of this decade were created came in part from a transnational, and particularly transatlantic, body of radical feminist and ecofeminist thinking. The work of American writers such as Mary Daly (1979) and Susan Griffin (1978), and the ecofeminist activism of the Spinsters and the Women's Pentagon Action (Linton and Whitham, 1982; King, 1983) were important sources of inspiration for Greenham. Not only were American feminist actions reported in British feminist newsletters and magazines, but individual women travelling between the US and Britain brought news of their own involvement in, for example, the Spinsters' weaving of a web to blockade the Vermont Yankee Power Station and the Women's Pentagon Action's encircling of the Pentagon.

The British context of Greenham rests in the particular configuration of traditions of political action and political discourses, both feminist and not, in the post-war period. Greenham's transformation from being a small, mixed peace camp in its first six months (albeit mostly women), into a large, open women's community of protest can only be understood in the light of critiques and practices developed within the

British women's liberation movement from the late 1960s until the early 1980s. Most importantly, the women's liberation movement articulated the necessity of women-only organization and social space, and established the women-only, locally-based, autonomous, non-hierarchical small group as the paradigmatic feminist form of organization. Radical and lesbian feminist strands of the movement created a women's culture in most of the major cities and a number of towns throughout Britain. This national feminist community helped to facilitate the transmission of news about Greenham through a potentially sympathetic audience.

The mixed peace movement of the late 1950s and early 1960s, in particular the Direct Action Committee against Nuclear War (DAC) and later the Committee of 100, established a precedent for non-violent direct action, and provided a nationally specific 'repertoire of action' (Tilly, 1978) on which Greenham was to draw. For example, the London–Aldermaston marches of this period suggested the form of protest with which Greenham began (the Cardiff–Greenham Women's Walk for Life, September 1981): the long-distance walk connecting a centre of population with a nuclear installation along the route of which public meetings were held and the issue publicized. Sit-downs organized by the DAC at military bases and attempts to board the supply ship for the Polaris submarine fleet at the Holy Loch were similar actions to the blockades, occupations and incursions in which women engaged at Greenham. The Committee of 100 spearheaded mass civil disobedience in 1961–62, including sit-downs in London and blockades and occupations of USAF bases around the country, and many activists were imprisoned; this too was not dissimilar to some of the actions at Greenham in the 1980s. The DAC and the Committee of 100's stress on the taking of individual responsibility for opposing nuclear weapons, and their opposition to the parliamentarian strategy of the Campaign for Nuclear Disarmament (CND) were also precursors of Greenham's ethos and mode of action in the 1980s.

A range of other movements during the 1960s and 1970s, some confined to Britain, others more transnational but strong in Britain, were also important intellectual precursors of Greenham. For instance, the Situationist movement advocated a politics of the 'spectacular' disruption, and reinvention, of everyday life (Erlich, n.d.; Plant, 1992), which presaged some of the more dramatic actions at Greenham. The Vietnam War called forth renewed and widespread peace protest, and directed the gaze of activists towards US imperialism in the Third World. At the beginning of the 1970s the Gay Liberation Front was formed, promoting a radical, confrontational politics of the personal. Also in the 1970s, provoked by the energy crisis of 1973, the environmental movement burst onto the political scene, challenging the post-war consensus on the desirability and possibility of continued economic growth. Environmentalists focused particularly on campaigning against the construction and extension of nuclear power plants, and large scale non-violent direct actions were held at Torness in Scotland. Another significant precursor of Greenham was the squatters' movement, which established a large number of alternative communal households and in some cities took over whole neighbourhoods of empty houses, legitimizing within the alternative culture the occupation of land which was not legally owned by those living there.

Together these movements bequeathed a legacy of anti-establishment attitudes, a strong strand of anarchist hostility to hierarchies, a critique of the materialism of industrial societies and of representative forms of democracy and the state, and a belief in the legitimacy and necessity of non-parliamentary forms of political action.

The importance of this national context of traditions of social protest can be seen by looking at the differences between Greenham and the women's peace camps which were set up, modelled on Greenham, in the USA and in Italy. The camp at Greenham was set up spontaneously at the end of the walk from Cardiff to the Cruise missile site, and was located on government-controlled land directly outside the base. Some of this land had once been common land, until requisitioned by the ministries of defence and transport for military use, whilst other places around the base where women set up camps still were 'common'. The acceptability of non-violent direct action in British traditions of collective action, the deep-seated attachment to a notion of common land in British culture which dates back to the time of the Enclosures in the sixteenth century, and the collective memory of protests such as the mass trespass by walkers of Kinder Scout in the 1930s to win public access to the countryside, made this occupation of land acceptable to those who did it, and to their supporters.

In upstate New York, however, the women's peace camp which was established outside the military depot at Seneca Falls, from which Cruise missiles were to be dispatched to Europe, had no similar tradition of struggle over land access on which to draw. Women in the United States chose to buy a piece of land close to the depot and to live there legally. Moreover, the actions which were taken at Seneca were less confrontational and less disruptive of the activities of the depot than was the case at Greenham; only a few hundred arrests were ever made, compared with many thousands at Greenham. Similarly in Sicily, where laws from the Mussolini era still required foreigners visiting for more than a few days to register with the police, and where the Mafia's presence was strongly felt, women also chose to buy land close to the proposed Cruise missile base on which to set up a camp, and to keep a much lower profile than at Greenham. Neither at Seneca nor at Comiso (Sicily) did it seem possible to just 'squat' a piece of land directly outside the target of the protest. Both the illegal and the legal occupation of land had their costs in terms of the time and energy of campaigners – the former involved evictions up to three times a day for much of the life of Greenham, the latter required fundraising and the organization of shareholding. But it was undoubtedly the case that the illegal and precarious positioning of the women's peace camp outside Greenham was a more potent symbol of resistance than the tidier, legal 'camps' on small plots of privately owned land some distance away from the subject of the protest. Images of the juxtaposition of the anarchic domestic life of the camp against a backdrop of barbed wire, soldiers, watchtowers and searchlights gave Greenham global recognition, unlike the camps at Seneca or Comiso.

The personal–local–global constitution of Greenham

The constitution of Greenham – the ongoing creation and re-creation of the camp and the wider women's peace movement over time – was dependent on personal, local and global processes, and on the interactions between these processes.

Like any form of collective action, Greenham was sustained over its eleven years of existence by the individual decisions of thousands of women to get involved and to stay involved. It was concern about the global politics of nuclear militarism which provoked the initial interest in Greenham of most of the participants.[5] For many women who were mothers, this concern was focused on the future of their children or grandchildren. For example:

> I had got involved because I did feel that the world was about to end if somebody didn't do something [. . .]. I had these terrible dreams about what would happen if my children were at school and nuclear war broke out. My whole life was absorbed in this fear that my children, not even that they might die, but that they might actually live and I might be crawling around in some half-life state.
>
> (Simone Wilkinson, aged 38)

Other women, particularly younger women without children, experienced deep psychological stress about nuclear war, and feared directly for their own future.

> I felt like the world is going to explode at any minute and why am I going to college? I mean, why go on with your life in this normal way when you feel like the world is about to blow up?
>
> (Liz Galst, aged 20)

> I remember when Reagan was elected I was still at university and we had an End of the World party because that was how we felt. I mean everybody just got roaring drunk for two days because we really felt like that was it, that none of us were going to live to see the end of our twenties.
>
> (Helen Mary Jones, aged 23)

Thus, events on the global stage precipitated action because they were experienced in a personal way.

However, it was not only the global situation which impelled women to get involved with Greenham. To understand Greenham as created only from the negative impulse of nuclear fear is to miss the centrality of the positive pull exerted by the camp as a women-only protest and community. Expressive, affective and cultural factors drew women to Greenham and sustained them in their involvement; in other words, factors local to Greenham, rooted in the social organization of the camp and the experience of being part of it, were an important motivation for involvement. For example, a sense of ownership and real participation was experienced by many women because the camp was women-only, and the opportunities provided by this women's space for developing close friendships with other women were highly valued. Other women were specifically attracted to Greenham by the large number of lesbians who were living there and the possibility this offered of being in a community in which lesbianism was the norm. But above all, women chose to live at Greenham and to continue living there or visiting because it was enjoyable, and because they found it personally satisfying.

> My reasons for going were that I thought I ought to go, because I felt that other people were doing something that I ought to be doing and I shouldn't be leaving this to other women to do [. . .]. But when I was there it was really different because I really loved it [. . .]. I loved

all the excitement and I loved to do all the actions and all that. It was great. And mixing with a big group of women which I'd not done before. I really had a good time and liked it and enjoyed it. And that's why I stayed.

(Penny Gulliver, aged 22)

Greenham was a place where women were able to engage in transforming and consolidating their self-identity.

The women weren't the only reason I was there, but they were certainly a big attraction [laughter . . .]. For the first time in my life I felt I'd found a place where I fitted in and whatever I was OK, and the same as the others.

(Jinny List, aged 20)

A hell of a lot of women grew through Greenham, in all sorts of ways. Your awareness of your own power and abilities. It broke our images of ourselves. We went with housewives' values, the values of real narrow-minded, narrow-, narrow-minded women from the Rhondda, and we broke this image of what we were. And then anything was possible.

(Christine King, aged 27)

Greenham was supported and sustained by networks of people, mostly but not exclusively women, which were national, local and global. Women went to live and to stay at Greenham not primarily from the surrounding area, but from all over Britain. Greenham was located close to the M4 motorway, allowing relatively easy access for those travelling from South Wales, the West Country, London, the Home Counties and the Midlands, and even for those coming from the north of England and Scotland, road connections were good.[6] The choice of USAF Greenham Common as a site for Cruise missiles had been made for operational reasons within the logic of global nuclear politics: good road networks would allow the movement of convoys of missile launchers about the countryside, in order to foil pre-emptive first strikes. However, this had the effect of locating Cruise in a place easily accessible to protesters living in the most populated parts of Britain.

Supporters often travelled hundreds of miles to visit Greenham for a few hours, bringing resources such as food, clothing, building materials, firewood and money, and for several years, there were hundreds of visitors to the camp each week. These flows of people around Britain not only provided essential woman-power and resources for the continuation of the camp, but also served to embed Greenham within the consciousness of the oppositional culture of the 1980s. Information and news about Greenham was carried by individuals from the camp to places throughout the country, bypassing the news media, which consistently produced inaccurate and hostile accounts of the movement (when it was not ignoring Greenham altogether).[7] Visitors to Greenham would report to their local CND group, trade union meeting, church group, Labour Party branch or women's group, and women who lived at Greenham travelled around Britain speaking at meetings of interested audiences. Money raised by Greenham support groups, women's peace groups and other organizations through local activities such as street collections and jumble sales provided the financial resources which bought food, materials for taking action against the base (such as boltcutters, ladders, paint), paid for petrol and camp vehicles, and supported women from overseas who were living at Greenham.

Local support for Greenham was also crucial to its survival. In the early days of the camp, it was the local anti-nuclear group, Newbury against the Missiles, which provided the tents, sleeping bags and cooking utensils which made it possible for the camp to be spontaneously set up at the end of the walk from Cardiff. Over the years a network of people who lived within ten miles of the camp opened their homes to the women who lived at Greenham, offering hot baths and a comfortable respite from the rigours of outdoor living. Some invited women to stay when they were sick, others let women store personal possessions in their homes to protect them from confiscation during evictions. The Society of Friends in Newbury gave Greenham women free access to their meeting house, which enabled meetings to be held in warmth and comfort, away from the interruptions occasioned by visitors and police at Greenham. The local Quakers also installed showers and set up a small office for the camp in their meeting house, providing an essential telephone contact point. Whilst the number of local supporters was small, their regular letters to the local papers and the constant pressure they exerted on local councillors and the local MP destabilized the hegemony of local hostility to Greenham, and gave Greenham some roots in the locality.

Although discussions of globalization have tended to focus on cities as global places (Harvey, 1990; Lash and Urry, 1994), the decision to site Cruise at Greenham made this rural space, four miles from the nearest (small) town, into a global locale. Although the US airforce was already stationed at Greenham, the upgrading of the base to house Cruise brought hundreds more American service personnel and their families to the area. Then as the camp organized its first large-scale actions such as the blockades of Easter 1982 and the 'Embrace the Base' demonstration of December 1982, which attracted over 30000 women, the world's media focused in on Greenham. Reporters and television crews from Europe, the US, the Soviet Union and beyond went to Greenham to interview the women, and to film and photograph the camp. By the time the first missiles were installed in November 1983, people in countries as remote as Nicaragua and South Africa knew about Greenham.

Greenham was outside local culture, and largely separate from the local community. Its culture was profoundly other to the conservative, small-town concerns of rural Berkshire. Greenham was cosmopolitan and looked outwards to a global community of anti-nuclear campaigners and feminists. The flows of women who came to Greenham from all over Europe, from Australia, the United States, Canada, some to visit, some to live, brought to the camp their previous experiences of political action and a range of political discourses and individual histories. An environment in which the exchanges of stories and personal experience was much valued, the praxis of Greenham was created out of these different traditions. For instance, Australian women brought information about the connection between uranium mining and aboriginal land rights, and introduced aboriginal mythology; from this grew Greenham's use of dragon and serpent imagery. Women from the United States raised concern about US intervention in Central America, which ultimately led to a number of Greenham women visiting Nicaragua, and to women from Nicaragua visiting Greenham. Women from overseas also 'carried Greenham home',[8] and spread the practices, ideas and actions of Greenham around the globe. Women's peace camps inspired by Greenham were set up in Australia, Canada, Denmark, West Germany, Italy, and the United States.

Thinking globally, acting locally, globally and personally

The oft-quoted injunction of the environmental movement to 'think global, act local' demands that a global conscience should be enacted within a local context, and implicitly suggests that local actions can be of global significance. Greenham held a similar belief. The ethos which guided action at Greenham was one of personal responsibility. It was believed that every individual has a responsibility to act according to her conscience, and therefore should engage in action to oppose nuclear militarism. Underlying this was a belief in the importance of individual agency in the production, reproduction and transformation of society. It was held that the cumulative power of thousands of individual, local actions could have an impact on the global situation.

The global collective conscience of Greenham produced action directed at the specific location of Cruise missiles in Britain. Blockades of the base, and many thousands of incursions into the base, as well as the constant tacit protest enacted by the camp's presence outside the base, were all local actions of resistance against global power. Reaching the point at which they felt able to break the law, cause criminal damage, and defy the police, British soldiers and armed American servicemen, was, for most women, a difficult process of internal dialogue and self-questioning, within a context of discussion with others. The taking of action at Greenham, which resulted in arrest and a court case, then often further underlined the global dimension of local and personal actions. In many of the thousands of court cases tried at Newbury Magistrates Court, women, usually defending themselves without a lawyer, would use international law, such as the 1969 Genocide Act, in their defence.

Greenham actions were not just located at Greenham: Greenham women roved across Britain and beyond. 'Greenham women are everywhere' was a slogan coined early in the life of the camp, to suggest that Greenham actions took place beyond that one corner of Berkshire, and were not confined to women who lived at Greenham. Whilst there was, at various times, considerable tension about the label 'Greenham women' and over the centrifugal pull of the camp, women's peace actions inspired by Greenham, and conducted by women who identified as 'Greenham women', took place all over Britain. Some of these were the actions of women who lived at the camp, but most were those of women whose primary commitment was to working in their home communities. It was particularly in taking action beyond Greenham that the project was pursued of 'making connections' between nuclear weapons, women's oppression, and other forms of global injustice. Roving actions can be divided into two main groups: those that related directly to Greenham, but which took place away from the camp; and women's peace actions in the style of Greenham, but not concerned primarily with Greenham.

The first group of actions was directed mainly at raising the profile of Greenham or at taking the protest about Cruise to other locations. For instance, women occupied the lobby of the House of Commons in

January 1983 to demand that the issue of Cruise be debated. Local women's peace groups throughout Britain regularly held demonstrations in town squares, set up peace camps on roundabouts and engaged in dramatic street theatre; and mass blockades were held in London and other cities to protest against and publicize the exercising of Cruise missile convoys. In 1985 there was a walk to 'reclaim Salisbury Plain' from military exercises; this passed over the firing range and the area in which convoys were exercised. This spreading of women's peace actions around Britain aimed to show how the problem of nuclear weapons was not confined to Greenham, but was an issue which affected everyone, everywhere.

Perhaps the most ambitious action in this category, and the one most clearly global in scope, was the court case brought in the New York Supreme Court by a group of Greenham women, their seventeen children and two US congressmen against Ronald Reagan, Defense Secretary Caspar Weinberger and US military chiefs of staff. The aim of this case was to get an injunction against the deployment of Cruise at Greenham, using international law and the US Constitution to argue that deployment was illegal.[9] The case attracted widespread support from the wider Greenham network and from the mixed peace movement in Britain and the United States, and for twenty four hours on 9 November 1983 camps were set up at all 102 US bases in Britain in support of the case, as well as outside the White House and the Supreme Court in New York.

The second group of actions was inspired by the distinctive ethos and style of protest of Greenham but went beyond the issue of Cruise, often aiming to draw attention to the connections between nuclear militarism and other issues, some global, others more specifically British. For instance, on the occasion of President Reagan's visit to London (7 June 1982), women from the camp and from the wider Greenham network performed a symbolic 'die-in' outside the Stock Exchange to highlight the huge profits made by the international arms trade. In March 1984, women demonstrated outside a seminar and sales conference for missile systems and technology, throwing red paint at the building in which it was held. Making links between militarism, the exploitation of animals in research and women's oppression there was also a women's camp at Porton Down (the chemical and biological weapons research establishment). To highlight the use of uranium mined in Namibia in the production of warheads for Trident nuclear submarines, a women's action was held at the British Nuclear Fuels plant, Springfields. Greenham women, working with Women against Pit Closure groups, also organized a series of women's walks from mining villages in South Wales to Hinckley Point nuclear power station, to demonstrate the relationship between the closing of coal mines, the expansion of nuclear power and the manufacture of nuclear weapons. The other major form of action in this category was the establishment of women's peace camps at other nuclear bases. Inspired by Greenham, there were, at different times, camps at military installations at Menwith Hill, Waddington, Morwemstow, Rosyth, Capenhurst, Fylingdales and Brawdy, amongst others, and blockades, fence-cutting and incursions took place at these and other bases.

Global–local–personal outcomes

Evaluating the influence of Greenham on global nuclear policy is fraught with difficulty. The impact of Greenham, in this area, is hard to disentangle from that of the wider peace movement, and, as Randle (1987) points out, commenting on non-violent direct action in the late 1950s and early 1960s, the secrecy which surrounds all government decisions, particularly about nuclear weapons, means that it is seldom possible to demonstrate beyond doubt that changes in policy may be attributed to social movements.

Obviously, Greenham did not achieve its initial aim of preventing the deployment of Cruise missiles in Britain. Unlike the Dutch and Belgian governments, the British government pushed ahead with NATO policy, unheeding of the mass protests and the opinion polls. But within four years of deployment, agreement had been reached between the superpowers to scrap cruise, and within ten years of the establishment of the camp, the last missiles were removed. Undoubtedly the most important factors which led to Gorbachev's disarmament initiatives were internal to the Soviet Union, and were primarily economic; the arms race was just not sustainable indefinitely. Commentators on the impact of the peace movement as a whole on this process are generally cautious, but argue that it contributed in a number of ways. Firstly, the peace movement heightened public consciousness about nuclear weapons, the arms race and NATO policy, galvanizing opposition to Cruise, which, according to opinion polls, ranged between 40 and 60 percent. The movement thereby contributed to the democratization of debate about defence (Carter, 1992; Wittner, 1988). Its assertion that people had a right to know and form opinions in this area constituted an important attack on the geo-political privacy of state elites and transnational blocs (Shaw, 1991). Secondly, in promoting debate about nuclear weapons and the implications of their use, the peace movement served to delegitimize them; Reagan's notion of a 'winnable' and limited nuclear war in Europe was publicly challenged, and its implications for Europe exposed. Wittner (1988: 287) suggests that this put a brake on the arms race and made nuclear war less likely.[10] Gleditsch (1990) concludes that the overall effect of the peace movement was to exert significant pressure on governments: 'it is questionable whether the breakthrough in the disarmament negotiations in 1986–87 would have occurred without the widespread moral revulsion against the nuclear arms race championed by the "new" peace movement' (Gleditsch, 1990: 73). Shaw (1991) is more specific about how this worked, suggesting that the movement indicated to Gorbachev that Brezhnev's European policy was outdated, and that there was a significant constituency in the West which was not actively hostile to the Soviet Union. This may well have contributed to his willingness to make the substantial concessions in the arms negotiations which eventually led to the INF treaty. The strength of the peace movement meant that NATO was impelled to listen seriously to Gorbachev. Finally, the Western peace movement stimulated the growth of the underground peace movements of Eastern Europe, contributing pressure for 'détente from below', and preparing the way for the revolutions of 1989 (Jahn, 1989; Shaw, 1991).

Greenham's role within the European and British peace movements was that of its most radical wing. Whilst Greenham's women-only policy was the subject of fierce debate within the peace movement, and was extremely unpopular in some sectors, Greenham undoubtedly influenced the forms of action in which other participants engaged. Mixed peace camps were set up at many other nuclear bases around Britain and in Italy and West Germany, following the model of Greenham, and gatherings and blockades, and disruption of military exercises became regular types of action there. CND initiated demonstrations which sought to replicate Greenham actions, such as the Aldermaston to Burghfield human chain of Easter 1983 which imitated Greenham's Embrace the Base gathering. The peace movement as a whole was never split over the issue of non-violent direct action in the way that it had been in the 1950s (Randle, 1987), and even the cutting of fences around military bases ('snowball actions') became a widespread practice in the years after it was first done at Greenham.

It was Greenham, spotlighted by the media during 1982 and 1983 because it was women-only and because of its imaginative and unusual forms of action, which seemed to be particularly effective at raising public awareness of Cruise. In 1980, 41% of those surveyed in Britain did not know that there were nuclear weapons in their country (Hastings and Hastings, 1982: 330), but by 1983, only 6% had never heard of Greenham (Hastings and Hastings, 1984: 323). Byrd (1985) suggests that there was a 'Greenham effect' on women, citing the significant gender gap in attitudes to Cruise, and the 32% of women who said that they had become more sympathetic to the campaign against Cruise as a result of Greenham, as against 50% who were unaffected (*Sunday Times*, 23 January 1983). A small non-random survey of women in *Spare Rib* also reported that one in three women had become more favourable to nuclear disarmament or more aware of the issue because of Greenham (*Spare Rib*, May 1984).

Whilst the contribution of the women's peace camp to the removal of Cruise from Greenham may be debatable, it is clear that what subsequently happened to the base and to the common has been profoundly influenced by the camp. An important strand of argument voiced by the camp highlighted the ecological destruction caused to the land of Greenham Common by the base (hundreds of trees were felled for instance), and evoked 'rural protectionist' sympathy amongst some local people who had enjoyed access to the common in their leisure time. When, in the mid-1980s, the government attempted to revoke all rights of access held by 'commoners' to Greenham Common, in an attempt to institute trespass laws which could be used against protesters entering the base, a campaign was begun by local residents to retain their rights of access to the common. Ultimately, commoners' rights were extended rather than rescinded, when, following the closure of the base, all but a hundred acres around the missile silos were sold back to Newbury District Council and returned to common land once more. Had there been no camp at Greenham, it is unlikely that the Ministry of Defence would have given up Greenham Common, or Newbury District Council bought it back.

At the individual and collective level, women at Greenham forged new identities and consciousness. It is beyond the scope of this chapter to explore the range of ways in which identities and consciousness were transformed through involvement with Greenham; in brief these included new identities as autonomous, empowered women, and as lesbians, and consciousness of women's oppression, state and police malpractice and of the global interconnectedness of political issues and peoples (Roseneil, 1995, 2000).

As I said earlier, although nuclear weapons are an issue of global significance, many of the women who were involved with Greenham had been impelled to act against them because of personal fear and concern for themselves and their families, rather than out of a global consciousness. Most had a fairly narrow British or Western European orientation to politics when they first got involved with Greenham. This was broadened through contact with visitors to the camp from all over the world, and by the camp's growing collective interest in global issues, which was manifested both in informal discussions and in meetings and actions about connections between political struggles in different parts of the world.

As these women explain:

> Whilst you were there a lot of other issues would click. There was the miners' strike and a lot of miners' wives used to come down [...]. And they'd ask us to go to the strike meetings and talk about nuclear weapons and the connection with the pits. And there was the American Indian from the Indian reservation. And he did a slide show about the uranium mines where they lived. And there were delegations from South Africa. And we were just dead ordinary working class women from the inner cities and we were talking to people who were directly involved in struggles from all over the world.
>
> (Trisha, aged 20)

> It made me feel connected to women from other places and other countries [...]. I met and spent time with women who were from other countries and had worked on connected issues.
>
> (Barbara Rawson, aged 52)

> One thing that was really historically and personally important to me was a visit of the South African Women's Theatre Troupe [...]. And they read the South African Women's Declaration of Demands and I remember that very high amongst them was the elimination of nuclear weapons from the world [...]. And I remember being so touched by that, and I felt that what we were doing at Greenham was this really revolutionary thing [...]. We really made a lot of connections.
>
> (Liz Galst, 20)

Many women moved beyond the confines of their own personal experience, which had been forged within fairly limited local and national contexts, to identify as global actors, members of a transnational movement of women working for peace, and linked to others struggling for peace and justice. After Greenham, many women became involved in and set up political projects with a global concern: examples include transnational campaigns against violence against women and against rape in war; Women's Aid to Former Yugoslavia; and the Women's Network for a Nuclear Free and Independent Pacific.

These are highly significant outcomes. Lash and Urry (1994) express concern that women are being excluded from the information and communication structures of the contemporary globalizing world. Yet the case of Greenham and the women's peace movement, whilst involving only a tiny proportion of the women of the world, shows that it has been possible for women to insert themselves as actors in the globalization process, and indeed to create themselves as actors of global significance with an understanding of events and politics in geographically distant places, and with connections to those engaged in similar political projects around the world.

Conclusion

Greenham and the women's peace movement of the 1980s were embedded within processes of globalization. They were at the same time both the product of globalization and productive of globalization. Emerging as resistance to the global threat of nuclear war and the globalization of nuclear militarism, the movement was composed of global flows of actors, ideas, and images, and it contributed to the creation of global identities and consciousness and to the formation of global networks of political activists. This discussion of the interconnections between the global, local and personal dynamics of Greenham suggests that Greenham was a movement characteristic of postmodernity. In an era of ever increasing global interdependence and high-consequence risks, in which processes of individualization mean that these changes and risks are experienced intensely personally (Giddens, 1991; Beck, 1994), Greenham engaged in a collective challenge to what were perceived as the negative aspects of postmodernity. But this challenge was inextricably bound up in those very processes of globalization, and was dependent upon them in its operation.

Notes

1. This chapter develops my earlier work on Greenham in which issues of globalization are considered only in passing (Roseneil, 1995).

2. For a more detailed discussion of the geopolitical context of Greenham, see Roseneil (1995).
3. The Belgian and Dutch governments later rejected the missiles, after intense peace movement opposition.
4. The source of the data referred to in this chapter is my ethnographic research on Greenham, which drew both on my own involvement and on interviews with 35 participants. For a discussion of the methodological issues involved, see Roseneil (1993), and for fuller reports on the data, see Roseneil (1994, 1995).
5. See note 4 above on the source of data.
6. Lash and Urry (1994) discuss the significance of the M4 corridor to economic development in the 1980s.
7. For discussion of the media reporting of Greenham, see Young (1990).
8. 'Carry Greenham Home' was a song written for Greenham by Peggy Seeger.
9. The case was eventually dismissed in 1985. See *Greenham Women Against Cruise Missiles* (1984), Hickman (1986) and Young (1990) for a more detailed discussion.
10. Randle (1987) makes a similar argument about the impact of the peace movement of the 1950s/1960s.

References

Beck, U. (1992) *Risk Society: Towards a New Modernity*, London: Sage.

Beck, U. (1994) 'The Reinvention of Politics', in U. Beck, A. Giddens and S. Lash, *Reflexive Modernization*, Cambridge: Polity Press.

Beck, U. (1998) *Democracy without Enemies*, Oxford: Polity.

Bunch, C. (1987) *Passionate Politics*, New York: St. Martin's Press.

Byrd, P. (1985) 'The Development of the Peace Movement in Britain', in W. Kaltefleiter and R.L. Pfaltzgraff (eds), *The Peace Movements in Europe and the United States*, London: Croom Helm.

Carter, A. (1992) *Peace Movements: International Protest and World Politics since 1945*, Harlow: Longman.

Castells, M. (1997) *The Power of Identity*, Cambridge, Mass: Blackwell.

Daly, M. (1979) *Gyn/Ecology: the Metaethics of Radical Feminism*, London: Women's Press.

Elworthy, S. (1989) 'Nuclear Weapons Decision-Making and Accountability', in C. Marsh and C. Fraser (eds), *Public Opinion and Nuclear Weapons*, London: Macmillan.

Erlich, C. (n.d.) 'Socialism, Anarchism and Feminism', in *Quiet Rumours: An Anarcha-Feminist Anthology*, London: Dark Star.

Friedman, J. (1994) *Cultural Identity and Global Process*, London: Sage.

Giddens, A. (1990) *The Consequences of Modernity*, Cambridge: Polity Press.

Giddens, A. (1991) *Modernity and Self-Identity: Self and Society in the Late Modern Age*, Cambridge: Polity Press.

Gleditsch, N.P. (1990) 'The rise and decline of the New Peace Movement', in K. Kodama and U. Vesa (eds), *Towards a Comparative Analysis of Peace Movements*, Dartmouth: Gower.

Greenham Women Against Cruise Missiles (1984) New York: Center for Constitutional Rights, Legal Education Pamphlet.

Griffin, S. (1978) *Women and Nature*, New York: Harper & Row.

Harvey, D. (1990) *The Condition of Postmodernity*, Oxford: Blackwell.

Hastings, E.H. and P.K. Hastings (eds) (1982) *Index to International Public Opinion 1978–1980*, Westport, CT: Greenwood Press.

Hastings, E.H. and P.K. Hastings (eds) (1984) *Index to International Public Opinion 1982–1983*, Westport, CT: Greenwood Press.

Hickman, J. (1986) 'Greenham Women Against Cruise Missiles and others versus Ronald Reagan and others', in J. Dewar et al. (eds), *Nuclear Weapons, the Peace Movement and the Law*, London: Macmillan.

Jahn, E. (1989) 'The Role of Governments, Social Organizations and Peace Movements in the New German and European Peace Process', in M. Kaldor, G. Holden and R. Falk (eds), *The New Detente*, London: Verso.

Kaldor, M. (1982) *The Baroque Arsenal*, London: André Deutsch.

Kaplan, F. (1984) *Wizards of Armageddon*, New York: Simon & Schuster.

King, Y. (1983) 'All is connectedness: scenes from the Women's Pentagon Action USA', in L. Jones (ed.), *Keeping the Peace*, London: Virago.

Lash, S. and J. Urry (1994) *Economies of Signs and Space*, London: Sage.

Liddington, J. (1989) *The Long Road to Greenham: Feminism and Anti-Militarism in Britain since 1820*, London: Virago.

Linton, R. (1989) 'Seneca Women's Peace Camp: shapes of things to come', in A. Harris and Y. King (eds), *Rocking the Ship of State: Towards a Feminist Peace Politics*, CO: Westview Press.

Linton, R. and M. Whitham (1982) 'With mourning, rage, empowerment and defiance', *Socialist Review*, 12(3–4): 11–36.

Mann, M. (1987) 'War and social theory: into battle with classes, nations and states', in C. Creighton and M. Shaw (eds), *The Sociology of War and Peace*, Basingstoke: Macmillan – now Palgrave.

Melucci, A. (1989) *Nomads of the Present: Social Movements and Individual Needs in Contemporary Society*, London: Hutchinson Radius.

Melucci, A. (1996) *The Playing Self: Person and Meaning in the Planetary Society*, Cambridge: Cambridge University Press.

Plant, S. (1992) *The Most Radical Gesture: the Situationist International in a Postmodern Age*, London: Routledge.

Randle, M. (1987) 'Non-violent direct action in the 1950s and 1960s', in R. Taylor and N. Young (eds), *Campaigns for Peace: British Peace Movements in the Twentieth Century*, Manchester: Manchester University Press.

Robertson, R. (1990) 'Mapping the global condition: globalisation as the central concept', *Theory, Culture and Society*, 7: 15–30.

Robertson, R. (1992) *Globalisation: Social Theory and Global Culture*, London: Sage.

Roseneil, S. (1993) 'Greenham Revisited: Researching Myself and My Sisters', in D. Hobbs and T. May (eds), *Interpreting the Field*, Oxford: Oxford University Press.

Roseneil, S. (1995) *Disarming Patriarchy: Feminism and Political Action at Greenham*, Buckingham: Open University Press.

Roseneil, S. (2000) *Common Women, Uncommon Practices: The Queer Feminisms of Greenham*, London: Cassell.

Shaw, M. (1991) *Post Military Society*, Cambridge: Polity Press.

Tilly, C. (1978) *From Mobilization to Revolution*, Reading, MA: Addison-Wesley.

Vellacott, J. (1993) 'A place for pacifism and transnationalism in feminist theory: the early work of the Women's International League for Peace and Freedom', *Women's History Review*, 2(1): 23–56.

Wittner, L. (1988) 'The transnational movement against nuclear weapons 1945–1986: a preliminary summary', in C. Chatfield and P. van den Dungen (eds), *Peace Movements and Political Cultures*, Knoxville: University of Tennessee Press.

Woolf, V. (1938) *Three Guineas*, London: Hogarth Press, reprinted 1977, Harmondsworth: Penguin.

Young, A. (1990) *Femininity in Dissent*, London: Routledge.

5

Transnational Feminist Networks: Collective Action in an Era of Globalization*

Valentine M. Moghadam

Introduction

Current theories of social movements have added much to our under-standing of the dynamics of collective action. This includes attention to the role of grievances, political opportunities and constraints, mobilizing structures, and framing processes (McAdam, McCarthy and Zald, 1996). However, there are gaps and biases: (i) a Western bias and a tendency to focus research on movements in Western countries; (ii) a gender bias and a tendency to ignore women's participation in social movements or theorize the gender dynamics of collective action; (iii) a national bias and a tendency to ignore global or world-systemic developments. Feminist sociologists have certainly advanced our under-standing of the social dynamics of women's movements and women's organizations (Katzenstein and Mueller, 1987; Ferree and Hess, 1995; Ferree and Martin, 1995), but this body of knowledge is based largely on research concerning single, Western societies. Studies that have had an international focus include Morgan (1985), Moghadam (1994), Stienstra (1994), and Basu (1995), but these have not explicitly addressed social movement theory; nor have they theorized women's movements as transnational or global social movements. (Basu [1995] explicitly rejects this proposition.)

This chapter builds on earlier research (Moghadam, 1996a), and seeks to contribute to feminist theorizing, to globalization studies, and to theories of social movements by discussing a new organizational form and a new form of collective action in an era of globalization: transna-

* This chapter was originally published in *International Sociology*, 15 (1) (March 2000): 57–86.

tional feminist networks and their activism. In this chapter I focus on the origins, objectives, and activities of four transnational feminist networks. They are: (1) Development Alternatives with Women for a New Era (DAWN), now based in Fiji (formerly in the Caribbean); (2) Network Women in Development Europe (WIDE), based in Brussels; (3) Women Living Under Muslim Laws (WLUML), based in Montpellier, France with an active branch in Lahore, Pakistan; and (4) the Association of Women of the Mediterranean Region (AWMR), based largely in Cyprus and Malta. In the course of this chapter, the following questions will be addressed: Are women's movements local, or can we speak of a global women's movement? Are women's movements oppositional and anti-systemic? Have feminism and the women's movement developed supranational constituencies, objectives, strategies and organizations?[1]

Social theory and transnational feminism

Social movements are organized initiatives aimed at effecting political change. Some theorists view social movements as a collective response to deprivation, or the availability of resources, or the contradictions of late capitalism. Some European studies cast social movements – and especially the so-called new social movements – as emancipatory projects, expressions of societal democratization and indicators of, and contributors to, civil society. Students of new social movements have argued that social movements in the late twentieth century are liberated from class, ideology, and economic concerns; that they employ new and creative forms of action; and that they focus on identity concerns rather than on strategy. It has been suggested that the women's movement, at least in the West, is one such 'identity politics' movement (Kriesi, 1996: 158).

Parallel to social movement research has been the emergence of scholarship on globalization (for example, Robertson, 1992), including the transnational capitalist class (Sklair, 1996) and international non-governmental organizations and their contributions to a global culture (Boli and Thomas 1997). Social movement theory has not yet incorporated the insights of globalization studies, but theorists are not unaware of the gaps. Tarrow (1996: 61) has raised the following question: 'Whether the increasingly global economy and supranational institutions that have been developing around it over the past few decades, has so thoroughly escaped the national state as to create transnational movements is a question students of political opportunity structure will have to face.' Kriesberg (1997) discusses how globalization processes may provide the basis for developing transnational identities, some of which may evolve into activist identities. McCarthy (1997: 243) notes that social movement theory is based on 'empirical evidence about nationally focused social movements operating within Western democracies'. He states that 'chronic social cleavages' such as 'class, religion, region, language, and ethnicity' may be the impetus for social movements; and he notes that 'there is great variation' in how social movement organizations are structured (245). He concludes that 'we lack systematic evidence about the scope and shape of transnational protest, and the transnational social sector is in its adolescence . . .' (258). Smith (1997: 48) mentions but does not elaborate on the fact that 'TSMOs [transnational social movement organisations] working for women's rights . . . multiplied over the decade'.

Neither the globalization literature nor the social movement literature examines feminism as a transnational social movement with transnational organizations linking women in developing and developed regions and addressing economic, social, and foreign-policy issues in supranational terms. (But see Keck and Sikkink, 1998.)

Introducing women, gender, and a global perspective

As important as current theories of social movements are, they pay little attention to women as actors in social movements, and to the ways that gender is built into political, organizational, and cultural processes. Gender ideologies may shape social movements in profound ways, deeply affecting the discourses, objectives, tactics, and outcomes of social movements. Within the same movement, women may be organized and mobilized differently from men. Recruitment patterns, leadership roles, and management styles may exhibit gender patterning. Gender roles, relations and ideologies may shape political opportunities – opportunities may exist for men but not for women, who may be less mobile or less able to respond to opportunities due to their greater involvement in family roles. Concomitantly, constraints are gendered. Constraints faced by women may be not only political but also cultural and familial. Within the same movement, women and men may have different objectives, priority concerns, or modes of protest (West and Blumberg, 1990). Outcomes are also gendered – social movement effects may be different for women than for men (Moghadam, 1997). More to the point, it is important to recognize the extent to which women have organized and mobilized politically, and the ways in which they have formed their own alternative movements and organizations – including transnational feminist networks, which are the organizational form of global feminism. These movements and organizations are based on a sense of collective identity, shared meanings, and common goals on the part of members.

Let us define our concepts: feminism, transnational feminist networks, global feminism. *Feminism* is a set of ideas, critiques and objectives predicated on the notion that women constitute a special category of people with certain traits and experiences in common, such as child-bearing and child-rearing, whether these be rooted in biology or in culture (Ferree and Hess, 1995: 32). Another essential premise is that women have a disadvantaged position in what is in effect a man's world. This disadvantage is manifested in the family, the economy, the polity, and cultural institutions, and it may be differentiated or exacerbated by historical era, or by economic or political system. Feminism offers a form of analysis and a critique of women's positions and of society as a whole, and a goal to effect social change through improvements in the legal status and social positions of women. The goals of equality, autonomy, empowerment, or social transformation may be emphasized and prioritized differently by women's organizations, depending on political and economic context.

International feminism has existed for over 100 years, international women's organizations have been in existence for decades, and links were established among women's movements in various countries in the early part of the twentieth century. Examples are the Women's International League for Peace and Freedom, the Women's International Democratic Federation, and the International Federation of Business and Professional Women (Rupp, 1998). However, international is not the same as *transnational*, which suggests a conscious crossing of national boundaries and a superseding of nationalist orientations. The phase of feminist organizing that began in the 1960s was, like many other social movements, initially nationally-based and nationally-oriented. In the 1970s clashes occurred among nationally- or regionally-framed feminisms, mainly due to disagreements between Western feminists, who tended to emphasize women's need for legal equality and for sex autonomy, and Third World feminists, who tended to emphasize imperialism and underdevelopment as obstacles to women's advancement. In the 1980s, and in the socio-demographic context of a worldwide growth in the population of educated, employed, mobile, and politically-aware women, feminist discourses and networking began to spread and to take on not only an international but a transnational form.

Today, feminist groups and women's organizations remain rooted in national or local issues, but their vocabulary, strategies and objectives have much in common with each other and have taken on an increasingly supranational form. Their encounter with UN-organized world conferences and regional meetings since 1975, their introduction to the new information technologies, and their experience with changing and increasingly harsh economic realities have broadened their horizons, resulting in considerable international networking and many joint initiatives. Four world conferences on women (Mexico City in 1975, Copenhagen in 1980, Nairobi in 1985, and Beijing in 1995), numerous regional preparatory meetings, and the participation of many women's non-governmental organizations (NGOs) in other UN conferences (such as the World Conference on Human Rights, held in Vienna in June 1993, the International Conference on Population and Development, held in Cairo in September 1994, and the World Summit for Social Development, held in Copenhagen in March 1995) have facilitated increasing interaction and co-operation among feminist organizations. The result has been the emergence of 'global feminism' and of transnational feminist networks.

Transnational feminist networks engage in information exchange, mutual support, and a combination of lobbying, advocacy and direct action towards the realization of their goals of equality and empowerment for women and social justice and societal democratization. Two examples may serve to illustrate this. First, concerted action since the late 1980s of networks including DAWN and WIDE in opposition to structural adjustment policies and the activities of the international financial institutions in developing countries, has forced the World Bank to take gender and social issues more seriously, and to form a Gender Consultative Group. Second, pressure from the Women's Alliance for Peace and Human Rights in Afghanistan (WAPHA), the National Organization for Women (NOW) and the Feminist Majority was instrumental in preventing US recognition of the Taleban regime in Afghanistan in 1997, and in prompting the December 1998 decision by Unocal to withdraw its bid for a gap pipeline through Afghanistan.

Global feminism may be defined as the discourse and movement of women aimed at advancing the status of women through greater access to resources, through legal measures to effect gender equality, and through the self-empowerment of women within national boundaries but through transnational forms of organizing and mobilizing. It is predicated upon the notion that notwithstanding cultural, class, and ideological differences among the women of the world, there is a commonality in the forms of women's disadvantage and in the forms of women's organizations worldwide. These organizations are increasingly networking and co-ordinating their activities, engaging in dialogue and forms of co-operation, solidarity, and mutual support, sending representatives to meetings in other countries and regions, and utilizing a similar vocabulary to describe women's disadvantage and the desired alternatives. As Sen and Grown (1987: 22) put it in a now-classic publication:

> We know now from our own research that the subordination of women has a long history and is deeply ingrained in economic, political, and cultural processes. What we have managed to do in the last few years is to forge grassroots women's movements and world-wide networks such as never existed before, to begin to transform that subordination and in the process to break down other oppressive structures as well.

A vivid demonstration of 'global feminism on the ground' was the myriad preparatory activities around the world for the Fourth World Conference on Women, and of course the participation of numerous women's NGOs at the conference itself. The *Beijing Declaration* and *Platform for Action* may be regarded as the 'manifesto' of global feminism (Moghadam, 1996a, 1996b). The passages below are taken directly from the *Platform for Action*, adopted in Beijing on September 15, 1995 (United Nations, 1996):

> The objective of the Platform for Action is the empowerment of women. The full realisation of all human rights and fundamental freedoms of all women is essential for the empowerment of women. While the significance of national and regional particularities and various historical, cultural, and religious backgrounds must be borne in mind, it is the duty of States, regardless of their political, economic and cultural systems, to promote and protect all human rights and fundamental freedoms . . .
>
> *(Platform for Action,* chapter II, para. 9)

> A world-wide movement towards democratisation has opened up the political process in many countries, but the popular participation of women in key decision-making as full and equal partners with men, particularly in politics, has not yet been achieved . . .
>
> (para. 17)

Recent international economic developments have had in many cases a disproportionate impact on women and children, the majority of whom live in developing countries . . .

(para. 20)

The growing strength of the non-governmental sector, particularly women's organisations and feminist groups, has become a driving force for change. Non-governmental organisations have played an important advocacy role in advancing legislation or mechanisms to ensure the promotion of women. They have also become catalysts for new approaches to development . . .

(para. 27)

The human rights of women include their right to have control over and decide freely and responsibly on matters related to their sexuality, including sexual and reproductive health, free from coercion, discrimination and violence . . .

(chapter IV, para. 97)

Transnational feminist networks

The proliferation of transnational feminist networks may be regarded as both a reflection of the multifaceted process of globalization and a response to and criticism of its vagaries. What began in the early part of the 1980s as the formation of a handful of small feminist networks comprised of individuals in a few neighbouring countries has been transformed into large, sometimes professionalized organizations with officers, publications, annual meetings, ties to national and international non-governmental organizations (such as human rights groups), consultative status with the United Nations, and so on. In many ways, this has changed the global political landscape. From a historical and sociological perspective, feminist organizations reflect the growth of the women's movement over the past two decades, the attainment of educational and employment experience by women, successful networking among women and between women and men, and the ambition to influence the direction of change. As such, women's organizations are able to take advantage of current technological advances in communications, making extensive use of, for example, the fax, Internet and e-mail.[2]

Some writings have singled out the Nairobi Conference as a turning point in national women's organizations and in the emergence of global feminism (Bunch and Carrillo, 1990). Regional research centres, feminist bookfairs, and international academic conferences on women began to proliferate as well. In 1981 the first International Interdisciplinary Congress on Women was held in Haifa, Israel. Subsequent ones have been held in the Netherlands in 1984, Ireland in 1987, the United States in 1990, Costa Rica in 1993, Australia in 1997 and Norway in 2000. Notable among the transnational feminist networks formed in the period after the Nairobi conference are those that serve mainly as a means of communication. These include the International Women's Information and Communication Service (ISIS), the International Women's Tribune Center (IWTC), and women's presses, such as Depthnews Asian Women's Feature Service (Stienstra, 1994: 106).

In recent years the IWTC has disseminated information on the 42nd session of the UN's Commission on the Status of Women. According to a 1998 dispatch regarding the Commission's meeting to discuss four items of the Beijing *Platform for Action*, a record number of women's NGOs attended the session. Lobbyists for actions outlined within the Women and Armed Conflict section of the *Platform for Action* called for a strengthening of implementation measures in eight areas. These were: (i) mainstreaming of a gender perspective into peace support activities at all levels; (ii) the creation of a culture of peace; (iii) the contribution of women to non-military peace-keeping operations, particularly in the protection of women and girls; (iv) the delegitimization (outlawing) of war and violence; (v) the implementation of commitments already made by governments to reduce military budgets and spending, and the diversion of the funds saved to social development programs; (vi) the establishment of a registry of production and export of all military equipment and components, to be maintained by the UN; (vii) the banning of all export of military equipment and components from all sources to countries where there are gross human rights violations and/or conflicts in progress or likely; and (viii) the elimination of all nuclear weapons and weapons of mass destruction (IWTC Globalnet no. 105, 10 March 1998, via Internet).

One of the best-known feminist networks to emerge after Nairobi was Development Alternatives for Women in a New Era (DAWN), currently based in Fiji and comprised largely of feminist groups from developing countries. The 'manifesto' of the DAWN group, now a classic in the field of women-in-development, is *Development, Crises, and Alternative Visions: Third World Women's Perspectives* (Sen and Grown, 1987). The feminist network WIDE was also formed after Nairobi, although it remained loosely organized and relatively fundless until 1990.

A number of feminist networks have focused their energies on structural adjustment and its social and gender effects, and on the biases and deficiencies of international development co-operation and assistance. For example, a feminist network in the United States, Alternative Perspectives on Women and Development (Alt-WID) was largely responsible for the publication of *Mortgaging Women's Lives: Feminist Critiques of Structural Adjustment* (Sparr, 1994). This feminist network offers critiques of current economic policies and environmental conditions and argues that increasing women's political power and participation in decision-making would resolve many of these problems. The Women's Environment and Development Organization (WEDO), co-founded by the late American lawyer and activist Bella Abzug, defines its goal as 'to make women more visible as equal participants, experts and leaders in policy-making from the community to the international level, and in formulating alternative, healthy, and peaceful solutions to world problems' (from its newsletter, *News and Views*). WEDO co-chairs are based in Brazil, Guyana, Norway, Egypt, Kenya, Nigeria, Costa Rica, India and New Zealand. Other feminist networks, such as the International Women's Health Coalition based in New York, focus on reproductive health and rights issues, mainly through policy-oriented research, publications, and advocacy. Women, Law and Development International, a network based in Washington, DC, includes prominent and internationally-known lawyers and judges from developing countries, as well as grass-roots-oriented regional and local groups that work on such issues as women's health and violence against women.[3]

Among the feminist networks that focus on women's human rights or legal status, WLUML provides an interesting example. Women Living under Muslim Laws (WLUML) 'took off' in the mid-1980s. It is a network of women who live in Muslim countries or who are from Muslim countries but live elsewhere. The network was formed mainly in response to the rise and spread of fundamentalism and of revisions in Muslim family codes that were formalizing the 'second-class citizenship' of women (for example, Iran, Algeria, Egypt). WLUML has a documentation centre in France, where its energetic founding member, Marie-Aime Hélie-Lucas, resides, and branches throughout the Muslim world. It also has an active affiliate in South Asia, Shirkat Gah, based in Lahore, and close ties with leading feminist networks and organizations in North America and Europe. Its most visible forms of action are its Action Alerts (petitions and campaigns reminiscent of Amnesty International), usually drawing attention to the plight of an individual or a group suffering from discrimination or unjust treatment in a Muslim country.

Although transnational feminist networks prioritize or emphasize objectives, they tend to have a broad political agenda. One transnational feminist network that is focused on a single issue, however, is the Women's Alliance for Peace and Human Rights in Afghanistan, based in Washington, DC. WAPHA was formed in 1996 in response to the Taleban take-over, and is led by Zieba Shorish-Shamley. This network of individuals in various countries who are concerned about the status of women in contemporary Afghanistan has forged links with two American feminist organizations – the Feminist Majority and the National Organization for Women – in an effective campaign to prevent the Clinton Administration from recognizing the Taleban government. It continues to agitate against support for any corporate activity in Afghanistan as long as the Taleban continue to practice 'gender apartheid'.[4]

A significant difference between feminist networks and other organizations lies in their non-hierarchical structure. The desire to avoid excesses of power and relations of domination and subordination within the organization leads to innovative ways of sharing responsibility. Feminist networks function to a great extent on the emotional and political commitment of their members and especially their staff, many of whom volunteer a considerable amount of their time. But what is a strength at one moment could become a weakness, especially if the organization expands and grows and management decisions become necessary. As Moser (1993) explains in her chapter on women's NGOs, unclear authority demarcation and defined responsibilities, and work overload on the part of some members could lead to conflict and dissent. This is true, of course, not only of feminist organizations but also of many voluntary organizations or political groups that have little funding and depend heavily on the work, time, and commitment of a core group of members.[5] It should also be noted that despite their non-hierarchical nature, feminist organizations frequently have strong and sometimes charismatic leaders. Strong leadership can be especially important in getting an organization started. But abuses of charisma have not been unknown in women's organizations.[6]

In sum, feminist networks have emerged in the context of the spread of global feminism, as an alternative to men's organizations, as a vehicle for political action, and as an expression of democratization and women's citizenship. Feminist networks provide information and support for members and other women, engage in advocacy and criticism of policies, and are moving effectively to take part in the formulation of policies and in the process of decision-making. The interaction and cooperation among feminist networks constitute a significant aspect of the phenomenon. Not only do the large networks have regular contact with each other (as in the case of the four examined in this chapter), but local groups that may belong to one network will also have members that belong to other networks. Feminist networks tap into each other in an almost seamless web, with many points of intersection.

We will now consider four such feminist networks: DAWN, WIDE, WLUML, and AWMR.

Development Alternatives with Women for a New Era (DAWN)

DAWN is an expanding network of women researchers and activists from developing countries promoting alternative approaches to economic development and more equitable gender systems. Its 22-member founding committee included prominent Third World activists and academics. Following an initial meeting in Bangalore, India in August 1984, on the eve of the third United Nations Conference on Women, the network prepared a platform document which was used as the basis of a series of panels and workshops at the NGO Forum in Nairobi in 1985. The network was formally launched the following year in Rio de Janeiro, where a secretariat was established. The secretariat rotated to the Caribbean in 1990, when a new general co-ordinator was selected, and it moved to Fiji at the end of 1995.

DAWN's specific contribution is to offer an alternative 'model' of socio-economic development, one which is people-centred, holistic, sustainable and which empowers women. In seeking an alternative paradigm for development, DAWN has developed a framework based on an analysis of the issues from the perspective of women in the South. DAWN's analysis attempts to reflect the diversity of regional experiences and to relate the experience of women at the micro level of the household and community to an understanding of macroeconomic policy and global trends. Its perspective has served as a catalyst for debates on key development issues.

Following the Nairobi Conference, a series of meetings and discussions resulted in the publication of *Development, Crises, and Alternative Visions*. DAWN's vision, now a staple of every publication, was first stated in that book:

We want a world where inequality based on class, gender and race is absent from every country, and from the relationships among countries. We want a world where basic needs become basic rights and where poverty and all forms of violence are eliminated. Each person will have the opportunity to develop her or his full potential and creativity, and values of nurturance and solidarity will characterize human relationships. In such a world women's reproductive role will be redefined: men will be responsible for their sexual behaviour, fertility and the well-being of both partners. Child care will be shared by men, women and society as a whole.

We want a world where the massive resources now used in the production of the means of destruction will be diverted to areas where they will help to relieve oppression both inside and outside the home. This technological revolution will eliminate disease and hunger, and give women means for the safe control of their lives, health, sexuality and fertility.

We want a world where all institutions are open to participatory democratic processes, where women share in determining priorities and making decisions. This political environment will provide enabling social conditions that respect women's and men's physical integrity and the security of their persons in every dimension of their lives.

(Sen and Grown, 1987: 80–1)

As stated in the book's preamble, the book was written following 'extensive debate and discussion with researchers, activists, and policy makers'. It was felt that by adopting an open and flexible process – one that drew on varied experiences – the group would be better able to come to a common perspective and objective. As the book's preamble states,

If we ourselves can evolve new working styles, new forms of co-operative organisation and practices, this will contribute to the search for genuine alternatives. To build a social order that is just, equitable, and life-affirming for all people, our methods must correspondingly be open and respectful of differences, and must try to break down hierarchies, power, and distrust.

(Sen and Grown, 1987: 10)

DAWN's affiliated organisations and individuals are from the Caribbean, Latin America, the Pacific, South Asia, South-East Asia, the

Middle East and Africa. Especially active are the Latin American members, who have produced a number of books, including *Alternatives, Volume 1: The Food, Energy, and Debt Crises in Relation to Women*, and *Alternatives, Volume 2: Women's Visions and Movements* (DAWN, 1991). Both books were published in Rio de Janeiro in 1991. A book on environmental issues was prepared for the UN Conference on Environment and Development and one on alternative economic frameworks was prepared for the World Summit for Social Development and for the Fourth World Conference on Women.[7] A number of studies were prepared for the International Conference on Population and Development, including one entitled *Population and Reproductive Rights: Feminist Perspectives from the South*, written by Sonia Correa and Rebecca Reichmann in association with DAWN.[8] The network was very prominent at the ICPD and at the Forum of the Non-Governmental Organizations that took place just before the Beijing Conference. Its activities took the form of participation in panels and workshops at the NGO Forum and, at the official conference, lobbying of government delegates and attendance at working groups formed to remove the brackets from contested paragraphs of the draft *Platform of Action*.[9]

Leading figures in DAWN include Gita Sen, an Indian economist and co-author of *Development, Crises, and Alternative Visions*, and Peggy Antrobus, a professor of women and development studies at the University of Barbados, who has become an active resource person in UN circles. Among the Founding Committee members, Noeleen Heyzer of Malaysia is now the Director of UNIFEM, while Lourdes Arizpe of Mexico is Assistant Director-General of UNESCO.

To support its various projects, DAWN receives funding from the major international development aid agencies, certain UN agencies, and universities and non-governmental organizations in various developing countries. According to one of its publications, DAWN 'counts on the participation of 4500 women throughout the Third World'.

Network Women in Development Europe (WIDE)

WIDE was established in 1985, immediately after the Nairobi Conference. Its focus was on development co-operation, with a feminist critique of aid. It saw its mandate as being responsive to women's needs in the South. Gradually, however, its focus shifted, especially as a result of Thatcherism in England and the spread in Europe of cutbacks in social spending and the expansion of labour market flexibility. This made the women of WIDE recognize in a more immediate and direct way the links between North and South economic and social processes. At the same time, they were very much inspired by DAWN's broad definition of development as spelled out in Sen and Grown (1987), and by its vision for an alternative form of development. Like DAWN, WIDE became involved in the international conferences of the 1990s: UNCED in 1992, the International Conference on Human Rights in 1993, the ICPD in 1994, the Social Summit in March 1995, and the Beijing Conference of 1995. WIDE's president, Helen O'Connell, was accredited to the official conference and presented a statement during the General Exchange of Views.

At the time of writing, WIDE consists of a network of 12 national platforms; each national platform consists of one or more women's groups. The oldest national platform is Ireland, and the most recent, Austria. The others are Spain, France, Italy, Belgium (with two platforms, one French and the other Flemish), Germany, England, Switzerland, Holland, Finland and Denmark. Each has its own program of work but shares information with the Brussels office. At its May 1995 General Assembly in Brussels, all 12 national platforms presented a report on their activities, and their plans for the Beijing Conference. The General Assembly was chaired by the President, had a financial report by the Treasurer, and a report by the Co-ordinator of the Brussels office.

In the first few years of existence WIDE was based in Dublin but in 1993 it moved its office to Brussels, so that it could carry out more effectively its lobby and advocacy work within the EU, the European Parliament, the Council of Ministers and to the delegations of member states. WIDE also co-operates and co-ordinates its activities with other networks in Europe, such as Protestant agencies, Catholic agencies, the European Network on Debt and Development (EURODAD), European Solidarity Towards Equal Participation of People (EUROSTEP) and others. WIDE is part of a new network called the Global Alliance for Alternative Development, which also includes DAWN and Alt-WID. The focus of the Global Alliance is alternative economics – an effort to critique economic theory from a feminist and gender perspective.

Much of WIDE's lobbying and educational efforts within the EU are geared towards identifying the contradictions and inconsistencies between the stated objectives of aid and development co-operation and the effects of structural adjustment. Despite its known critiques of the currently fashionably neoliberal economic policies, WIDE's funding is principally from the EU and it was invited by the Dutch government a few years ago to submit an application for a large grant. WIDE has been invited to take part in and prepare position papers for the EU

Committee on Women's Rights, the UNDP Human Development Report 1995, the OECD/DAC/WID group, and the prepcoms for the Social Summit and the Beijing Conference. According to the WIDE Annual Report for 1994–95, its work for 1996 had five aims:

- to influence the debates in the field of gender during the Intergovernmental Conference of the EU in 1996;
- to monitor the implementation of the Platform for Action of Beijing by the EU and its member states;
- to elaborate and publish a gender mapping of the EU trade policies;
- to plan the installation of four regional consultation groups (North Africa, Sub-Saharan Africa, Latin America, Asia) on EU policy and the impact on women;
- to follow-up on Lomé IV (a trade agreement with African countries).

In her remarks at the General Assembly in Brussels in May 1995, WIDE's president mentioned two tensions in the organization's structure. One was the tension arising from the need to have a good working relationship with EU officials, and being able to express criticism of EU policies. The other tension was that between having a central office and being a network. At the time, the tension was resolved through information exchange among the national platforms and between the national platforms and the WIDE office in Brussels.

The day before its General Assembly, WIDE held a conference in Brussels to discuss ideas around its draft position paper for the Beijing Conference, which began with an examination of the assumptions behind neoclassical economics and their links with misguided neo-liberal policies. One book that had inspired this effort is *Male Bias in the Development Process* (1991), edited by the British economist Diane Elson. Elson defines male-biased development outcomes as those that result in more asymmetry and inequality between men and women, and identifies the proximate causes in terms of male bias in everyday attitudes and decisions, in theoretical analysis, and in the process of defining and implementing public policy. The key structural factor shaping these attitudes and policies is the social and economic organization of access to resources and to childcare. For this reason, WIDE feminists place a great emphasis on women's reproductive activities, much of which is unpaid (if it is domestic and based in the home) or under-paid (if it is occupational and within the labour market). A major criticism from the alternative-economics feminists within the WIDE network is that structural adjustment does not take into account the interdependence between the 'productive economy' and the 'reproductive economy' (also called by some'the economy of care'). They point out that programmes of expenditure cuts are frequently designed in a way that undermines the ability of women to respond to new price incentives in agriculture and job opportunities in export-oriented manufacturing (in that women have to compensate with their labour-time for cuts in social sectors) and that jeopardize human development targets. Their recommendation is that all programmes for macro-economic policy reform should include not only targets for monetary aggregates and policy instruments for achieving them but also targets for human development aggregates and policy instruments for delivering them. The relation between the policy instruments and the targets should be analysed in gender-desegregated terms that recognize the inputs of unpaid labour as well as paid labour. In terms of economic analysis and economic policy prescriptions, WIDE feminists are sympathetic to the UNDP's concept of human development.

Many feminist organizations are critical of masculinist organizations and of policies that reflect a predominantly male standpoint. As such, WIDE is a feminist network par excellence. For example, a 1994 briefing paper jointly prepared by EURODAD and WIDE was entitled 'Male Chauvinist SAPs: Structural Adjustment and Gender Policies', and highlighted the inherent male bias of structural adjustment policies. A 1995 press release on another publication, called *Gender Mapping the European Union*, began thus:

> European Union policy is 'gender blind', concludes a new report jointly published by WIDE and EUROSTEP. The report entitled *Gender Mapping in the EU* pinpoints who pulls the strings in the EU institutions in relation to gender. The report was commissioned to penetrate the institution's lack of procedural transparency, and to identify those responsible for policy design and implementation.
>
> 'The EU claims to be gender sensitive in its work,' commented Mieke van der Veken of WIDE, 'but there is no clear gender policy formulated in the aid system and even less in foreign and trade policy departments.' Although there is compulsory gender training in some parts of the Commission in effect there are no equal gender opportunities in recruitment,' says Brita Schioldan Nielsen of EUROSTEP. 'Without a policy of positive discrimination for women the grey-suited masculine culture of the Commission will remain.'

WIDE's 1997 annual meeting, held in Finland, was attended by some 130 participants from 20 countries. The focus was on globalization, the role of international financial institutions, and impacts on women. Examples of how economic transformation has affected women focused on Russia, the Nordic welfare states, and India. According to the conference report, entitled *Trade Traps and Gender Gaps: Women Unveiling the Market*, 'the globalisation of markets has unleashed the forces of deregulation of national financial and labour markets, accelerating the onslaught of inequality, poverty, social disintegration and environmental degradation. These negative effects of the global market will only further be exacerbated by current attempts on the part of transnational corporations and their political supporters to modify and improve rules for the operation of the market on their own terms.' The report highlighted 'the lack of transparency and accountability in economic life in all levels, . . . the lack of accountability to citizens of global economic structures', contrasting these with 'the accountability which is built into the locally based economic and trading initiatives of which examples were presented during the conference'.[10]

Women Living Under Muslim Laws/International Solidarity Network (WLUML)

In July 1984 an Action Committee of Women Living Under Muslim Laws was set up by nine women from Algeria, Sudan, Morocco, Pakistan, Bangladesh, Iran, Mauritius and Tanzania. The committee was established in response to situations arising out of 'the application of Muslim laws in India, Algeria, and Abu Dhabi that resulted in the violation of women's human rights' (Kazi, 1997: 141). It evolved in January 1985 into an international network of information, solidarity and support. In April 1986, the first planning meeting of the network, gathering together ten women from Algeria, Morocco, Tunisia, Egypt, Sudan, Nigeria, India, Pakistan and Sri Lanka, set the tasks for the network. These were:

- To create international links between women in Muslim countries and communities;
- To exchange information on their situations (similarities and differences), struggles and strategies, in order to strengthen and reinforce women's initiatives and struggles through various means (publications, exchanges, etc.);

- To support each other's struggles through various means including an Alert for Action system. (Hélie-Lucas, 1993a: 225)

The network receives appeals and responds to as well as initiates campaigns pertaining to violations of human rights, including women's human rights. All requests from groups or individuals representing varied opinions and currents from within the movement for reform or defence of women's rights seeking support and urgent actions are forwarded throughout the network. As Hélie-Lucas (1993a) herself explains, these actions range from campaigns concerning the repeal of discriminatory legislation; the end of oppressive practices; the enactment and/or enforcement of legislation favourable to women; cases of systematized or generalized violations of human rights; to individual cases where, for example, inhuman sentences have been given, women have been forcibly married against their will, fathers have abducted their children or women's lives have been threatened.

Action Alerts are initiated or disseminated by the head office in Montpellier or by the South Asia office, Shirkat Gah Women's Resource Center, based in Lahore, Pakistan. A sample of Action Alert efforts between 1990 and 1995 that were either initiated by WLUML or disseminated by them on behalf of other organizations include the following: an alert on the campaign to end the trafficking of Burmese women and girls into Thai brothels; an alert on the campaign to prosecute three war criminals of the Bangladesh War of Liberation, now citizens and residents of the UK; an alert regarding violation of women's human rights in Kurdistan (in this case 'committed by the relatives of women or even by members of the autonomous government of Kurdistan'); an alert regarding the appeal by a Pakistani fanatical group for the murder of four prominent citizens for alleged blasphemy; an appeal by Amnesty International regarding the torture of a nine-year-old Indonesian boy detained on suspicion of stealing a wallet; an alert regarding the rape of an 11-year-old Bangladeshi girl by police in northeast Delhi; an alert regarding the campaign to save the lives of a 13-year-old Christian Pakistani boy and his uncle who had been sentenced to death under blasphemy charges in Pakistan; an alert regarding the abduction, torture and killing of Marinsah, an Indonesian female factory worker and trade union activist; an appeal from the group Women for Women's Human Rights in Turkey calling for the revision of Turkey's Family Code; many appeals regarding the situation of Algerian women and fundamentalist terror; a condemnation of female genital mutilation; many appeals regarding Bosnia; an appeal by the Union of Palestinian Working Women Committees regarding ill-treatment of Palestinian women fighters in Israeli jails; an alert regarding the Egyptian government's closure of the Arab Women's Solidarity Association; the campaign for the International Day of Protest against the continued presence of US military bases and facilities in the Philippines; an alert regarding the situation of women in Iran; and an alert regarding the reinstatement of a law allowing 'honour killings' in Iraq.

Besides the Action Alerts, the activities of the network entail documenting and disseminating information in the form of Dossiers, which describe the situation of Muslim women and legal codes in various countries and report on the activities of women's organizations. In addition, there is a news sheet published by Shirkat Gah in Lahore. During 1997 and 1998, many articles were devoted to describing the plight of women in Algeria and in Afghanistan. The news sheets do not focus exclusively on Muslim women, but address themselves to women's human rights situations throughout the developing world. Shirkat Gah also devotes its resources to translating and publishing books, including two on the gender implications of the changing political economy of Uzbekistan and Central Asia.[11]

Collective projects on topics related to women in the Muslim world have also occasionally been organized by WLUML. These included an exchange program in 1988 that allowed 18 women from 15 countries to meet for the purpose of exchanging information on strategies used in different parts of the Muslim world by women activists. According to Hélie-Lucas (1993a: 227):

> We realised that many local customs and traditions practised in the name of Islam in one part of the world were in fact unheard of in others. It also became evident that not only are the varied and contradictory interpretations of the Koran monopolised by men but they are also the only ones who have so far defined the status of Muslim women.

This realization led to the initiation of a project on Koranic Interpretation by Women (started in July 1990), which brought together 30 women activists and resource persons from ten countries to read for themselves the verses of the Koran relating to women. 'The meeting allowed participants to see just how differently the same verses of the Koran have been interpreted (both through translations and explanations, or tafsir) by Islamic scholars and various schools of thought'

(Hélie-Lucas, 1993a: 227). This effort led to the initiation of yet another project, called the Women and Law Project (1991–94), which involved women in 20 Muslim countries who examined legislation, especially the Muslim family codes, that discriminate against women and indeed contradict clauses regarding equality in countries' constitutions. The stated objective of the Women and Law Project was: 'to empower women living under Muslim laws through knowledge of their rights in their societies and to strengthen their capacity to understand their situations, to act locally, and work together towards meeting their needs. As well, it aims to enhance the participation of Muslim women in the development of their societies.'

Finally, WLUML has involved itself in an effort to broaden the scope of development conditionally to benefit women:

> . . . linking aid to the democratisation of our countries gives us little hope, since there is no sign that the fate of women will be seen as a valid indicator of democracy by the international community. What we see instead is a narrow interpretation of democracy in the exclusive sense of parliamentary democracy. This never prevented Hitler from being elected!
>
> Rather than leaving women to the 'goodwill' of their (male) political leaders, states should be obliged by donors to direct a percentage of their aid money to women's projects. A women's lobby group is presently working towards having the EC adopt such a policy vis-à-vis the North African countries. (Hélie-Lucas, 1993b: 62)

By 1994 some 25 countries were associated with WLUML through various projects (Kazi, 1997: 145). According to Shaheed (1995: 320)

> over two thousand women in several continents are linked through WLUML. These women have diverse professional and academic backgrounds, organisational frameworks and political perspectives but share a commitment to expanding women's autonomy. Most are actively involved in the women's movement in their own countries or place of residence. In addition, many are engaged in general advocacy initiatives.

Like WIDE, DAWN, and other feminist networks, WLUML stresses information exchange, mutual support and international solidarity toward the realization of its essential goal. Through its projects and its documentation and dissemination activities, WLUML has expanded the creative use of scarce resources and helped individuals and groups to form contacts and exchange knowledge, thereby increasing their effectiveness. Such a strategy 'strengthens our local struggles by providing support at the regional and international levels, at the same time as our local struggles strengthen the regional and international women's movement in a mutually supportive process' (Hélie-Lucas, 1993a: 226).

The Association of Women of the Mediterranean Region (AWMR)

The AWMR unites women from Albania, Algeria, Cyprus, Egypt, France, Gibraltar, Greece, Israel, Italy, Lebanon, Libya, Malta, Morocco, Palestine, Spain, Syria, Tunisia, Turkey, and the former Yugoslavia. It was founded in Malta in 1992 'after seven years of meeting, networking, and joint work'.[12] The AWMR has a 19-person Board of Directors, elected for a period of three years, who are 'dedicated to justice, equality, and peace'. The current president and founding member is Yana Mintoff-Bland. She happens to be the daughter of the veteran socialist leader of Malta, Dom Mintoff, whose early support for the Palestinian cause set him apart from other European leaders. The General Secretary, Ninetta Pourou-Kazantzis, is from Limassol, Cyprus. During 1998, board members from Malta, Morocco and Tunisia had recently been elected or appointed to legislative positions in their countries. Board members, and other AWMR members, have been active in various progressive causes, and some have been members of left-wing political parties. This common political background allows for consensus and co-operation of women across different conflict regions.[13] Thus members can agree on such resolutions as: 'We condemn the use of embargoes and military intervention against defenceless populations. These actions deprive children of their basic human right to health.'[14]

AWMR's stated aims are the following:

- just and peaceful resolution of regional conflicts;
- regional demilitarization and global disarmament;
- elimination of discrimination, poverty, and violence against women;
- human rights, real democracy, and sustainable development;
- the welfare and rights of children;
- education for peace through the family, schools, and media;
- common action to end environmental degradation of the Mediterranean Region.

Among its actions and achievements have been petitions to end the violence in Bosnia; the sale of Palestinian women's crafts in the USA; joint activity by Jewish and Palestinian women against Israeli aggression; the initiation of dialogue between Greek Cypriot women and Turkish Cypriot women; joint activity among women in Zagreb, Sarajevo, and Belgrade; a visit by Italian delegates to Albania in support of women's rights; actions in defence of Algerian women; and a 1997 petition for Education for Peace in the Mediterranean. The association puts out a newsletter, publishes the proceedings of its annual conferences, and sends copies of its resolutions to governments and to the United Nations Secretariat.

The first six annual conferences – held in either Malta or Cyprus – were on women's rights, colonialism, militarism, health, refugees and immigrants, and education for peace. Each conference ends with a set of resolutions and is followed by a conference report and the publication of a book. In July 1998 the seventh conference was on 'Women and Work in the Mediterranean'. The local organizing committee from the southern Italian region of Lecce was in charge of the arrangements, which included an opening ceremony and social events. The main panel discussions were on: the right to work in the context of women's human rights; exploitation, unemployment, and ways to organize; and country analyses of women and work. There was also a workshop on globalization, the presentation of position papers and resolutions, and a general assembly. Panel presentations were on subjects such as immigrant working women in Italy and elsewhere; women, work, and the changing political economy in the Middle East and North Africa; the problems and prospects of women and work in Algeria; women and structural adjustment in Turkey; women and the legal profession in Italy; the economic empowerment of women victims of domestic violence and war refugees; and women and work in Cyprus, Greece, Israel, Serbia and Bulgaria. Short papers on the above subjects were available to the participants.

Resolutions were passed on the violence in Algeria; on a parliamentary proposal in Greece to introduce military conscription for women; on the continuing problems in Israel/Palestine and its implications for women; on the special problems of persons of mixed marriages in the former Yugoslavia; on women's rights and violence against Kurds in Turkey; on the conflict in Kosovo; and on the continuing division of Cyprus. The final conference resolution – subsequently sent to government bodies of the region, and to the UN – consisted of four paragraphs on the economic and political situation of the region, and a list of 12 'minimum conditions necessary to safeguard women's right to work'. The introductory paragraphs highlighted the adverse effects of globalization on national economies, the feminization of poverty in countries of the region, rising unemployment, and the growing inequalities within and between countries. The minimum conditions emphasized the state's responsibility to provide work opportunity for the unemployed, 'the right to work in dignity and safety and without sexual harassment', good wages, an end to huge income inequalities, conducive social policies for working mothers, and 'the right of all women workers, including home-workers, agricultural workers, and housewives, to pensions and benefits in their own name'.[15]

The Association has no paid positions and is based entirely on voluntary work. It has received funding from a generous private source and some from the governments of Cyprus and Malta, but most of its revenues come from membership fees and from the sale of books. In early 1999 it set up a website and was planning its eighth conference, to be held in Athens and to focus on the environment.

Transnational feminist networks and the future of collective action

Feminist networks, including the four case studies, offer an alternative to male-dominated political organizations; they are an expression of the political awakening of women; and they exemplify the maturation of feminism and the interaction of women's activists around the world. Feminist networks have actively responded to negative global processes, including economic restructuring and the expansion of fundamentalism; and they are taking advantage of other global processes, including new information technologies. They engage in information exchange, mutual support, and a combination of lobbying, advocacy and direct action towards the realization of their goals of equality and empowerment for women and social justice and democratization in the society at large. They seem to have devised an organizational structure that consists of active and autonomous local/national women's groups but that transcends localisms or nationalisms. Their discourses and objectives are not particularistic but are universalistic. As such, these transnational feminist networks are situated in the tradition of progressive modernist politics, rather than in any new wave of postmodernist or identity politics. The organizational form is not a federative or international one; rather, it is transnational and, indeed, supranational. As such, it is the form that the labour movement should have adopted, but never did. Whether the world's labour movement will follow the organizational form and collective action strategies of the world's women's movement is a pertinent question.

This chapter has not focused on the internal structures of the four feminist networks analysed in the case studies, but suffice it to say that they are run according to democratic principles and by consensus rather than in the form of a hierarchical bureaucracy. Although there is a certain degree of professionalization in the networks – especially in WIDE and WLUML, which have a few paid positions – none of the four networks displays any bureaucratization or centralization in decision-making. Within the AWMR, the preferred method of decision-making is consensus of the members, but sometimes votes are taken and a resolution is passed by a simple majority. WLUML has been described as having 'a fluid structure and rejection of hierarchies' (Shaheed, 1995: 324). This is not to say that women's organizations, or the transnational feminist networks described here, do not experience internal problems.[16] Rather, it is to say that the network form of a feminist organization may be the one most suited to transnational organizing, mobilizing, policy-oriented research and advocacy that also includes non-hierarchical and democratic objectives. It may also be the most effective form of feminist organizing and mobilizing in an era of globalization.

Like many other feminist networks and women's organizations, the members and activists of DAWN, WIDE, WLUML, and AWMR are largely middle-class, highly educated women. In some cases, this class profile can be a disadvantage, inasmuch as the women may be distanced from the concerns of working-class and poor women. But many feminist networks and organizations in fact have extensive connections with women of the popular classes. For example, WLUML includes locally-based activist member groups that work at the grass-roots level. AWMR includes trade unionists and other activists who work at the local, 'grass-roots' level. At the same time, given that an important objective of these feminist networks is to challenge the ideas, attitudes, policies, and decisions of large sophisticated organizations – including international financial institutions and state agencies – the presence of highly-educated women advocates of alternative economics and of women's rights is necessary and effective.

The four feminist networks examined in this chapter have somewhat different emphases. DAWN and WIDE focus on development and economic issues; WLUML devotes its energies toward legal and political rights of women in Muslim countries; AWMR has a broad and holistic approach. And yet these concerns necessarily overlap at the equity and empowerment nexus, and all four networks share the goals and strategies of feminist networks as I have described them. Although there will continue to be a diversity of feminisms, framed by local issues, problems, needs, opportunities and constraints, this need not refute the proposition that there seems to exist a worldwide women's movement with common goals and strategies. The four transnational feminist networks that I have described would seem to validate this. These and other feminist networks should be understood as so many webs within the larger net of global feminism.

Finally, the study of transnational feminist networks has several implications for social theory, including theories of social movements and globalization studies. The first point is that transnational feminist networks have emerged in a multifaceted context of opportunities and constraints: (i) a growing population of educated, employed, mobile, and politically-aware women around the world; (ii) increasing opportunities afforded by UN conferences; (iii) economic crisis and restructuring; (iv) continued discrimination, oppression, and gender inequality; and (v) economic, political, and cultural globalization. The second point is that 'new social movements' such as the women's movement are not necessarily non-economic and identity-focused. All four of the case-study transnational feminist networks organize around issues pertaining to the economy, the political system, and foreign policy, as well as reproductive rights, family laws, and violence against women. The third point is that the transnational nature of feminist networks calls into question theorizing that begins and ends with single societies. One may continue to argue the need for nationally-oriented research and point out the continued salience of nation-states and domestic organizations. But nation-states, national economies, and cultural formations – including social movements and organizations – are increasingly affected by global processes, with the result that the appropriate unit of analysis must combine global, regional, and local. The fourth point is that transnational feminism calls into question sociological research that remains focused on the West. If the concentration of modern capitalism in the West was once a justification for sociology's exclusive focus on Europe and the United States, the existence of a global capitalism, and the transnational flows of labour, capital, and ideas, necessitate a broader perspective. Finally, the network form of transnational organizing may be the one most conducive to the era of globalization. It appears to be flexible, efficient, and non-hierarchical. More research is needed, however, on the strengths and weaknesses of decentralized networks versus more formal organizations.

Notes

1. Research for this chapter was begun in 1995. It is based on a variety of methods: participant observation at two annual meetings (WIDE, Brussels, May 1995 and AWMR, Gallipoli, Italy, July 1998); a close reading of the publications of the transnational feminist networks; and relevant secondary sources. In addition, my participation as a UN staff member at two UN conferences (the Social Summit, Copenhagen, March 1995 and the Fourth World Conference on Women, Beijing, September 1995), several pre-Beijing regional preparatory meetings of governments and of non-governmental organizations, and the annual UN Ad-Hoc Inter-Agency Meeting on Women in Development (which always preceded the annual meeting in March of the Commission on the Status of Women) all gave me insights into the growth of women's organizations worldwide and into their global linkages.
2. An example was the flood of protests against the change of venue for the NGO Forum, the planned parallel meeting of the Fourth World Conference on Women. Protests were sent to the UN by fax and e-mail from women's organizations around the world in May 1995. This very effective method of global feminist communication was co-ordinated by the International Women's Tribune Center, based in New York. In another, more recent example, the Women's Alliance for Peace and Human Rights in Afghanistan has been disseminating information and circulating petitions over the Internet.
3. Based on author's observations and interviews during the network's international conference, 'From Basic Needs to Basic Rights', held in Kuala Lumpur, Malaysia in October 1994, and the network's literature.
4. For an analysis of the situation in Afghanistan, see Moghadam (1999).
5. This observation is based in part on the author's experience in the Iranian student movement in Canada and the US during the late 1970s and early 1980s.
6. See, for example, Dwyer (1991) on disputes and splits in women's organizations in Egypt and Tunisia.
7. UNCED took place in Rio de Janeiro in 1992. The Social Summit was held in Copenhagen in March 1995. The FWCW convened in Beijing in September 1995.
8. The ICPD took place in Cairo in 1994.
9. Based on author's observations and discussions at the NGO Forum and the Fourth World Conference on Women, Beijing, September 1995.
10. WIDE, *Trade Traps and Gender Gaps: Women Unveiling the Market: a Full Report of WIDE's Annual Conference Held at Jarvenpaa, Finland, 16–18 May 1997*. Brussels: WIDE, 1998.

11. The two books are Marfua Tokhtakhodjaeva, *Between the Slogans of Communism and the Laws of Islam: the Women of Uzbekistan* (Lahore: Shirkat Gah Women's Resource Center, 1995), and Marfua Tokhtakhodjaeva and Elmira Turgumbekova (eds), *The Daughters of Amazons: Voices from Central Asia* (Lahore: Shirkat Gah Women's Resource Center, 1996).
12. From its brochure.
13. Personal observation at the seventh annual conference, held in Gallipoli, Italy, in July 1998. At one point during the conference I was asked to help draft a resolution on the Kosovo conflict by delegates from Serbia and Albania. I was impressed by the principled and civil nature of the differing views expressed, as well as by the capacity of the women to agree on a statement condemning the violence and calling for negotiations.
14. A resolution of the 1994 conference on Militarism in the Mediterranean, held in Malta.
15. From AMWR, *Final Resolution*, Gallipoli, Italy, 11 July, 1998.
16. These could include lack of coordination, poor management, competitiveness, leadership abuses, and activist burn-out.

References

Basu, A. (ed.) (1995) *The Challenge of Local Feminism*, Boulder, CO: Westview Press.

Boli, J. and G.M. Thomas (1997) 'World culture in the world polity', *American Sociological Review*, 62(2) (April): 171–90.

Bunch, C. and R. Carrillo (1990) 'Feminist perspectives on women in development', in I. Tinker (ed.), *Persistent Inequalities: Women and World Development*, New York: Oxford University Press, pp. 70–82.

DAWN (1991) *Alternatives, Volume 1: The Food, Energy, and Debt Crises in Relation to Women, and Alternatives; Volume 2: Women's Visions and Movements*. Rio de Janeiro.

Dwyer, K. (1991) *Arab Voices: the Human Rights Debate in the Middle East*, Berkeley: University of California Press.

Elson, D. (ed.) (1991) *Male Bias In the Development Process*, Manchester: Manchester University Press.

Ferree, M.M. and B.B. Hess (1995) *Controversy and Coalition: the New Feminist Movement across Three Decades of Change*, revised edition. NY: Twayne.

Ferree, M.M. and P. Yancey Martin (eds) (1995) *Feminist Organizations: Harvest of the New Women's Movement*, Philadelphia: Temple University Press.

Hélie-Lucas, M.-A. (1993a) 'Women's struggles and strategies in the rise of fundamentalism in the Muslim world: from entryism to internationalism', in H. Afshar (ed.), *Women in the Middle East: Perceptions, Realities, and Struggles for Liberation*, London: Macmillan.

Hélie-Lucas, M.-A. (1993b) 'Women living under Muslim laws', in J. Kerr (ed.), *Ours By Right: Women's Rights as Human Rights*, London: Zed Books, in association with the North–South Institute.

Katzenstein, M.F. and C. McClurg Mueller (eds) (1987) *The Women's Movements of the United States and Western Europe*, Philadelphia: Temple University Press.

Kazi, S. (1997) 'Muslim law and Women Living Under Muslim Laws', in M. Afkhami and E. Friedl (eds), *Muslim Women and the Politics of Participation: Implementing the Beijing Platform*, Syracuse, NY: Syracuse University Press, pp. 141–6.

Keck, M. and K. Sikkink (1998) *Activists Beyond Borders: Advocacy Networks in International Politics*, Ithaca, NY: Cornell University Press.

Kriesberg, L. (1997) 'Social movements and global transformation', in J. Smith, C. Chatfield and R. Pagnucco (eds), *Transnational Social Movements and Global Politics*, Syracuse, NY: Syracuse University Press, pp. 3–18.

Kriesi, H. (1996) 'The organizational structure of new social movements in a political context', in D. McAdam et al. (eds), *Comparative Perspectives on Social Movements*. Cambridge University Press, pp. 152–84.

McAdam, D., J.D. McCarthy and M.N. Zald (eds) (1996) *Comparative Perspectives on Social Movements*, Cambridge University Press.

McCarthy, J.D. (1997) 'The globalization of social movements', in J. Smith, C. Chatfield and R. Pagnucco (eds), *Transnational Social Movements and Global Politics*, Syracuse, NY: Syracuse University Press, pp. 243–59.

Moghadam, V.M. (1994) *Identity Politics and Women: Cultural Reassertions and Feminisms in International Perspective*, Boulder, CO: Westview Press.

Moghadam, V.M. (1996a) 'Feminist networks North and South: DAWN, WIDE and WLUML', *Journal of International Communication*, 3(1) (July): 111–26.

Moghadam, V.M. (1996b) 'The Fourth World Conference on Women: dissension and consensus', *Indian Journal of Gender Studies*, 3(1): 93–102.

Moghadam, V.M. (1997) 'Gender and revolutions', in J. Foran (ed.), *Theorizing Revolutions*, New York and London: Routledge, pp. 137–67.

Moghadam, V. (1999) 'Revolution, religion and gender politics: Iran and Afghanistan compared', *Journal of Women's History*, 10(4) Winter.

Morgan, R. (ed.) (1985) *Sisterhood is Global*, New York: Anchor Books.

Moser, C.O.N. (1993) *Gender Planning and Development: Theory, Practice and Training*. London: Routledge.

Robertson, R. (1992) *Globalization: Social Theory and Global Culture*, London: Sage.

Rupp, L. (1998) *Worlds of Women: the Making of an International Women's Movement*. Princeton, NJ: Princeton University Press.

Sen, G. and C. Grown (1987) *Development, Crises, and Alternative Visions*, New York: Monthly Review Press.

Shaheed, F. (1995) 'Linking dreams: the network of Women Living Under Muslim Laws', in M.A. Schuler (ed.), *From Basic Needs to Basic Rights: Women's Claim to Human Rights*, Washington, DC: Women, Law, and Development International, pp. 305–25.

Sklair, L. (1996) 'Social movements for global capitalism: the transnational capitalist class in action', paper presented at RC 49: Conference on *Globalisation and Collective Action*, University of California, Santa Cruz (May).

Smith, J. (1997) 'Characteristics of the modern transnational social movement sector', in J. Smith, C. Chatfield and R. Pagnucco (eds), *Transnational Social Movements and Global Politics*, Syracuse, NY: Syracuse University Press, pp. 42–58.

Smith, J., C. Chatfield and R. Pagnucco (eds) (1997) *Transnational Social Movements and Global Politics*, Syracuse, NY: Syracuse University Press.

Sparr, P. (ed.) (1994) *Mortgaging Women's Lives: Feminist Critiques of Structural Adjustment*, London: Zed Books.

Stienstra, D. (1994) *Women's Movements and International Organisations*, New York: St. Martin's Press.

Tarrow, S. (1996) 'States and opportunities: the political structuring of social movements', in D. McAdam et al. (eds), *Comparative Perspectives on Social Movements*. Cambridge University Press, pp. 41–61.

United Nations (1996) *Platform for Action and the Beijing Declaration*, New York: UN.

West, G. and R. Blumberg (eds) (1990) *Women and Social Protest*. New York: OUP.

6
Global Feminist Theorizing and Organizing: Life-Centred and Multi-Centred Alternatives to Neoliberal Globalization

Angela Miles

Introduction

As Alain Touraine (1971) pointed out decades ago, to warrant the name, a social movement must go beyond opposition to existing structures to propose alternatives. However, theorists of 'new social movements' today tend to focus on forms of struggle rather than on content. They have tended to abandon the dialectical historical materialist project of reciprocally understanding and assessing complex social struggles and the alternatives they represent in and through their social contexts. But this remains as important today as it ever was. In other words, to begin to understand the role of any particular social movement (and they must be analysed in all their complexity and particularity) we need to go beyond an analysis of the neoliberal agenda and processes of globalization to analyse underlying structural shifts in industrial relations of production.

Social movements cannot be explained in terms of changing material conditions alone, and their politics are not determined by these conditions. Material conditions nevertheless provide the boundaries of possibility within which social movements attempt to create history and reinvent the world. The shape of social movements must be understood in terms of the conditions in society which give rise to them. These conditions are, in turn, illuminated and shaped by the social struggles which attempt to change them. Social movements and the society they resist must be read in each other and analysed with reference to each other if we wish to recognize political activists as producers of social change as well as its product.

I cannot undertake such a full-blown analysis in this chapter.

However, I want to look selectively at alternative life-centred values and multi-centred forms of organizing that are emerging in global feminist movements as women around the world respond to and expose the pressures and potentials of a changing world. Of interest here is autonomous women's activism, whether or not it is self-defined as feminist, whether or not it is around issues generally understood in popular discourse as 'women's issues', and whether or not men also participate. This is activism whose means, aims, forms, strategies, and alliances are determined by women in relation to women's needs, also defined by them.

Life-centred values and visions

I have written elsewhere about the post-industrial context of what are called the 'new social movements' (Miles, 1979, 1992). There, I have argued that the emergence of new productive forces beginning in the 1920s has meant, as Marx predicted, that 'the surplus labour of the masses has ceased to be a condition for the development of wealth in general' (McLellan, 1971: 142) and that labour power has been displaced as the key source of value.[1] Science, technology, information and the organization of production have come to play that role. With the emergence of these new productive forces the development of production and human self-development become compatible; the industrial dichotomy between reproduction and production and the dominance of production is breached. What have been women's marginal and dependent life-sustaining activities of individual and community reproduction become central.

In the current period this shift is contained and distorted within the same industrial, patriarchal, colonial relations it threatens. The growing potential to move beyond alienated industrial relations of production is met by an intensification of commodification and an extension of industrial forms and instrumental rationality throughout society into areas previously relatively immune. The end of the indirect control of private and cultural life through the economic discipline of the materially based wage is met by the ordering of the whole of life in support of now artificial wage dependence. So the newly defining role of human development in production becomes alienated mass consumerism, exploitative sexual and cultural libertarianism, and controlling social (or, increasingly, privatized) services. Potential leisure becomes the scourge of unemployment.

Women from the economic South have made a formative contribution to feminist understanding of the deeply negative aspects of the global economy and the 'growth' and 'development' pursued as an unquestioned good in its name.[2] But feminists from the economic North increasingly share this understanding and have contributed to it.[3] 'Modernization'/'development' has brought not only an enormous increase in production for profit, but also, and equally centrally, the relative and/or absolute deprivation of women, colonies, and marginal groups and communities. For expansion of the market and production for exchange at the expense of production for use (i) removes the means of subsistence from individuals and communities; (ii) institutionalizes men's dependence on wages and women's dependence on men (and increasingly also on wages); (iii) reduces all of human and non-human life to a commodity, valuable only in so far as it contributes to profit for a few; and (iv) fuels the concentration of wealth and power in fewer and fewer hands, ultimately a few non-accountable transnational corporations.

The intensification of this process of homogenization, control and commodification is the real agenda of the 'globalization' we hear so much about today. Everywhere, the exigencies of global competition and the global market are used to enforce policies which put absolute priority on unfettered transnational profit-making at the expense of people and the planet. The emerging centrality of human development and its suppression thus coincides with the increasing importance of defending endangered human and non-human life in a period when the very survival of the planet is at risk (Milani 2000).

Over the last decades just such life-centred priorities have become the defining values of much feminist analysis.[4] Feminists all over the world have come to reject the profit-based market system which (i) compels private ownership of all the earth's goods, (ii) recognizes as valuable only what is sold for profit on the market, and therefore (iii) fails, by definition, to acknowledge the value of nature and of women's work. Asian feminists at a regional meeting said of this system:

> Far from promoting broadly-based human development, this model has resulted in gross violations of human rights, continuing depletion of natural resources, increasing destitution of local communities and violence against women.
>
> (Second Asian and Pacific Ministerial Conference
> on Women 1994: 31)

Feminists globally are committed not only to resist the worst consequences of this system and its spread but also to work towards totally different equal, co-operative, life-sustaining, communal forms of social and economic organization. This involves recognizing the worth of women's work[5] and of nature and the importance of women's and other traditional knowledges, all of which are currently denied, devalued, marginalized and rendered invisible. Feminists not only recognize the worth of these things but do so in terms of an alternative logic grounded in the value of life rather than profit.

Finding ways to include these things in economic measures of value, production, growth and so on can be a useful consciousness-raising exercise. For it can help make their worth visible and reveal the irrational ideological underpinnings of measurements which deny their value. However, changing accounting practices to include measures of value of women's work and nature simply extends the logic of exchange relations and increases opportunities for profit if it is done as an end in itself. Done alone, it becomes a rationalization rather that a repudiation of the existing system.

Measuring value in terms of what contributes to the sustenance of human and non-human life, on the other hand, reveals the absurdity, even criminality, of the current system which measures only production for the market and for profit (Waring, 1988). It makes it possible to see that what is called progress/growth/modernization/development has been a centuries-long process, in both the economic North and economic South, of often violent colonization of nature, women, workers, indigenous peoples, and traditional cultures and communities.

If we understand women's autonomous local and global struggles for community survival and transformation in this context, we can see that women are not only reacting to the depredations of global capital, patriarchy, neocolonialism and militarism (although they are doing that). Many women/feminists in all regions of the world are also responding to post-industrial possibilities. For women's struggle for survival and liberation today is necessarily a struggle to realize new life/reproduction-centred alternative values and social organization – a transformative and visionary project.

Women in advanced industrial settings are fighting for recognition of the value of the goods and services they produce in the home; for men's equal participation in this work; for its social support in the form of child care, income support, health and education services; and for decent wages for chronically underpaid 'women's' clerical, service, and caring work. At the same time, women in embattled communities in both the economic South and North are struggling to maintain traditional patterns and capacities of subsistence in the face of devastating 'development' processes.

In all these ways and many more in every region of the world, women in all types of communities are challenging the marginalization and trivialization of paid and unpaid reproductive work and responsibility and its relegation to women. They are resisting the neoliberal agenda which, through free trade, currency devaluations, privatization, and cuts in government spending, is forcing the continued shift of economic resources from individual and social production for local use to production for transnational profit, in the process undermining local communities' ability to provide for themselves in sustainable ways and women's ability to care adequately for their children and old people.[6]

Hilkka Pietila's research confirms the historical and visionary importance of feminist opposition to this economic agenda and defence of local production for local use.[7] When she divided the Finnish economy into three spheres (which she called Free, Protected and Fettered) and calculated the proportion of time spent and value created in each, she found that:

- The Free Sphere, made up of all non-monetary production for local use, accounted for 54% of the total work time and 35% of the total value of production;
- The Protected Sphere, which includes all production for the home market, including such services as transportation, health, and education, accounted for 36% of work time and 46% of the value; and
- The Fettered Economy, which is production for international exchange subject to the exigencies/fetters of international competition, accounted for only 10% of work time and 19% of the value of production.

The fact is that, far from being the bulk of economic activity even in advanced industrial societies, production for international exchange is a tiny shell of activity around a large core of local market and non-market production for local use. The tyranny of policies which sacrifice all other interests and needs to the dictates of international competitiveness becomes evident. Neoliberal policies and resulting 'globalization' stand revealed as the concentrated and ruthless attempt of transnational corporations and their national (G-7) and multilateral (World Bank, International Monetary Fund and World Trade Organization) governmental allies to capture all possible production for the 'fettered' section of the economy and push whatever production cannot be captured for profit onto women in the 'free' sector, regardless of the social and environmental cost.[8]

Women around the world bear the first and greatest burdens of this agenda. So it should come as no surprise that they are not seeking simply to integrate women into these destructive processes on a more equal basis, but to transform them. Many aim to recentre and generalize concerns and work that are marginalized, trivialized, devalued and relegated to women in the process of industrialization, modernization and development. Their struggle for power as women in both the economic North and economic South is nothing less than a bid to transform patriarchal, colonial, and capitalist social priorities and social relationships. In 1979 US feminists Barbara Ehrenreich and Deirdre English expressed this vision as an affirmation of use-values and the value of human life over exchange-value and the requirements of profit:

> We refuse to remain on the margins of society, and we refuse to enter that society on its own terms . . . The human values that women were assigned to preserve [must] become the organising principle of society. The vision that is implicit in feminism [is] a society organised around human needs . . . There are no human alternatives. The Market, with its financial abstractions, deformed science, and obsession with dead things . . . must be pushed back to the margin. And the 'womanly' values of community and caring must rise to the centre as the only human principle.
>
> (Ehrenreich and English, 1979: 342)

Since then, the transformative feminist commitment to life has become explicitly ecological with a commitment to non-human as well as human life, as illustrated in the following quotation from Indian feminist Vandana Shiva:

> The recovery of the feminine principle allows a transcendence and transformation of patriarchal foundations of maldevelopment. It allows a redefinition of growth and productivity as categories linked to the production, not the destruction of life. It is thus simultaneously an ecological and a feminist political project which legitimises the way of knowing and being that creates wealth by enhancing life and diversity, and which delegitimises the knowledge and practice of a culture of death as the basis for capital accumulation.
>
> (Shiva, 1989: 13)

This life-centred feminist vision is grounded in alternative values whose very articulation requires the reconceptualization of such key concepts as work, value, wealth, development, nature and progress and whose realization would require the re-integration and re-definition of the economic, political, cultural, social, ecological and spiritual realms of life fragmented in industrial society. This holistic project speaks directly to the emerging post-industrial potential for a less alienated life outlined at the beginning of this chapter.

Multi-centred movement

This approach involves the rejection of the dominant dualistic hierarchical and androcentric view of the world. Static antagonistic and unequal industrial oppositions between, for instance, society and nature, ends and means, reason and emotion, mind and body, individual and community, production and reproduction, political and personal, public and private are rejected in favour of more holistic and less violent ways of viewing and living in the world.

> [Women's] experience of continuity and relation with others, with the natural world, of mind and body – provide[s] an ontological base for developing a nonproblematic social synthesis, a social synthesis that need not operate through the denial of the body, an attack on nature, or the death struggle between self and other, a social synthesis that does not depend on any of the forms taken by abstract masculinity.
>
> (Hartsock 1983: 246–7)

Diverse women's work, embodied life experience, powerlessness, and existential 'otherness' are all mined as material resources for holistic, egalitarian aspirations, and therefore possibilities for the world. But these are not pre-existing possibilities embedded in nature or in women, essential relations simply to be uncovered. They are the political and personal achievement of entirely new ways of being and living to be envisioned and created by free women (and men) in the dynamic and passionate process of making history and re-making the world:[9]

> The Feminine is no longer the same nor the opposite of the Masculine. Neither is it an essence linked to an immobile nature, but rather experience linked to a historical nature, a becoming. In this way, femininity is entering a region of freedom. . . . Femininity's freedom

to define itself in due course will relate to nature, not as essence but as experience. It will not deny the body as its original point of departure for living in and thinking about the world, but will integrate this thinking into the world. . . . This plan to integrate the history of female Nature into the design for femininity's future is both feminist and ecological.

(Oliviera, 1992: 71/1)

Simple survival for many women and children requires protection from inherently violent practices and institutions. Beyond this, the lives feminists are inspired to fight for are free and dignified, equal and autonomous. The families and communities and world they aspire to are diverse, egalitarian, co-operative, and peaceful:[10]

One cannot speak of a democratic state if it does not take into account women's perspectives, interests and demands in a direct and permanent way. But democracy from [a feminist] perspective goes even further, reaching into domestic life. You can't talk about democracy in homes filled with authoritarianism, violence, impositions, physical and psychological abuse, blackmail, and arbitrary, absolute hierarchies.

(Maria Teresa Blandon, coordinator of the National Feminist Committee of Nicaragua, quoted in Aleman, Miranda and 1993: 21)

This involves resistance to power at every level (from the most personal to the most public) and of every kind (class-, colonial-, and race-, as well as gender-based):

To accept the existence of class, race, ethnicity and generational differences among women and to devise multiple fronts of struggle in order to eliminate domination in any of its forms is what gives feminism its vitality. By broadening the concept of political, to include all spheres of power from the 'natural' state of hierarchies to the power of language to the ensemble of intra-household relations and showing how these institutions perpetuate the ideologies of domination, feminism brings a new vision and breadth to social movements.

(Alya Baffoun (1985: 4) – an African feminist)

It is an aspiration to transform power itself:

> If we continue . . . to use the same concept of power that exists, then we would have changed nothing: Power to use, to manipulate, to dominate, to control, to coerce, is the masculine understanding of power. . . . We women, coming as we do from the peripheries of power, may together with other oppressed people find through our powerlessness a redefinition of power, an alternative concept of power that encourages and enhances the potential of each one, and then perhaps collectively we may find new human strengths that will help us to find new possibilities.
>
> (D'Souza, 1992: 49)

Through the affirmation of the least advantaged, least powerful and most despised:

> The rejection of dualism, of the positive–negative polarities between which most of our intellectual training has taken place, has been an undercurrent of feminist thought. And rejecting them, we reaffirm the existence of all those who have through the centuries been negatively defined: not only women, but the 'untouchable,' the 'unmanly,' the 'nonwhite,' the 'illiterate': the 'invisible.' Which forces us to confront the problem of the essential dichotomy: power/powerlessness.
>
> (Rich, 1976: 48)

The affirmation of political identities and the claiming of political voice by diverse individual women and women's groups long silent and (often) despised, is an important part of this struggle. It is far from the crude essentialism so widely suspected and loudly denounced in academe. Nor does it generally lead in practice and on the ground to the fragmentation/balkanization often predicted and imagined in theoretical critiques of 'identity politics'.[11]

As more women win the power to be heard at local and global levels, the resulting articulation of more types and levels of difference among women has not narrowed self-defined groups. Rather it has revealed powerful competing identities and ever richer cross-cutting specificities. The identities of Black, Jewish, lesbian, indigenous, Third World, Muslim, old, working-class, or disabled women are neither exclusive nor expendable. Active women/feminists are claiming complex multiple identities and links with diverse groups who share varied important aspects of self. As more of women's particular experiences and perspectives are named, the recognition of diversity necessarily involves discovering the richness of shared specificities and complex politically constructed subjectivities. It is very rarely the construction of high walls between static 'insider' and 'outsider' groups based on single reified characteristics or conditions. The articulation of specific identities, then, paradoxically becomes a militant refusal of rigid, limiting concepts of self; it is the conscious rejection of essential identity for the complexity of political identity.[12]

'Welfare Warriors', 'WHISPER' (Women Hurt in Systems of Prostitution Engaged in Revolt), 'The National Black Women's Health Project', and 'Women Living Under Muslim Laws' are all examples of autonomous women-positive identity-based groups with large and inclusive visions of social change grounded in their own experience. As you will see from the descriptions below, shared identity is a political achievement for these groups, not a given condition. It helps their members find and celebrate each other, become present to other feminists, and participate in constructing the wider women's movement. All these groups presume to make theoretical and political contributions of general relevance to women from the particular location and experience of their members. These groups and the political identities that define them are foundations to reach out from, not walls to hide behind.[13]

Welfare Warriors,[14] founded in 1986 in the USA, is a group of poor mothers concerned to:

> put an end to stereotypes immobilizing us . . . Welfare myths not only serve to justify sexist, racist and classist abuse of women, they also work to keep us divided and conquered. Poor mums distrust each other, fearing that the other mothers really fit the stereotypes of dependent, lazy, loose, lying, child abusing and drug addicted. Working and middle class people are conned into using us as scapegoats for society's failures. Thus the myths serve to keep people from uniting to fight for justice in their community and developing effective strategies in this war of the rich against everybody else.
>
> (Gowens, 1993: 33)

The group insists that *all* people are dependent on each other and society, not just mothers of children who depend on community child support (welfare). These mothers are, in fact among the most independent mothers in the nation but they *should not have to be*: 'As long as dependence is a dirty word, all groups of dependent people will continue to be oppressed. As a nation we must once again strive for a society based on interdependence' (Gowens, 1993: inside back cover).

This alternative vision of a co-operative and caring community and society, with respect and resources for raising children and supporting people, is the ground from which the Welfare Mothers reach out 'to forge global connections with other poor mothers – and to develop alliances with other feminist groups' (Welfare Warriors, 1991: 20). They articulate the specific needs and terrors of mothers living poverty[15] around the world as extreme instances which can throw light on the condition experienced by all women:

> Like all women, poor moms must live in fear of rape and battery (more frequent for us since we often live with angry men, take buses, and walk in war zones) . . . All mothers in patriarchy lose our children, in some degree, to the Fathers. But impoverished mothers suffer wrenching, heart breaking, violent, literal losses of our children – disappeared in El Salvador, gunned down in Milwaukee, legally snatched *whenever, wherever they will bring in a profit for the Fathers*.
> (Welfare Warriors, 1991: 20. Emphasis in the original.)

They draw attention to poor women's particular possibilities of solidarity around the world and across differences and, therefore, of major contribution to all women's struggle:

> Impoverished mothers are the largest group of women in the WORLD – and possibly the most multi-racial, multi-cultural, multi-able group of women that exists. We have great differences but one thing in common: *we are MOTHERS raising children in systems that do NOT work for mothers and our children and which are very HOSTILE to us*.
> (Welfare Warriors, 1991: 20. Emphasis in the original)

The [US] National Black Women's Health Project[16] was founded by Byllye Avery in 1983 following two years of meetings and discussions with African American women. The First National Conference on Black Women's Health Issues that year, co-sponsored by the National Women's Health Network, drew 2000 women to Spelman College and began a process of networking and organizing that has resulted in 150 chapters in 31 states in the US and numerous groups in the Caribbean and Africa (six groups in Kenya, and one each in the Barbados and Belize in 1990).

The Group's Newsletter, *Vital Signs*, radically challenges the sexist and racist ideology and structures of the dominant culture and society while putting Black women at the centre of an alternative, inclusive, caring, sisterly, cultural, spiritual, political Afrocentric, yet universal, perspective.

Angela Davis, who is a member of the board of directors of the Project stresses the power of this frame for working across diversity:

> Our work focuses on physical, mental and spiritual health needs of Black women. Until recently, the emphasis has been on 'self-help', as adapted from the larger feminist health movement, but geared to the particular needs of Black women. The most exciting aspect of this organisation is its ability to unify Black women beyond the limitations of age, social class, occupation and geographical origin. A typical gathering includes girls as young as thirteen and women as old as seventy-five, rural women on welfare and women who are lawyers or university professors, women from the most rural areas of the South and women from urban centres like New York.
>
> (Bhavnani, 1989: 77–8)[17]

The National Black Women's Health Project is built around a core process of Black women sharing their lives and experiences, naming their own health needs and providing for them through self-help groups. Mutual support and validation are stressed. Love and nurture are affirmed and Black women are urged to love themselves first, a truly radical and empowering spiritual as well as political message. The group's developing analysis recognizes both social inequality and oppression and personal power and responsibility. Their practice is designed to help Black women value themselves, to recognize the ways that adversity has built them up as well as worn them down, and to become active agents in their own lives and in social change. In a speech in Toronto Byllye Avery made the challenging point that 'whether life grinds you or polishes you depends on what you are made of'. Her accompanying message was that we are all made of the right stuff if we know how to call on it.

The National Black Women's Health Project organizes and supports local groups, does public education, runs large and innovative health projects, and participates in protests and pressure to change policy. The main aim of the group is to develop the specific voices and power of Black women to define and tackle Black women's health needs, including the social and economic structures of class as well as race and gender oppression that put their health at risk:

> Our analysis, which will be put into practice around effective coalition building, must always be done around the sisters who are forced to function at the bottom of the society – that is, the sisters who have

the lowest income, who have the least access to services, who have the hardest time. They are who we need to hear from.

(Avery, 1990b: 308)

The group's practice is built on the premise that a culturally specific, rather than an abstract approach, is needed for success. But it is not isolationist. The National Black Women's Health Project grew out of both the limitations and the strengths of the National Women's Health Movement, and has become a powerful force shaping a more inclusive, racially aware, and multicentred feminist health politics in general; a politics and power which was further challenged and enriched by the subsequent founding of the National Latina Health Organization in 1986 and the Native American Women's Health Education Resource Centre in 1988;[18] and by increasing global networking. Members of the group, for instance, were at the International Conference on Women in Africa and the African Diaspora in July 1991, networking with Women in Nigeria (WIN) and WAND (The Women's and Development Unit of the University of the West Indies).

Women Hurt in Systems of Prostitution Engaged in Revolt (WHISPER)[19] was founded in 1985 in Minnesota:

WHISPER is an organisation of women who have survived systems of prostitution and women who are committed to ending this form of violence. We are women of diverse, racial, ethnic, and economic backgrounds, and all affectional orientations. Together we are creating change in our personal lives and our communities.

('When you can't stand turning one more trick turn to us.' n.d.)

Systems of prostitution are defined broadly by the group as 'any industry in which women's and children's bodies are bought, sold, or traded for sexual use and abuse . . . (including) pornography, live sex shows, peep shows, international sexual slavery, and prostitution as it is commonly defined'. Members' common experiences and identities as victims and survivors of various aspects of the sex industry provide an inclusive frame for participation by otherwise extremely diverse women. The identity basis of membership in this group, like the other groups described here, is used consciously and explicitly to reach out and build support among women across deep divisions:

For every real difference between women (like culture, religion, race, class, sexual orientation, disability), prostitution exists to erase our diversity, distinction and accomplishment while reducing all of us to meat; to be bought, sold, traded, used, discarded, degraded, ridiculed, humiliated, maimed, tortured and too often murdered for sex.

The acronym WHISPER is used to highlight the fact that women in systems of prostitution do name and share their experiences, although their knowledge is drowned out by the dominant myths that are 'shouted out in pornography, in mainstream media and by self-appointed experts'. The main focus of the group is to reach and support and empower prostitutes and ex-prostitutes for individual and social change. But they are also concerned to link with other women's groups, educate other women and the wider public, and contribute their members' particular knowledge to the development of general feminist analyses and practice. The statement of purposes and principles at the beginning of the first issue of the group's newsletter *WHISPER* says, for instance:

WHISPER is written by and for women who are either currently in systems of prostitution or who have escaped. Occasionally we will print articles that we believe are important, written by non-prostitutes (such as a health column by a medical worker). We also hope that WHISPER will be used as an educational tool for non-prostitute women to learn the truth about prostitution. Primarily, this forum exists for us to speak out about the realities of our lives. We want this forum to be used by prostitutes and ex-prostitutes to explore ideas for change. We expect it to be a tool for change in our lives, in our lifetime. In this forum we will speak for ourselves. We will think about our lives and we will write the truth. Our purpose is to make the sexual enslavement of women HISTORY.

(Emphasis in the original)

As well as its newsletter, the group has an oral history project with prostitutes and ex-prostitutes; runs Radical Education Groups 'where women can examine the impact of prostitution on their lives, explore new ideas and together create change in both our personal lives and communities' ('Before you turn another trick', n.d.: frontispiece); produces educational and informational material for prostitutes; organizes and participates in educational forums across North America; presses for legislative change; advocates increased services for survivors; participates in local, national and, increasingly, international consultation – for instance, WHISPER was an active participant at the 16th session of the United Nations Working Group on Contemporary Forms of Slavery in Geneva in 1991 (Reports in *WHISPER*, VI 1–2 Winter/Spring 1992).

WHISPER is developing the specific voices and presence of survivors of systems of prostitution as a basis from which to participate in and influence wider feminist struggle. The group analyses prostitution in the context of all women's dependence and vulnerability to patriarchal power, and includes attention to the special vulnerabilty of women subject also to race and class power. Members bring a 'blend of passion, personal experience, commitment to feminism, and a history of organising against violence against women' (Before you turn another trick', n.d.: 9) to their claims that systems of prostitution can best be understood as forms of violence against women. Group members' own experience of prostitution and their research enables them to document convincingly the ways that prostitution is a particular form of rape and the significant ways that prostitutes' situation parallels that of trapped and battered wives. Members of WHISPER, like feminists everywhere, are refusing the definitions of experts and taking power into their own hands to name and change their lives. In doing so they are providing new understandings, not only of prostitution, but of wife beating and rape and the structures and processes of male power generally. Their involvement has helped activists in the battered women's movement develop more radical and inclusive analyses and shown them the importance of extending services to survivors of prostitution as well as marriage.

WHISPER is convinced that only feminisms which speak to the experience of its members are worthy of the name. In developing the *particular* voices of prostitutes and sharing their knowledge and analysis of the sex industry they are contributing to the *general* development of feminism as the inclusive movement it must be. The group provides a place from which prostitutes can reach out to both prostitutes and other women as the centre of their own politics and struggle. Increasingly this outreach/dialogue includes a global component. The newsletter carries information about global structures of prostitution, their relationship to international economic and military arrangements and the growing resistance of women around the world.[20] And group members participate in international dialogue, learning from and contributing to the ways these struggles are understood and defined for legal, policy and political purposes.

The International Solidarity Network of Women Living Under Muslim Laws (WLUML), emerged in 1984 from initiatives by nine women from

Algeria, Morocco, Sudan, Iran, Mauritius, Tanzania, Bangladesh, and Pakistan who were concerned to respond to issues requiring urgent action:

> The case of three feminists arrested and jailed without trial, kept incommunicado for seven months in Algeria for having discussed with other women the 'Family Code,' which was highly unfavourable to women.
>
> The case of an Indian Sunni woman who filed a petition in the Supreme Court arguing that the Muslim minority law applied to her in her divorce denied her the rights otherwise guaranteed by the Constitution of India to all citizens, and called for support.
>
> The case of a woman in Abu Dhabi, charged with adultery and sentenced to be stoned to death after delivering and feeding her child for two months.
>
> The case of 'mothers of Algiers' who fought for custody of their children after divorce.
>
> *(Women Living Under Muslim Laws Dossier*, n.d.)

The network maintains active links among women and women's groups in Muslim countries and communities 'to increase women's knowledge about both their common and diverse situations in various contexts, and to strengthen their struggles and create the means to support them internationally from within the Muslim world and outside' (ibid.). To this end it produces information kits, working papers, and a series of dossiers; facilitates contact, communication, and exchanges; builds links and initiates campaigns among women from different geographical regions; works with other feminist networks and organizations such as FINRRAGE (Feminist International Network of Resistance to Reproductive and Genetic Engineering), ISIS, AAWORD (African Association of Women on Research and Development), and Women Against Fundamentalism.

The Network welcomes participation by women with very different relationships to Muslim experience, identity, and faith. It seeks to support both the more and the less devout in the particular struggles they each face rather than to define what these struggles should be. The network addresses itself to women living where Islam is the religion of the State, as well as to women who belong to Muslim communities ruled by minority religious laws; to women in secular states where Islam is rapidly expanding and where fundamentalists demand a minority religious law, as well as to women from immigrant Muslim communities in Europe and the Americas; and to non-Muslim women, either nationals or foreigners, living in Muslim countries and communities, where Muslim laws are applied to them and to their children' (ibid.). The wide variety of viewpoint, circumstance, and experience among participants means that the fact of living under Muslim laws delimits not so much sameness as a useful frame for co-operation across difference. The identity that is shared is one of struggle and resistance that does not deny but rather affirms as it transforms specific cultural, traditional, and/or religious existence and contexts.

WLUML enables diverse women to offer and accept support from each other in the knowledge that they are all contesting power in their own communities. It provides a space for women to develop alternative interpretations of the Koran and the world and to act on these. Its explicit focus on Muslim laws provides a way for women of Muslim heritage and/or faith to be strongly present in global dialogue as *Muslim women* even while challenging their diverse Muslim cultures and conditions; it enables them to seek support from women not living under Muslim laws without risking diminution or loss of their specifically Muslim identification and voice. This is the articulation of strategic identity as a basis for struggle and a place to move out from.

These four and all the many other local and global groups and networks based on political (as opposed to essentialist) expressions of identity name their particular experience (as poor mothers, prostitutes, disabled/Black/Third World/lesbian/indigenous/Muslim women) in the expectation that this will deepen the general understanding of all women's reality: not because all women's experience is the same, but because women share a complex reality which only the experience and insights of diverse women can reveal in its entirety. They presume to speak for particular groups of women in voices with universal significance and to be central in a movement with many centres. The identity base of membership in these groups is designed to foster connections and inclusion across differences, to sustain collective action, and support the myriad voices necessary for a broader multi-centred movement. These groups all see their members' specific lives and struggles to be connected to the fate of women around the world. They understand themselves as being central to the wider women's movement, but not *the* centre. They are insistent on the importance of their particular perspectives and practices without being vanguardist or sectarian; they actively support and celebrate the coming to voice of other groups of women everywhere.

Recent decades have seen an enormous expansion of activism at the local and global level among feminists in all regions[21] much of it informing and informed by these transformative perspectives. Participation in the non-governmental forums accompanying the United Nations Conferences at the beginning, midpoint, and end of the UN Decade for Women rose from 6000 in Mexico City in 1975, to 7000 in Copenhagen in 1980, to 14000 in Nairobi in 1985. The Fourth World Congress of Women, held ten years later in Beijing, attracted over 30000 women and was the culmination of intensive feminist participation in a series of prior UN Conferences on Environment and Development in Brazil 1992, Human Rights in Vienna 1993, Population in Cairo 1994, Social Development in Copenhagen 1995.

Because these Conferences involve formal lobbying along with exciting informal contacts and cutting-edge exchanges, they have generated documents which clearly reveal the breadth and depth of global feminist consensus around transformative perspectives in all issue areas.[22] The deeply radical analyses and shared holistic and life-centred values that underlie this consensus were forged in political dialogue within and among well-developed activist networks with strong links to local issues and local practice.[23] These include:

- Identity-defined networks such as the Third World Women's Network, Indigenous Women's Network, The Network of Women Living Under Muslim Laws and international networks, among many others, of disabled women, lesbian women, Catholic women and so on;
- Regionally-defined networks (much less developed in the North than the rest of the world) such as AAWORD (Association of African Women on Research and Development), AWRAN (Asian and Pacific Women's Research and Action Network), CAFRA (Caribbean Association for Feminist Research and Action), and Latin American Feminist Encuentros held every two years;
- Issue-defined networks such as The Coalition Against Trafficking in Women, DAWN (Development Alternatives with Women for a New Era, a Third World women's network), FINRRAGE (Feminist International Network of Resistance to Reproductive and Genetic Engineering), International Commission for the Abolition of Sexual Mutilation (Female Genital Mutilation), Mujer a Mujer (a collective of Mexican, Canadian, US and Caribbean women addressing the North American Free Trade Agreement and structural adjustment policies more generally), Women Against Fundamentalism, Women's Environment and Development Organization (WEDO), Women's

Rights are Human Rights Network, and networks, among many others, around health, peace, external debt and structural adjustment, and violence against women.

In all these contexts feminists are building consensus around shared values and political perspectives while eschewing homogeneity. Power differences among women are named and seriously (though not always successfully) resisted, while other differences are honoured. Varied priorities and strategies, and diverse cultures and histories are seen as important strengths. As a feminist from Bangladesh explained at a conference of the Canadian Research Institute for the Advancement of Women in 1990:

> We believe in the concept of spinning local threads, weaving global feminism. We may have different threads both in colors and texture from many local areas. But we are rich with experiences from various parts of the world, from Africa, Latin America, Asia and Pacific, Australia, Europe and America. We have experiences where women are fighting against poverty, against external domination, against the business corporate exploitation, against racism, against patriarchal social and cultural systems. The experiences are diverse and sometimes far from each other even in terms of understanding. We do not think that there can be only one design to be followed as an 'answer.' The diversity in design and color but woven in a single cloth will make us united and strong.
>
> (Das, 1991: 17)

The challenge of weaving this cloth, of communicating across differences and of deepening one's analysis and vision to encompass the interests of all women, is being taken up directly by feminists in a myriad of contexts. For instance, the theme of the first Asian Indigenous Women's Conference in Baguio City, the Philippines was 'Sharing Commonalities and Diversities: Forging Unity towards Indigenous Women's Empowerment.' In 1993 Israeli feminists organized a national conference, 'Together Beyond Our Differences.' Nicaraguan feminists entitled their first national conference 'Seeking Unity in Diversity.' In South Africa in April 1992, 67 national organizations founded the National Women's Coalition within which women across the political spectrum developed collective positions on the ongoing Constitutional debate and wrote a common Woman's Charter.

Building solidarity that honours the specificity of individuals, communities, and struggles is no easy task. Conceiving of equality and commonality apart from sameness is a major departure from the dominant dualistic Western discourse of equality which opposes individual to community and accords individual rights on the basis of abstract human qualities which in practice construct white western man as the norm and compel the denial of all particularity and context. Naming the need to move beyond these limits without losing the benefits of the Western liberal tradition is an important first step. But the work of conceiving and actually creating new possibilities must be done in tandem. Feminists all over the world are striving to find ways in practice to build egalitarian and co-operative relations and to identify and defend common interests and values through the proud affirmation of their particularities.

The resulting multi-centred feminist movement foreshadows an emerging social capacity for what Corinne Kumar (D'Souza 1992: 44) has called a 'new universalism':

> not a universalism that denies the many and affirms the one, not a eurocentric universalism; not a patriarchal universalism. . . . A new universalism that will challenge the universal mode, the logic of our development, science, technology, militarization, the nuclear option. A new universalism that will respect the plurality of different societies – . . . one that will be rooted in the particular, one which will develop in the context of the dialectics of different civilisations, birthing a new cosmology.

Thus transformative feminisms today hold the seeds of the world they want to create. Feminists' responses to alienated and exploitative globalization have generally not been simple withdrawal, refusal, or reaction but the creation of autonomous, democratic, and empowering global relations in the struggle for alternative life-centred social organization – a project which speaks in particularly appropriate ways to post-industrial possibilities.

Notes

1. Drawing on a ground-breaking Czechoslovakian report (Richta 1968), Fred Block and Larry Hirschhorn (1979) have done valuable work in documenting this historical shift in the role of labour power in value creation in advanced industrial nations.

2. Anand 1980, Antrobous 1983, Bhasin 1992, Dakar 1982, D'Souza 1992, ISIS 1983, Corral 1992, Sen and Grown 1987, Shiva 1989.
3. Boulding 1980, Bunch and Carillo 1990, Leghorn and Parker 1981, Mies 1986, Mies and Shiva 1993, Moraga 1993, Pietila 1993, Waring 1988.
4. Although a marked radical consensus around life-centred values has emerged among feminists globally, this does not include all feminists. In my book, *Integrative Feminisms: Building Global Visions, 1960s–1990s* (1996), I draw a distinction between equality frame feminisms shaped essentially by the aim of assimilation and what I call 'integrative feminisms' which reflect the alternative rationality and life-centred values described here. The book documents integrative feminist developments in 'First' and 'Two Thirds' Worlds in much more detail and discusses their significance more fully.
5. 'Women's work' is used loosely here to refer to the enormous amount of diverse and changing subsistence work associated with women and done, with or without (low) pay, in dependent circumstances in hugely varied societies.
6. These policies are called 're-structuring' in the North and 'structural adjustment' in the South. For a more detailed account of the policies and their impact on women in both North and South see Isla (1993a) and Isla, Miles and Molloy (1996).
7. These findings of Hilkka Pietila are reported in Waring (1988: 301–2).
8. For a discussion of the connected economic and environmental costs of 'restructuring' and 'structural adjustment' policies see Isla (1993b).
9. The attention of these feminists to nature and the body and to diverse women's characteristics and concerns is very far from the essentialism and determinism it is often taken to be. For they are naming and drawing on what is specific to diverse women's lives in the conscious political project of imagining and creating new futures. See Miles (1996) for a more developed discussion of post-structuralist and other anti-essentialist critiques of transformative feminisms which fail to see this distinction.
10. 'We cannot talk of democracy outside the family yet allow male dictatorship inside it. In fact we believe that real democracies and egalitarian societies can only be established if we practice democracy, equality and mutual respect within the family. Real peace can only be established if we experience peace at home' (Bhasin and Kahn, 1986: 14).
11. Closed and essentialist expressions of identity are not unknown in feminist practice. However, the all too prevalent blanket condemnation of 'identity politics' dismisses, with this, the crucial transformative political articulation of identity by diverse groups of women that lies at the heart of feminism's growing capacity to re-vision solidarity and universality in multi-centred movement.
12. 'What am I? a third world lesbian feminist with marxist and mystic leanings. They would chop me up into little fragments and tag each piece with a label.

    You say my name is ambivalence? Think of me as Shiva, a many armed and legged body with one foot on brown soil, one on white, one in straight society, one in the gay world, the man's world, the women's, one limb in the literary world, another in the working class, the social, and the occult worlds. A sort of spider woman hanging by one thin strand of web.

Who, me confused? Ambivalent? Not so. Only your labels split me.'
(Anzaldua, 1983: 205)

13. Albrecht and Brewer, 1990; Anzaldua, 1990; Cardinal, 1992; Peters and Samuels (eds), 1976; Telling It Collective, 1990.

14. Their publication *Welfare Mothers' Voice*, a national bilingual publication, is available for $15 ($4 for low-income mothers) from 4504 North 47th, Milwaukee, WI, 5318.

15. I first heard the phrase 'women living poverty' used in preference to the term 'poor women' by Carolyn Lehmann, a founding member of Casa Sofia, a women's centre in the barrios of Santiago, Chile.

16. The information here comes from (Avery, 1990a, 1990b, 1990c, The Boston Women's Health Collective 1992, *Vital Signs*), talks and workshops I have heard by Byllye Avery over the years, and periodical reports in the feminist press. National Black Women's Health Project, 1237 Ralph Abernathy Blvd., SW Atlanta, GA, 30310. Tel. 404-758-9590.

17. Byllye Avery also emphasizes the importance of diverse participation when she says of the first Conference: 'responding to the rallying cry "We're sick and tired of being sick and tired," they came with Ph.D.s, M.D.s, welfare cards, in Mercedes and on crutches, from seven days old to 80 years old – urban, rural, gay, straight – to find something' (1990b: 78).

18. National Women's Health Network, 1325 G St., N.W., Washington, DC, 20005; 202-34701140. National Latina Health Organization, P.O.Box 7667, Oakland, CA, 94601; 510-534-1362. Native American Women's Health Education Resource Centre, P.O.Box 572 Lake Andes, South Dakota, 57356; 605-487-7072.

19. The information provided here is from the group's newsletter *WHISPER* and its educational materials: 'When you can't stand turning one more trick, turn to us', and 'Before you turn another trick . . .'. Unless otherwise indicated the quotations here are taken from the statement of principles on the first page of Volume I Number 1 of *WHISPER* (Winter 1985/86). The group's address is: Lake Street Station, Box 8719, Minneapolis, Minnesota, 55408. Tel. 612-644-6301. For more information on the development of the group see a long interview with founder member Evelina Giobbe by Anne Mayne and Rachel Wingfield (1993).

20. *WHISPER* has carried reports, to name just a few, on the Nairobi Conference; UNESCO Conferences and resolutions on prostitution; prostitution laws in Moscow; trafficking in Asian women; sex tourism between Norway and Thailand, and between Japan and the Philippines; articles on Peru, China, and Kenya; a large overview of global trafficking in women; and information about the anti-prostitution struggles of Gabriela in the Philippines and the Rainbow Project in Thailand.

21. For reports of local feminist projects in many parts of the world see: Albrecht and Brewer 1990, Davies (ed.) 1983, 1987, Kerr (ed.) 1993, Match International Centre 1990, Morgan (ed.) 1984, Schuler (ed.) 1986, 1990, 1992.

22. One example of these documents is the Report of the World Women's Congress for a Healthy Planet, held in Miami 1991, where fifteen hundred feminists from 84 countries, active in diverse networks in all regions of the world, met to 'develop policy goals and actions, for use in this decade

and into the next century' and to guide women's interventions at the UN Conference on Environment and Development in Brazil 1992. The Report includes: testimonies from women all over the world on a wide variety of topics including violence against women, human rights, militarism, external debt and so on; Regional Caucus Statements from Africa, Europe, International Indigenous Women, Latin America and the Caribbean, the Middle East, North America, Pacific, Women of the South, and Women of Color of North America; and Women's Action Agenda 21, a collectively written statement expressing powerful consensus on transformative perspectives. The Report is available from: WEDO (Women's Environment and Development Organization), 845 Third Avenue, 15th Floor, New York, NY, 10022, USA.

23. These activist networks also have research projects, published position papers, conference reports, manifestos, statements, newsletters and journals that clearly reflect transformative feminist perspectives. See, for instance, AAWORD (1985), Coalition Against Trafficking in Women (1993), DAWN Toronto (1986), FINRRAGE (1989), Indigenous Women's Network (1995), Sen and Grown (1987), South Asian Workshop on Women and Development (1989), Tauli-Corpuz (1992), WAND/APCD (1980), Women Against Fundamentalism (1990), Women Living Under Muslim Laws (n.d.), Women's Rights are Human Rights (n.d.).

References

AAWORD (1985) 'Feminism in Africa,' *Echo, AAWORD Newsletter*, 2/3: 1–11.

Albrecht, L. and R.M. Brewer (eds) (1990) *Bridges of Power: Women's Multicultural Alliances*, Philadelphia: New Society.

Anand, A. (1980) 'Rethinking women and development', written in 1980 published in ISIS (ed.) (1983) *Women in Development: a Resource Guide for Organization and Action*, Rome and Geneva: ISIS International.

Antrobus, P. (1983) 'Equality, development and peace: a second look at the goals of the UN decade for women', address to the Associatied Country Women of the World, Vancouver, British Columbia, 18–29 June.

Anzaldua, G. (1990) *Making Faces, Making Soul: Haciendo Cara: Creative and Critical Perspectives by Women of Color*, San Francisco: Aunt Lute.

Avery, B. (1990a) 'Breathing life into ourselves: the evolution of the National Black Women's Health Project', in E.C. White (ed.), *The Black Women's Health Book*, Seattle, WA: Seal Press, pp. 4–10. (From a talk given in Cambridge, Massachusetts, July 1988.)

Avery, B. (1990b) 'Reproductive rights and coalition-building', in M. Gerber Fried (ed.), *From Abortion to Reproductive Freedom: Transforming a Movement*, Boston, MA: South End Press, pp. 307–8.

Baffoun, A. (1985) 'Future of feminism in Africa', *Echo, AAWORD Newsletter*, 2/3: 4–6.

'Before you turn Another trick . . . ' (n.d.) Pamphlet published by WHISPER.

Bhasin, K. (1992) 'Alternative and sustainable development', *Convergence*, 25(2): 26–35.

Bhasin, K. and N.S. Khan (1986) *Some Questions about Feminism and Its Relevance in South Asia*, New Delhi: Kali for Women Press.

Bhavnani, K.-K. (1989) 'Complexity, activism, optimism: an interview with Angela Y. Davis', *Feminist Review*, 31 (Spring): 67–81.

Boulding, E. (1980) 'Integration into what? Reflections on development planning for women', *Convergence*, 12(1–2): 50–9.

Boston Women's Health Collective (1984) *The New Our Bodies Ourselves: a Book By and For Women*, New York: Simon & Schuster. (First edition first published in 1971.)

Boston Women's Health Collective (1992) 'When yogurt was illegal', *Ms*, (July/August): 38–9.

Block, F. (1987) *Revising State Theory: Essays in Politics and Postindustrialization*, Philadelphia: Temple University Press.

Block, F. and L. Hirschhorn (1979) 'The new productive forces and contradictions in contemporary capitalism,' *Theory and Society*, 7: 363–95.

Bunch, R. and R. Carillo (1990) 'Feminist perspectives on women and development', in I. Tinker (ed.), *Persistent Inequalities*, New York: Oxford University Press, pp. 70–82.

Cardinal, L. (1992) 'La recherche sure les femmes francophones vivant en milieu minoritaire: un questionnement sur le féminisme', *Recherches féministes*, 5(1): 5–29.

Coalition Against Trafficking in Women (1993) 'Convention on the Elimination of All forms of Sexual Exploitation of Women: A Proposal for a New Convention.'

Dakar (1982) 'The Dakar Declaration on another development with women', *Development Dialogue*, 1(2): 11–16.

Das, S. (1991) 'Women with diverse designs: feminism from the perspective of real experiences of women in Bangladesh', *CRIAW Newsletter*, 12(1): 15–17.

Davies, M. (ed.) (1983) *Third World, Second Sex: Women's Struggles and National Liberation*, vol. 1, London: Zed Press.

Davies, M. (ed.) (1987) *Third World, Second Sex: Women's Struggles and National Liberation*, vol. 2. London: Zed Press.

DAWN, Toronto (1986) 'An Open Letter from the DisAbled Women's Network D.A.W.N. Toronto to the Women's Movement', Toronto: DAWN.

D'Souza, C.K. (1992) 'The South Wind', in R.D. de Oliviera and T. Corral (eds), *Terra Femina*, Brazil: IDAC and REDEH, pp. 24–53.

Ehrenreich, B. and D. English (1979) *For Her Own Good: 150 Years of the Experts' Advice to Women*, New York: Anchor Press/Doubleday.

FINRRAGE (1989) 'Declaration of Comilla', *Resources for Feminist Research*, 18(3) (September): 84–6.

Gowens, P. (1993) 'Welfare Warriors', *Equal Means*, 7(4) (Winter): 33.

Hartsock, N. (1983) *Money, Sex and Power: Toward a Feminist Historical Materialism*, New York: Longman.

Indigenous Women's Network (1995) 'Statement from Beijing'.

ISIS (ed.) (1983) *Women in Development: a Resource Guide for Organization and Action*, Rome and Geneva: ISIS International.

Isla, A. (1993a) 'Women, development and the market economy', *Canadian Woman Studies*, 13(3) (Spring): 28–33.

Isla, A. (1993b) 'Debt crisis in Latin America: an example of unsustainable development', *Canadian Woman Studies*, 13(3) (Spring): 65–8.

Isla, A., Miles, A. and S. Molloy (1996) 'Stabilization/structural adjustment/

restructuring: Canadian feminist issues in a global framework', *Canadian Woman Studies*, 16(3) (Summer).

Kerr, J. (ed.) (1993) *Ours By Right: Women's Rights as Human Rights*, London: Zed Press with the North–South Institute.

Leghorn, L. and K. Parker (1981) *Women's Worth: Sexual Economics and the World of Women*, London: Routledge.

McLellan, D. (1971) *Marx's Grundrisse*, London: Macmillan.

Match International Centre (1990) *Linking Women's Global Struggles to End Violence*, Ottawa: Match.

Mayne, A. and R. Wingfield (1993) 'Women Hurt in Systems of Prostitution' (an interview with Evelina Giobbe), *Trouble and Strife*, 26 (Summer): 22–30.

Mies, M. (1986) *Patriarchy and Accumulation on a World Scale: Women in the International Division of Labour*, London: Zed Press.

Mies, M. and V. Shiva (1993) *Ecofeminism*, London: Zed Press.

Milani, B. (2000) *Designing the Green Economy: the Postindustrial Alternative to Corporate Globalization*, Boston: Rowman and Littlefield.

Miles, A. (1979) 'The Politics of Feminist Radicalism: a Study in Integrative Feminism', Ph.D., University of Toronto.

Miles, A. (1992) 'Le féminisme, la gauche et la politique industrielle', in G. Boismenu, P. Hamel and G. Labica (eds), *Les formes modernes de la démocratie*, Montreal: Les Presses de l'Université de Montréal.

Miles, A. (1996) *Integrative Feminisms: Building Global Visions, 1960s–1990s*, New York: Routledge.

Miranda, C. and V. Aleman (1993) 'National Feminist Committee: with ideas of their own', *Barricada Internacional*, 13(365, September): 20–1.

Morgan, R. (ed.) (1984) *Sisterhood is Global: the International Women's Movement Anthology*, Garden City, NY: Anchor Press/Doubleday.

Oliveira, R.D. (1992) 'Women and nature: an ancestral bond, a new alliance', in Oliveira and Corral (eds), *Terra Femina*, pp. 70–83.

Oliviera, R.D. de and T. Corral (eds) (1992) *Terra Femina*, Brazil: IDAC and REDEH.

Peters, B. and V. Samuels (eds) (1976) *Dialogue on Diversity: a New Agenda for American Women*, New York: Institute on Pluralism and Group Identity.

Pietilä, Hilkka (1993) 'A new picture of human economy: a woman's perspective', paper presented to the Fifth Interdisciplinary Congress on Women, San José, Costa Rica, 22–6 February.

Rich, A. (1976) *Of Woman Born: Motherhood as Experience and Institution*, New York: Norton.

Richta, R. (1968) *Civilization at the Crossroads: Social and Human Implications of the Scientific and Technological Revolution*, Czechoslovakia: International Arts and Science Press.

Schuler, M. (ed.) (1986) *Empowerment and the Law: Strategies of Third World Women*, Washington, DC: OEF International.

Schuler, M. (ed.) (1990) *Women, Law, and Development: Action for Change*, New York: OEF International.

Schuler, M. (ed.) (1992) *Freedom from Violence: Women's Strategies from Around the World*, New York: OEF International, UN Development Fund for Women, Women Ink.

Sen, G. and C. Grown (1987) *Development, Crises, and Alternative Visions: Third*

World Women's Perspectives, Analysis developed by the Third World women's network, DAWN (Development Alternatives with Women for a New Era), New York: Monthly Review Press.

Shiva, V. (1989) *Staying Alive: Women, Ecology and Development*, London: Zed Press.

South Asian Workshop on Women and Development (1989) *Pressing Against the Boundaries*, Report of an FAO/FFHC/AD Workshop, including 'South Asian Feminist Declaration'. Bangalore, New Delhi: FAO.

Tauli-Corpuz, V. (1992) 'Keynote Address: First Asian Indigenous Women's Conference', *Chaneg*, 4(1) (January–March): 9–14.

Telling It Collective (1990) *Telling It: Women and Language Across Cultures*, Vancouver: Press Gang.

Touraine, A. (1971) *The Post Industrial Society: Tomorrow's Social History: Classes, Conflicts, and Culture in the Programmed Society*, trans. Leonard F.X. Mayhew. New York: Random House.

Vital Signs: News from the National Black Women's Health Project.

WAND/APCD (1980) *Developing Strategies for the Future: Feminist Perspectives*. Report of the International Feminist Workshop held at Stony Point, New York 2–25, April 1980 and the Report of the International Feminist Workshop held in Bangkok 23–30 June 1979. New York: International Women's Tribune Center.

Waring, M. (1988) *If Women Counted: a New Feminist Economics*, San Francisco: Harper & Row.

Welfare Warriors (1991) 'Letter to the Editor', *Off Our Backs: a Women's Newsjournal*, 20.

White, E.C. (ed.) (1990) *Black Women's Health Book: Speaking for Ourselves*, Seattle, WA: Seal Press.

Women Against Fundamentalism (1990) 'Women Against Fundamentalism Statement', *Women Against Fundamentalism Newsletter*, 1(1): 2.

Women Living Under Muslim Laws (n.d.) 'Statement of Principles', published at the beginning of every *Women Living Under Muslim Laws Dossier.*

Women's Rights are Human Rights (n.d.) 'Women's Rights are Human Rights', Petition circulated by women's networks and groups around the world and presented at the United Nations Conference on Human Rights in Vienna, 1993.

World Women's Congress for a Healthy Planet (1992) *Official Report, Including Women's Action Agenda 21 and Findings of the Tribunals*, New York: Women's Environment and Development Organization (WEDO).

7
Globalization and the Mobilization of Gay and Lesbian Communities

Barry D. Adam

Any consideration of linkages between globalization processes and the development of gay and lesbian movements necessarily raises two questions: (i) a structural question concerning ways in which globalization shapes movements; and (ii) a question about how movements respond, thrive, and intervene in globalization processes, perhaps by developing global aspects themselves. These questions are complicated by the ambiguity of the idea of 'globalization' itself. Like many other scholarly 'buzzwords', globalization has proven to be a fruitful concept precisely because its lack of clarity invites creative speculation about the historical moment. Writing about globalization has tended to pursue two tracks of thought, one focused on cultural aspects of the changes occurring at the end of the twentieth century, the other on political economy, often with little connection between the two. A cultural-structural divide has been salient in new social movement theory as well. Since lesbian and gay movements tend often to be placed on the cultural side of the binary – by new social movement theory, by cultural studies, and by queer theory in particular – the question of how they might be articulated with the modern world-system has tended to be lost. What may be incontrovertible in all of this is that gay and lesbian movements have become increasingly global in the post-war period, especially in the last 25 years – at least in the sense that local organizations have been emerging in countries around the world. Just how and why gay and lesbian movements have become global raises many of the issues in current globalization debates.

Globalization as culture

If 'globalization' refers to the accelerating realization of Marshall McLuhan's prediction of a coming 'global village' – brought about by the mass media, and telecommunication innovations from the fax to the Internet – then gay and lesbian movements do show a global dimension. There has been a good deal of favourable commentary by journalists and scholars about the rush toward a global village. Their approach has been simply to explore (and sometimes to celebrate) the implications of dissolving the barriers of space and time in contemporary societies (Robertson, 1992; Spybey, 1996). This notion of cultural globalization tends to follow in the tradition of the older, anthropological idea of 'cultural diffusion' where contact among cultures results in a (generally benign) adoption and exchange of cultural elements, broadening horizons, and an overcoming of parochialism.

More critical approaches challenge this somewhat anodyne version of globalization. They discern a political face to international communication, concluding that much cultural diffusion may better be termed 'cultural imperialism' because cultural diffusion happens largely on terms set by the advanced industrial nations and by the multinational corporations that dominate the means of producing and distributing culture. News about world events, popular tastes, and youth cultures typically flow from a few power centres among news agencies, MTV, and the advertising industry, blanketing and submerging indigenous traditions. In its colonial form, military and missionary coercion enforced European ideologies on indigenous populations. In its postcolonial form, the hegemony of Hollywood, Associated Press, Reuters, the Murdoch chain, and a few other multi-billion-dollar enterprises dominate the world information order.

The application of these versions of globalization to gay and lesbian movements is not straightforward. There are no lack of examples of cultural diffusion. An American soldier of German extraction made the first (failed) attempt to found a gay movement organization in the United States in the 1920s after witnessing the early gay movement in Germany as a member of the US occupation forces (Adam, 1995: 46). The founders of the first gay movement group in Canada in the 1960s included two Dutch participants who had been used to having a community-run clubhouse in Amsterdam (Kinsman, 1996). Expatriate Chinese, Indian, and Arabic people in the European Union, North America, and Australia have been influential in organizing their compatriots around gay and lesbian identities in recent years. The gay and lesbian press has had far-flung subscribers since the days of the small circulation, trilingual Swiss journal, *Der Kreis* (1932–67) to mass circulation magazines of today. Those with access to the World Wide Web can easily find a wealth of gay, lesbian, bisexual, and transgender resources. Gay and lesbian people and organizations are aware of, and in contact with, each other in unprecedented ways, especially in the advanced industrial nations. The International Lesbian and Gay Association brings together gay, lesbian, bisexual, and transgender organizations from every continent and connects them through its bulletin and internet listserve.

The colonial/postcolonial proposition of globalization raises more difficult issues. Certainly the colonial propagation of European ideas was overwhelmingly anti-homoerotic. European conquistadors, missionaries, and colonists, from the fifteenth to the twentieth centuries, systematically and violently suppressed indigenous forms of same-sex affection and sexuality in the Americas, Asia, Africa, and Melanesia. Today homosexually-interested people in independent, postcolonial states still often have to contend with ingrained colonial legacies of anti-homosexual criminal law enforced by state elites and supported by authoritarian Christian or Islamic clerics. In addition, the contemporary world military order is dominated by the singularly homophobic US military with its lengthy record of support for authoritarian regimes around the world (Scott and Stanley, 1994; Chomsky and Herman, 1979).

Scholars of contemporary gay and lesbian studies have, since its inception, debated the politics of the postcolonial spread of Western ideas of the 'gay', 'lesbian', 'bisexual', and 'transgendered'. Debates over essentialism and social constructionism have centred around the degree of (dis)continuity or (un)commonality among various forms of same-sex bonding in history and across cultures. The invention of 'the homosexual' as a species apart appears to be a peculiarly Western construction. For contemporary queer theorists, who dream of a deconstruction of the boundaries that channel the flows of desire, the internationalization of gay and lesbian identities is scarcely a thing to be celebrated; rather, it is the diversity of indigenous forms of homoeroticism that merits recognition and affirmation. This utopian dream, however, tends to deconstruct an idea rather than its material conditions. The absence of gay-lesbian categories more often signifies the repression or denial of same-sex bonding than sexual or affective freedom, and people in Asia, Africa, and Latin America who seek to defend same-sex desire continue to find inspiration and pragmatic strategies in gay and lesbian models.

Mechanisms of the spread of gay and lesbian forms of homosexuality can scarcely be identified with imperial cultural flows that some have termed 'McDonaldization'. Gay and lesbian cultures of the advanced industrial nations have, at best, tangential or interstitial relations with hegemonic centres of cultural production. Hollywood, the major television networks, and the news organizations, with occasional exceptions, present distorted-mirror versions of lesbian and gay cultures, rarely permitting voices from gay communities to speak for themselves. The cinema, theatre, and artistic representations rooted in gay and lesbian cultures only infrequently break into 'mainstream' distribution networks that persist in reproducing cultural products that position 'the homosexual' as the object of ridicule or deserved victim of violence (Epstein and Friedman, 1995). Still, the gay 'meccas' of Amsterdam, New York, San Francisco, and Sydney exert a worldwide influence through the migration of workers, travellers, students, writers, and artists both from Asia, Africa, and Latin America into the metropoles and the reverse. There can be little doubt that the indistinguishability of gay discos in San José, Costa Rica, from their equivalents in the United States, or the adoption of the latest fashions in gay Tokyo by young men strolling along the Bund in Shanghai, show the effect of external models of how to be gay. Indeed, it is very often the middle-class, literate, and well-travelled strata of major Latin American cities who have adopted 'First World' categories of gay or lesbian identity, while indigenous forms of homoeroticism continue in the streets and small towns.

What cultural theories cannot explain, however (despite the ambitions of some discourse theorists), is local receptivity or resistance to new cultural forms. Ideas, examples, and fashions from the First World do not inevitably acquire adherents elsewhere – nor, when they are adopted, do they necessarily assume the same form; rather, they often become adapted and synthesized into local frameworks. Gay and lesbian identities and movements presume a myriad of structural prerequisites. It may be that the increasing pervasiveness of gay and lesbian social forms has less to do with cultural diffusion, or worse, imperialism, than with changes in the modern world-system that have created the social conditions for new forms of sexual expression.

Globalization as political economy

The increasingly visible, global presence of gay and lesbian communities and movements is not simply due to cultural homogenization, but rather to shifting structural conditions where indigenous traditions of same-sex bonding are changing with the social conditions around them. This sense of 'globalization' refers to a half millennium (or more) historical process where local cultures have been drawn into the modern world-system, eventually becoming reshaped in their fundamental socio-logics by their relationships with global capitalism. As characterized by Immanuel Wallerstein (1989) and others, the incorporation of new societies (peripheries) into the realm of the dominant economic powers (metropoles) has resulted, over the long term, in the fundamental reorganization of their systems of production and distribution, in their class systems and political organization, and the composition of their populations through labour migration. The process of incorporation into the modern world-system has also impacted family and household formation as the centrality of kinship relations in determining life chances has typically become subordinated to the capitalist labour market (Alderson and Sanderson, 1991; Smith and Wallerstein, 1992).

There has been a strong tendency to treat gay and lesbian communities and their movements as cultural artefacts unrelated to structure, political economy, or the modern world-system (Seidman, 1996). This tendency gives gay and lesbian people over to the 'globalization-as-culture' school virtually by default. A good deal of contemporary social movement theory has assimilated lesbian and gay mobilization into the 'new social movement' camp, and into 'identity politics' in particular. New social movements now supposedly 'seem to exist independently from ... structural and cultural conditions' (Eder, 1993: 44) and gay movements are, somewhat inexplicably, all about affirming and expressing identities (Dudink and Verhaar, 1994). What is missing from this view are the ways the changes wrought by the world-system articulate with the historical rise of gay and lesbian forms of same-sex connection and how lesbian, gay, bisexual, and transgender identities have become 'necessary fictions' (Weeks, 1993) in contemporary political environments.

The 'gay' and 'lesbian' categories of the modern world, when compared to cross-cultural and historical forms of same-sex relations, show several specific characteristics:

1. In societies where kinship has declined as a primary organizing principle determining the survival and well-being of their members, homosexual relations have developed autonomous forms apart from dominant heterosexual family strictures.
2. Exclusive homosexuality has become increasingly possible for both partners and a ground for household formation.
3. Same-sex bonds have developed relatively egalitarian forms, characterized by age and gender 'endogamy', rather than involving people in differentiated age and gender classes.

4. People have come to discover each other and form large-scale social networks because of their homosexual interests and not only in the context of pre-existing social relationships (such as households, neighbourhoods, schools, militaries, churches, and so on).
5. Homosexuality has come to be a social formation unto itself characterized by self-awareness and group identity (Adam, 1995: 7).

These characteristics presume a sociological infrastructure characteristic of the modern world-system:

1. *The financial 'independence' of wage labour.* In societies where access to the means of production depends on kin ties and inheritance, homosexuality is either integrated into the dominant kinship order (through gender redesignation or limitation of homosexual ties to a life stage) or subordinated to it as a hidden and 'unofficial' activity.
2. *Urbanization and personal mobility.* The growth of cities, the invention of public spaces, migration away from traditional settings and from the supervisory gaze of families have all created new opportunities, especially at first for men, to form new, non-traditional relationships.
3. *Disruption of traditional gender rules.* As minorities and women have been entering wage labour in increasing numbers, often occupying newly created locations in the division of labour, more of the choices taken for granted by men have become available.
4. *Development of the welfare state.* The creation of social services in health, education, welfare, employment insurance, pensions, and so on have supplemented traditional family functions, providing alternatives to reliance on kin.
5. *Liberal democratic states.* Legal guarantees of basic civil liberties also facilitate the ability of people to love and live with those of their choice, though most liberal democratic states have lengthy histories of violating basic constitutional freedoms of conscience, assembly, and free speech in order to suppress their gay and lesbian citizens, and gay and lesbian communities have also carved out small spaces for themselves in the hostile environments of authoritarian states.

Having enumerated some of these factors, it is important to note that these are structural underpinnings of contemporary gay and lesbian worlds, not of homosexuality itself, which is best conceived as a universal human potential with a wide range of expression across cultures. Even though gay and lesbian worlds (as defined above) have now been documented for at least three centuries in Europe, these social conditions do not in themselves determine that same-sex relationships will necessarily take gay/lesbian forms. Medieval constructions of sodomy (Jordan, 1997), Judaeo-Christian obsession with narrowing legitimate sexuality to its procreative form, and the Western tendency to force sexuality to 'confess truth' about the nature of persons (Foucault, 1978) all enter into Western constructions of the 'gay' and 'lesbian'. Japan offers an example of a society with the political economy of an advanced, industrial society but none of the history of religious or state persecution of homosexuality. Though Japan has developed gay (and to a very limited degree, lesbian) public spaces similar to those to be found in its Western counterparts, the formation of a popular sense of identity and movement has been less evident (Lunsing, 1999). Finally, even among the citizens of advanced industrial societies, many more people have homosexual experiences than identify as 'gay', 'lesbian', or 'bisexual' and these identities may, as well, be less widespread among non-white and working-class people who nevertheless have homosexual interests and practices (Laumann et al., 1994).

Still, where this sociological infrastructure is lacking, gay and lesbian identities, and the movements built out of a sense of commonality signified by these identities, are also unusual. As Badruddin Khan (1997) remarks about urban Pakistan, widespread practices of sexuality among men tend not to lead to gay identities where family networks remain major determinants of one's well-being, families make sure their progeny marry regardless of sexual orientation, and very few young people have the financial ability or freedom to form households of their own choosing. Similar conditions apply to much of Latin.America, with the partial exception of the urban middle classes. The Communist states of Eastern Europe, on the other hand, showed a different array of social conditions that both facilitated and inhibited the growth of gay and lesbian cultures. State socialism typically pursued a development model founded on industrialization, resulting in urban migration, conversion of much of the population to wage labour, and improved opportunities for women. As in capitalist societies, state socialism displaced kinship as the primary determinant of people's life chances, disestablished churches, and devolved decisions about family and reproduction to the individual level (Adam, 1995: 166). It is not surprising, then, that gay and lesbian bars and coffee-houses became part of the urban scene in Eastern European capitals well before the fall of Communism and movement organizations came into existence in several countries despite the power of central bureaucracies to control the mass media and administer labour migration, commercial meeting places, and housing (Hauer et al., 1984). When the Communist states collapsed in the early 1990s, gay and lesbian movement organizations rapidly emerged across the region in a pattern similar to Western Europe because the sociological infrastructure was already in place.

Globalization and neoliberalism

Contemporary fascination with 'globalization' arises, in particular, from attempts to make sense of the current transition (evident especially in advanced, industrial nations but also strongly impacting developing nations) from state-regulated economies with extensive provision of social welfare services, to neoliberal economies characterized by shrinkage of the welfare establishment (Cox, 1994, 1996). Much of this transformation appears to be underpinned by the intention of the multinational capitalist class to extend and facilitate its ability to wield capital across borders by abolishing trade barriers through the World Trade Organization (Overbeek and van der Pijl, 1993; Arrighi, 1994; Teeple, 1995). 'Globalization' has become a shorthand referent for the profound social and political effects that are unfolding as a result of the enhanced power of multinational capitalist elites to outflank nation-states and labour unions in setting social, political, and economic agendas around the world.

Bowles and Gintis (1986: 58–9) contend that the welfare state was founded on an implicit social contract among three key sectors (that they call the Keynesian compromise) consisting of:

- state economic regulation where state-supported demand impelled economic growth and profit, and regulated class conflict through trade union legislation;
- continued capitalist control of investment; and
- workers' ability to partake of the wealth generated by post-war growth through unionization; a social wage through the state provision of health, education, and welfare; and the promise of individual (rather than collective) social mobility for their children, if not for themselves.

This system was maintained in the context of a Cold War imperium over the Third World.

As Gary Teeple (1995: 26) argues, the welfare state was intended

to counter the extremes of the business cycles, to provide unprofitable but necessary economic services, to defend and promote the

interests of national capital in domestic and overseas markets, to
ensure the reproduction of the working class, to act as guarantor
of social order, to mitigate working-class interest in revolutionary
socialism, and so on.

The Keynesian compromise began to unravel in the 1970s; the Reagan
and Thatcher governments, in particular, accelerated and promoted
the shift toward neoliberalism, that Carl Boggs (1986: 129) sums up as
a: 'return to the mythic free-enterprise economy, with its glorification
of unfettered individualism, self-regulating market forces, and private
incentives, and to traditional values embodied in an old-fashioned
work ethic, the neighborhood, religion, patriarchal sex roles, and
patriotism.'

Neoliberalism has moved to rework the Keynesian compromise by
paring back both the real and social wages of workers, managing social
discontent by: (i) investing heavily in police and prisons at the same
time as health, education, and welfare have been cut back (Chambliss,
1994; Davey, 1995); (ii) propagating a neo-conservative ideology of
lowered expectations and 'family values' (Hall, 1988a; Smith, 1994); and
(iii) weakening workers' organizations by facilitating the almost instant
worldwide transfer of capital to locations with quiescent and amenable
populations.

In the midst of this transition, new social movements have come
to prominence (though it is important to note that most, including
gay and lesbian movements, have much older antecedents). They
came about not simply as defensive movements preserving community in the face of commodification, but as movements resisting
the ways in which race, gender, sexuality, and the environment
have been taken up and reproduced in advanced capitalist societies
(Adam, 1993). They are movements grounded, not only in the workplace, but, as the post-Althusserian regulation school might term it,
in the arena of the reproduction of the relations of production –
that is, in the social organization of family, education, law, communication media, religion, and social services. And they have faced formi-
dable obstacles in challenging the neoliberal agenda by: (i) exposing and
challenging the availability of environmental and social inputs taken
for granted by capitalist production and expansion; (ii) deconstructing the neoconservative disciplinary ideology of receiving less while
working more; and (iii) resisting right-wing populism rooted in the
resentment of those whose social status has declined in neoliberal
economies.

The global movement

Today the International Lesbian and Gay Association federates movement organizations and attempts to monitor civil rights around the world, twin established organizations with new, and link international efforts around asylum, the military, churches, youth, ableism, health, trade unions, AIDS, and prisoners.[1] A primary objective of national movements has been to win legal recourse against discrimination. Beginning with Norway in 1981, sexual orientation has been included in the human rights legislation of Canada, Denmark, Ecuador, Finland, France, Iceland, Luxembourg, Netherlands, New Zealand, Slovenia, South Africa, Spain, Sweden and Switzerland, as well as ten of the fifty United States, five states in Australia, and 73 cities in Brazil (as of 2001).[2] Ireland and Israel also legislated workplace protection in the 1990s. Even more recent is legislation recognizing the spousal status of same-sex relationships. Norway, Sweden, Netherlands, France and Iceland have followed the precedent set by Denmark in 1989, and a supreme court decision in Hungary has included same-sex couples in common-law spousal status. Canada legislated same-sex relationship recognition in 2000 and breakthroughs have occurred in the US states of Hawaii and Vermont. With the exception of the law adopted in the Netherlands in 2001, all of these laws fall short of full equality, often barring gay and lesbian couples from full-fledged marriage, adoption, or access to artificial insemination.

Gay and lesbian movements have emerged along with (and sometimes in explicit coalition with) democratic movements to oppose authoritarian rule in Spain (after the death of Franco), South Africa (in overcoming apartheid), in Eastern Europe (with the fall of Communism), and Brazil, Argentina, Uruguay, and Chile (in ending military dictatorships). Once these precedents are in place, gay and lesbian communities may take the opportunity to mobilize in neighbouring countries. With the African National Congress in power in South Africa and sexual orientation entrenched in the new constitution, groups in Zimbabwe (1990), Botswana (1996), Namibia (1996) and Swaziland (1997) have declared themselves often in the face of virulent homophobia enunciated by local rulers. The struggle against AIDS has created the first opening for gay mobilization in even less hospitable places such as Kenya, Malaysia, and Ecuador.

This record of civil emancipation must be viewed in the context of ongoing homophobic practices of states and their agents, of reactionary civil and religious movements, and of those in control of cultural reproduction from the schools to television programming. Amnesty International (1994) documents the incarceration or murder of homosexual people in several countries – most notably, Iran, Turkey, and Romania. Movement groups continue to face repeated police raids on gay gathering places and death squad activity in many cities of Latin America, especially in Colombia, Peru, Mexico, and Brazil. Gay and transgender Argentines were among the targets of the 'dirty war' perpetrated by the police and death squads and sanctioned by the military and Roman Catholic hierarchies (Jauregui, 1987). Sweeping police powers continued after the fall of the military dictatorship into the 1990s, resulting in numerous bar raids and arbitrary arrests. The work of the Comunidad Homosexual Argentina, in collaboration with other democratic organizations, resulted in 1996 in the revocation of police powers and inclusion of sexual orientation as legally protected categories in Buenos Aires and Rosario.

Globalization processes, then, have affected the mobilization of gay and lesbian communities in a wide variety of ways. Insofar as globalization refers to processes of incorporation of local communities into the political and economic networks of the capitalist world-system, then globalization has accelerated processes of proletarianization, urbanization, family change, and democratization. These processes have created social conditions where indigenous forms of same-sex adhesiveness (to use Walt Whitman's term) have tended to evolve toward gay and lesbian social forms. Contemporary gay and lesbian communities and movements have also, in turn, provided fertile ground for the defence, growth, and reworking of older, more traditional bisexual and transgendered forms of sexual life. Where globalization refers to the faster and easier circulation of cultural practices and ideologies, gay and lesbian movements have been participants here as well. Though gay and lesbian cultural forms usually have an uneasy or oppositional relation with the established, institutional ideological circuits of religion, nationalism, and 'family values', an international gay and lesbian culture has emerged throughout the metropoles and, increasingly around the world, through personal contacts, the gay press, and now more formal, if fragile, organizations like the International Lesbian and Gay Association. Pride celebrations, which originated in political demonstrations against repression, have become so massive, in such cities as Sydney, Toronto, and San Francisco, that they have changed the cultural landscape and attracted commercial interests intent on making inroads into a new market of consumers.[3]

Globalization, as a political and economic process underlying the transition from the welfare state to neoliberalism, has consequences for the well-being and potential mobilization of numerous social movement constituencies. Neoliberal governments, particularly in the United States and the United Kingdom, have drawn on conservative ideologies of work discipline, delayed gratification, racial and national supremacy, and patriarchal definitions of gender and family to 'sell' wage restraints and the withdrawal of social services, as well as to re-attribute blame for the declining quality of life. As Stuart Hall (1988b: 48) remarks, Thatcherism combined 'organic Toryism – nation, family, duty, authority, standards, traditionalism – with the aggressive themes of a revived neoliberalism – self-interest, competitive individualism, anti-statism.' Neoconservative governments thereby encouraged and exploited the resentment of social classes damaged by the world economy, channelling their anger toward traditional lightning rods of popular prejudice, including lesbians and gay men (Adam, 1995: ch. 6). The global economy has struck hard at some social groups – typically rural people, small business people, and workers employed in heavy industries. Declining or beleaguered ethnic and class groups have proven to be especially susceptible to right-wing mobilization, from the anti-Semites of the early twentieth century to the homophobes and xenophobes of the late twentieth century.

At the same time, gay and lesbian movements, with the other 'new social movements', have flourished in the neoliberal age. The welfare state both changed and reinforced family and gender requirements in the 1950s by (i) relieving families of some of the functions they could not always fulfil but also by (ii) restoring the home as the women's sphere and by overtly suppressing gay and lesbian life. The social policies of neoliberal governments of the 1980s tended to press for the 'restoration' of traditional gender and family scripts (restoring to some degree a family that never was (Coontz, 1992)) while reducing the social services available to them. Gay and lesbian mobilization, like the women's movement, is part of the larger wave of 'antisystemic' movements since 1968 (Wallerstein, 1990), building on and expressing some aspects of structural change – such as women's increasing participation in wage labour – while resisting others such as explicitly conservative social policy. And as capital has gone global, social movements as well have sought unprecedented world-wide networks.

Notes

1. The International Lesbian and Gay Association can be contacted at: Antenne Rose and FWH, 81, rue Marché-au-charbon, B-1000 Bruxelles 1, Belgium;

website: http://www.ilga.org. The International Gay and Lesbian Human
Rights Commission is at: 1360 Mission Street no. 200, San Francisco,
California, USA 94103; website: http: //www.iglhrc.org.
2. Much of this section draws on Adam (1995) and recent issues of the *Bulletin
of the International Lesbian and Gay Association*.
3. For a critique of the commercial cultivation of gay consumerism, see the early
work of Dennis Altman (1982) and the more recent work of Mark Simpson
(1995).

References

Adam, B. (1993) 'Post-Marxism and the new social movements', *Canadian Review
of Sociology and Anthropology*, 30(3): 316–36.
Adam, B. (1995) *The Rise of a Gay and Lesbian Movement*, revised edition. New
York: Twayne/Simon & Schuster Macmillan.
Adam, B. (1999) 'Moral regulation and the Canadian state', in B.D. Adam, J.W.
Duyvendak and A. Krouwel (eds), *The Global Emergence of Gay and Lesbian
Politics*, Philadelphia: Temple University Press, pp. 12–29.
Alderson, A. and S. Sanderson (1991) 'Historic European household structures
and the capitalist world-economy', *Journal of Family History*, 16(4): 419–32.
Altman, D. (1982) *The Homosexualization of America*, New York: St. Martin's.
Amnesty International (1994) *Breaking the Silence*, New York: Amnesty Interna-
tional Publications.
Arrighi, G. (1994) *The Long Twentieth Century*, London: Verso.
Boggs, C. (1986) *Social Movements and Political Power*, Philadelphia: Temple
University Press.
Bowles, S. and H. Gintis (1986) *Democracy and Capitalism*, New York: Basic Books.
Chambliss, W. (1994) 'Policing the ghetto underclass', *Social Problems*, 41(2):
177–94.
Chomsky, N. and E. Herman (1979) *The Washington Connection and Third World
Fascism*, Boston: South End.
Coontz, S. (1992) *The Way We Never Were*, New York: Basic Books.
Cox, R. (1994) 'Global restructuring', in R. Stubbs and G. Underhill (eds),
Political Economy and the Changing Global Order, Toronto: McClelland and
Stewart, pp. 45–59.
Cox, R. (1996) 'A perspective on globalisation', in J. Mittelman (ed.), *Globaliza-
tion*, Boulder, CO: Lynne Rienner, pp. 21–30.
Davey, J. (1995) *The New Social Contract*, Westport, CT: Praeger.
Dudink, S. and O. Verhaar (1994) 'Paradoxes of identity politics', *Homologie*,
4(94): 29–36.
Eder, K. (1993) *The New Politics of Class*, London: Sage.
Epstein, R. and J. Friedman (dir.) (1995) *The Celluloid Closet* [film].
Foucault, M. (1978) *The History of Sexuality*, New York: Pantheon, volumes
1–3.
Hall, S. (1988a) 'The toad in the garden', in C. Nelson and L. Grossberg (eds),
Marxism and the Interpretation of Culture, Urbana, IL: University of Illinois Press,
pp. 35–57.
Hall, S. (1988b) *The Hard Road to Renewal*, London: Verso.

Hauer, G. et al. (1984) *Rosa Liebe unterm roten Stern*, Hamburg: Frühlings Erwachen.

Jauregui, C. (1987) *La homosexualidad en la Argentina*, Buenos Aires: Tarso.

Jordan, M. (1997) *The Invention of Sodomy in Christian Theology*, Chicago: University of Chicago Press.

Khan, B. (1997) 'Not-so-gay life in Pakistan in the 1980s and 1990s', in S. Murray and W. Roscoe (eds), *Islamic Homosexualities*, New York: New York University Press, pp. 275–96.

Kinsman, G. (1996) *The Regulation of Desire*, second edition. Montreal: Black Rose.

Laumann, E., Gagnon, J., Michael, R. and S. Michaels (1994) *The Social Organization of Sexuality*, Chicago: University of Chicago Press.

Lunsing, W. (1999) 'Japan', in B.D. Adam, A. Krouwel and J.W. Duyvendak (eds), *The Global Emergence of Gay and Lesbian Politics*, Philadelphia: Temple University Press, pp. 293–325.

Overbeek, H. and K. van der Pijl (1993) 'Restructuring capital and restructuring hegemony', in H. Overbeek (ed.), *Restructuring Hegemony in the Global Political Economy*, London: Routledge, pp. 1–27.

Robertson, R. (1992) *Globalization*, Thousand Oaks, CA: Sage.

Scott, W. and S. Stanley (1994) *Gays and Lesbians in the Military*, Hawthorne, NY: Aldine de Gruyter.

Seidman, S. (1996) *Queer Theory/Sociology*, Cambridge, MA: Blackwell.

Simpson, M. (1995) *Antigay*, London: Cassell.

Smith, A.M. (1994) *New Right Discourse on Race and Sexuality*, New York: Cambridge University Press.

Smith, J. and I. Wallerstein (1992) *Creating and Transforming Households*, New York: Cambridge University Press.

Spybey, T. (1996) *Globalization and World Society*, Cambridge, MA: Blackwell.

Teeple, G. (1995) *Globalization and the Decline of Social Reform*, Toronto: Garamond.

Wallerstein, I. (1989) *The Modern World-System*, volumes 1–3. San Diego: Academic Press.

Wallerstein, I. (1990) 'Antisystemic movements', in S. Amin, G. Arrighi, A. Gunder Frank and I. Wallerstein (eds), *Transforming the Revolution*, New York: Monthly Review Press, pp. 13–53.

Weeks, J. (1993) 'Necessary fictions', in J. Murray (ed.), *Constructing Sexualities*, Windsor, Ontario: University of Windsor Humanities Research Group, pp. 93–121.

Part III
The Multiplicities of Globalization

8
Cross-Border, Cross-Movement Alliances in the Late 1990s*

Aaron Pollack

Introduction

In the middle and late 1990s, a trend toward 'cross-border, cross-movement' organizing, in many parts of the world, has become visible. Though what are arguably the strongest movements presently active around the globe – those of a religious or 'ethnic' nature – do not participate in these developments, these initiatives represent a new type of political action that has important implications. They are beginning to negotiate the limits created by national frontiers and the boundaries between social movements that have historically constrained their actions. More importantly, because many of the groups which participate in these initiatives do not share the epistemological bases of modernity, the existence of different worldviews must (or at least should) be confronted. In these situations, the dominance, or hegemony, of the modern epistemology can be brought into question.

What can be presently observed in the field of international organizing is an increased cross-movement co-ordination as well as a greater focus on regional and 'global' efforts that is a response to global economic restructuring and both the regionalization and the globalization of the world economy that this entails. These initiatives involve a number of interchanges between 'advocacy movements' led by non-governmental organizations (NGOs), 'livelihood movements'[1] and some strands of organized labour.

The principal reasons for this convergence are the marginalization of much of the world population through continued global neoliberal restructuring; an increasing frustration on the part of many NGOs regarding their new and contradictory roles; and the continued weak bargaining position of labour unions that organize alone and only on a national level. By the late 1990s, these three factors were already established facts and different forms of 'cross-border, cross-movement' organizing were being tested.

The newest factor to enter into these alliances is the presence of many diverse groups that do not necessarily subscribe to modern conceptions of 'liberalism', 'Marxism', 'radical democracy', or 'civil society'. While these groups are active in the present forms of international organizing, they are marginalized within the new initiatives, recognized but still outside the mainstream of discussions. Thus while women, indigenous people and other 'others' are invited to participate, it is usually understood that they act as specific groups, with group-specific goals, not easily integrated into the 'political' and 'economic' issues which are almost always seen as most important and somehow separable from those of the 'others'.

A key factor in the recent growth in the strength and capacity of these various organizations and networks is improved technology which permits more rapid transfer of information. This change could be observed in the solidarity and human rights movements during the 1970s, 1980s, and 1990s that used first fax and then e-mail both to pass information among themselves and as a means of putting immediate pressure on state and interstate actors regarding concrete and urgent actions. These technological innovations have vastly changed the possibilities for international organizing, particularly in situations where public outcry can have the effect of changing state policy.[2] The quick passing of information among NGOs and other organizations also simplifies the definition of common positions for lobbying purposes (Lins Ribiero, 1998: 341). The new technologies also speed up the availability of counter-information which can be used to counteract false (or the absence of) reporting in mainstream news services.

Access to this new technology tends to reflect already existing relations of power, both internationally and within organizations – particularly in the poorer parts of the world (Lins Ribiero, 1998: 342). However, in those *few* contexts where all have relatively equal access to technology,[3] it can make for a more horizontal sharing of information among organizers and movement members.

At the same time, the use of e-mail and the Internet reinforces the tendencies toward individualization within modern societies, allowing each person to take political action from his or her home or worksite, without the need for any 'personal', human interchange. This trend builds upon the already existing 'membership organizations' *cum* social movements developed in the US and expanded to Europe which consist of donors who may also take on the role of 'letter writers' and 'voters'. The creation of 'social movements' that express themselves through e-mails, faxes, and (every so often) votes, is reflective of the 'deperson-alization' of the modern world. After years of mass movements, and calls for 'direct democracy' and so on, it seems that capitalism and modernity have succeeded in commodifying and rationalizing the 'new social movements' as well.

The use of e-mail and Internet sites as means of information exchange are nonetheless incredibly important in the increasing use of 'network' forms of organizing which are more horizontal in nature. This can imply a network of people that form a single group or organization, and also a network of groups and organizations. This type of organizing is by no means original to the Internet, and can be found in anarchist, and more recently, Western feminist forms of organization.[4] Nonetheless, the new technologies have made it possible for groups which are highly dispersed geographically to 'network' in ways that were previously impossible.

This chapter will look at four particular phenomena in present 'cross-border, cross-movement' organizing, identifying them as parts of a trend toward increased global/international social movement inter-change and co-ordination. These four phenomena are each unique, but all come from trajectories which are, in some part, common. The Encounters and Network against Neoliberalism and for Humanity,[5] NGO networks and the International Forum on Globalisation (IFG),[6] the Santiago Counter-Summit[7] and the People's Global Alliance (PGA)[8] all represent moments of co-ordination/interchange by social movements in response to neoliberal economic restructuring. The first three of these are rooted in the Americas and can all claim a common root in orga-nizing against the North American Free Trade Agreement (NAFTA) in the early 1990s. The PGA, in turn, can claim some of its own roots in the Encounters.

Encounters Against Neoliberalism and for Humanity

For one week, during the summer of 1996, the First Encounter Against Neoliberalism and for Humanity was held in Chiapas, Mexico, orga-nized by the Zapatista Army of National Liberation (EZLN) and attended by about 3000 participants, principally from Europe, Mexico and the US, with significant representation from the rest of Latin America, and very little from the remainder of the world. The Second Encounter was held one year later in different parts of the Spanish state,[9] with approximately 2000 people, primarily from Europe again, but on this occasion with participants from approximately 70 nations (Simoncini, 1998: 167).

The EZLN and 'civil society' – background to the first Encounter

The first Encounter was planned and organized by the EZLN, principally to increase pressure on the Mexican government, with whom they were at that time holding peace negotiations, but also to promote an interchange among those who shared the idea(l)s reflected in the title of the Encounter. Inasmuch as it was part of the political strategy of the EZLN, it followed on a number of similar events involving Mexican and international 'civil society'.

The EZLN, and their supporters, both nationally and internationally, had slowly constructed a network, with a great deal of participation from Mexico, North America, Europe and a significant amount from Latin America, all built upon the already existing networks related to indigenous issues, human rights networks, Central American solidarity networks and, in North America, on the anti-NAFTA organizing of the early 1990s.[10] After the initial mainstream press coverage of the uprising, it was the networks, built principally upon e-mail and the Internet,[11] that kept information flowing and allowed for popular, national and international responses to particular events which, on several occasions, prevented the Mexican Army from militarily eliminating the EZLN (Castells et al., 1995–96: 23; Wager and Schulz, 1995: 34–5).

By the time of the first Encounter in mid-1996, the EZLN had long been maintaining public interactions with different social movements and 'civil society' groups to maintain themselves in the public spotlight, to look for possible alliances, and to push forward a broad-based 'grassroots' campaign for democratizing Mexico.

The Encounters

In addition to providing a show of international solidarity for the EZLN, the First Encounter succeeded in creating a space for interchange between activists, and a bit of hope in the dark days of the consolidating new world order. The first Encounter was able to establish and strengthen ties between different groups which previously had little knowledge of each other's work. It was not designed to create a new organization, but rather to allow for discussion, disagreement and a free flow of information among participants.

The discussions at the First Encounter were dominated by the West, both in terms of participants and in terms of content. This was also reflected in the Latin American presence, which was primarily of European extract and worldview. The presence of the members of the EZLN, who participated minimally in discussions, preferring to listen (or sleep, at times),[12] did little to change the overwhelmingly Western tone of the discussions in which I participated.[13] Nonetheless, the communities in which the Encounter was physically located had some effect on the ambience of the event as a whole.

The organizers of the event had tried to make sure that all potential categories of the 'marginalized' could have a chance to discuss their specific issues. In this sense the Encounter was inclusive, if not always successfully, and not without a great deal of discussion and disagreement.[14] Though it was organized in a 'democratic' manner, in the sense that enough tables and sub-tables were arranged such that all could have a chance to participate, many forms of exclusion were to be found within the Encounter itself. The European tone of the discussions meant that often those who spoke were those who were most willing to interrupt, while those who would politely wait their turn would never have an opportunity to express their opinions.[15] Additionally, the traditional hierarchies of power (male/female, North/South, modern/non-modern) were present, with the obvious but nonetheless striking twist that any Mayan with a bandanna or ski mask was accorded considerable respect, giving credence to the Zapatista slogan: 'we cover our faces in order to be heard'.[16]

The operative conclusions of the First Encounter were three fold: 'to create a network against neoliberalism and for humanity'; to realize a global poll on agreement or disagreement with the baseline ideas of the Encounter; and to organize a Second Encounter, somewhere in Europe, the following year. The first conclusion was already in place, the second was almost universally ignored and the third was to prove a burdensome task.

Over the next year, different European organizations, principally Chiapas solidarity committees, came together to discuss the organization of the Second Encounter. Before these meetings began, however, the solidarity movement itself started to split, and was weakened, principally because of differing ideas regarding the type of relationships the solidarity committees should have with national political parties in France, Italy and Spain, the three countries which had sent the most participants to the First Encounter (Albertani and Ranieri, 1998).

The prevailing opinion among the European organizers was that the Second Encounter should be 'self-organized', implying no funding from institutional sources, and therefore greater freedom of expression.

Among those involved in planning the Encounter, there were different ideas of what it should have been centred around. There were those who supported a continued focus on Chiapas, those who wanted to emphasize the negative aspects of the idea of 'Europe' as it was being promoted by the Maastricht Treaty of the European Union, others who considered the situation of immigrants in Europe to be a priority, and some who, 'going against the accusation of abstraction', wanted to discuss new forms of 'social and political action' *(agire politico)* (Albertani and Ranieri, 1998: 20). In the end, the invitation to the Encounter was broad, allowing for the discussion of a variety of themes, including all of those mentioned above.

The Second Encounter itself was again heavily dominated by Europeans (at least this time we were in Europe) and, although the theme of this Encounter was 'A World in Which Many Worlds Fit', the discussion was yet more overridingly European. One weakness in the first Encounter, the limited number of participants from outside Europe and Latin America, was improved upon, but not enough to change the general dynamic. The 'traditional' forms of doing politics and types of discussion were even more visible than in the previous Encounter. Those who adopted these strategies (controlling the microphone, controlling the translations, behind closed doors negotiations to reach particular goals, and so on) had a relatively easy time of it, as many others present not only weren't playing by those rules, but weren't even aware that anyone else was. The general sense after the Encounter was one of disappointment (mixed with appreciation that it had occurred), partially because of unrealistically high expectations, but also because of some poor organizing decisions and the 'traditional' forms of politics mentioned above.

The greatest frustrations centred around very different ideas of what the Encounter was about. While for some it was to be an encounter, a meeting, an interchange, for others it should have been a step, a movement toward the construction of an organization, however nebulous that might be. The Second Encounter had taken as a general theme, to be discussed at all tables, the construction of the 'network against neoliberalism and for humanity' agreed upon at the end of the First Encounter. The ongoing discussions about this, and the eventual conclusion that the already existing networks should continue to function, without any form of centralization or greater co-ordination, reflected a consistent tension throughout the Encounter between those who wanted to create structures and those who opposed that initiative.

The 'intergalactic encounters' (as they have been affectionately called) were, in the end, only that. They were initiatives toward interchange, without any designs at unification. On a political level, there is no organization, no one to be 'included' or 'co-opted'; nor is any participant responsible (morally or otherwise) for the actions of any other. The lack of a centralized decision-making structure should make unified action more difficult, but between December 1997 and February 1998, protests against the Acteal massacre[17] took place in over fifty countries, made possible through the 'network' (Simoncini, 1998: 10).

NGO networks

Many of the larger European- and US-based NGOs have played the principal roles in the appearance and growth of NGO-led advocacy movements, both because of their greater access to financial resources and because of the traditional North–South power imbalances which are equally present in the NGO world (Krut, 1997: esp. 13–17), largely a result of the monetary inequalities. Many NGOs, whether large or small, local or transnational, are faced with serious contradictions brought on by their change in roles over the past fifteen years. The most important of these are: their greatly increased work as service providers at both international and national levels, filling in some of the gaps left by state withdrawal; and their increased access to centres of decision-making, acting in an 'advocacy' role on an international level, having gained entrance to United Nations (UN)-sponsored conferences, and to the processes of World Bank project planning and implementation (Nelson, 1996). The strength of the NGOs in both of these areas is based on their ability to network internationally, and the capacity to take advantage of the political space that has become open to them as a result of global economic restructuring, which has handed them some of the political power regarding resource distribution that had previously been under the control of national governments.

The different advocacy networks (environmental, women's, human rights, development-related, among others) have grown in parallel fashion over the past twenty years, taking advantage of both increased possibilities for communication and increased funding from private foundations and governments. NGO networks have expanded through contacts made during specific campaigns, as well as, particularly during the past decade, through participation in UN conferences and the NGO forums that have accompanied them.

The focus of the campaigns of the 'development-related' NGO networks has tended to be against multinational corporations or the World Bank (Nelson, 1996; Rich, 1994: esp. 107–47), the latter often organized through pressure on the US Congress. Although the historical dominance of US-based NGOs at the apex of many of these networks (Nelson, 1996: 608–9), particularly those focused on the Bretton Woods Institutions (BWI) located in Washington, has recently been somewhat weakened as organizations from other parts of the world have begun to take on lobbying roles in Washington, they still retain a great deal of power (Jordan and van Tuijl, 1998; Nelson, 1996: 616). This situation is one of many that feeds into the generalized impression of a power imbalance between Northern and Southern NGOs mentioned above.

The histories of the 'development-related' networks and the environmental networks have at times overlapped, though the environmental network grew out of specific campaigns which brought together advocacy NGOs working through international channels and grass-roots organizations working locally.[18] 'Development-related' NGOs have formed networks that draw on experiences of North–South co-operation and have often allied with environmental NGOs in anti-World Bank campaigns (Nelson, 1996: 615). Some of the strongest internationally oriented environmental NGOs became closely engaged with the 'development-related' networks during the 'Fifty Years is Enough' campaign in the mid-1990s against the BWI (Nelson, 1996: 615–16; Danaher, 1994).

During the 1970s and 1980s human rights networks grew incredibly after financial support for this type of organization expanded initially from North American foundations and was later supported by European NGOs. This paralleled the high level of interest in the subject shown by the Carter administration, joining its voice to that of some Western European countries already active on these issues within the UN system. The Ford Foundation made human rights one of its 'program priorities' beginning in 1977 (Keck and Sikkink, 1998: 101), at the same time that, then US President Carter began to use human rights language in foreign relations. While the Carter administration was closely connected to the Trilateral Commission (Center for Rural Studies, 1979: 52–3), the Ford Foundation was one of its founders (Gill, 1990: 264 note 37) and Foundation members have observer status with the Commission (Gill, 1990: 148).[19] International human rights networks have since continued to be closely intertwined with national governments (Keck and Sikkink, 1998: 102).

Women's networks have been primarily built upon the many contacts made at the various UN Conferences on Women since 1975 (Chen, 1995; Keck and Sikkink, 1998: 169). Much funding for women's organizations has also come from the Ford and other foundations, primarily based in the North, resulting both in accusations from within the Latin American movement of external dependence (Alvarez, 1998: 311–15) and by others of the existence of unequal power relations that favour Northern NGOs (Keck and Sikkink, 1998: 183). Amongst women's organizations, a number of issue-specific networks have been formed internationally (Keck and Sikkink, 1998: 167–70) and a great deal of emphasis has been placed on the participation of women in the various conferences organized by the UN during the 1990s.

The overlap between networks/movements has increased over the last decade, both because of cross-participation in the various UN conferences and because of co-ordination between networks during certain campaigns. One example of cross-over has been the unification of international women's organizing around the issue of violence against women, tying it to the idea that 'women's rights are human rights'. In other situations, such as the Ogoni struggle against Shell Oil in Nigeria, and that of the rubber tappers and indigenous people of the Brazilian Amazon against continued capitalist expansion and state development programmes, issues of development, environment and human rights are all present, as are issues regarding indigenous peoples.

International Forum on Globalization

In 1994, a number of advocates and activists, working in different organisations, particularly those connected to 'development-related' and environmental networks, formed the International Forum on Globalization (IFG), which traces its own roots to the struggles against NAFTA and the General Agreement on Tariffs and Trade (GATT) (IFG, n.d.). The principal work of the Forum seems to be that of a network, interchanging information and participating in campaigns, though it does produce some of its own materials about 'corporate rule' and social movement organizing. The Forum's understanding of 'globalization' is closely related to a vision of 'corporate rule' according to which corporations have *recently* taken political power from states. In its documents, the Forum directs itself to social movements, and states that 'we can no longer apply a piecemeal approach to what has become a systemic problem' (Clarke, n.d: par. 6). The task of dismantling corporate rule requires 'enabl(ing) social movement activists to develop their own analyses and strategies for tackling systems of corporate rule in their own countries and regions.' (Clarke, n.d.: par. 7). The role of the IFG in that particular process is to provide the tools that local organizations can use to understand corporate rule.

The People's Global Alliance against Free Trade and the World Trade Organization[20]

The People's Global Alliance against Free Trade and the World Trade Organization (PGA) is a broad alliance of social movements which held its first general conference in February of 1998, to plan actions in protest of the biannual World Trade Organization (WTO) meeting in May of the same year. The widely disparate groups present at the first meeting, coming from 54 nations,[21] were similar to those present at the Encounters described above, with the difference that the organizations present were less likely to use violent forms of struggle, principally because one of the four guiding principles of the PGA is non-violence. The non-OECD countries were well represented at the meeting, with 22 Third World countries present, and eight nations from Eastern Europe and the former Soviet Union.

The Conference was marked by a division among Marxists, liberals and others, resulting in long discussions about terminology, and the 'manifesto' of the PGA shows that mix. Though the Marxist elements dominate, 'corporate rule', 'patriarchy', and 'cultural homogenization' are also discussed in the final document (PGA, 1998).

While the PGA draws on many sources, including NGO networks, the Encounters against Neoliberalism and grass-roots movements from many parts of the world, it is much more centralized than the Encounters,[22] or the previous campaigns organized by NGO-led groups. The degree of organizational structure desired was another point widely discussed during the meeting, with some groups even promoting symbols and slogans to be adopted by the Alliance. The tension within the PGA around the issue of centralization is an ongoing one, reflected in the difference between these proposals and the initial convocation of the Conference which called for the creation of 'a global instrument of communication and co-ordination for those who fight against the destruction of humanity and the planet by "free" trade and construct local alternatives to globalisation' (PGA, 1997). Nonetheless, in terms of discussion, the PGA meeting was much more structured and goal-oriented than the Encounters, putting ideological disagreements onto a different terrain because the results were to be used to form part of the Alliance's manifesto. Whereas the Encounters had been almost solely a question of interchange, networking and discussion, the PGA meetings had those elements plus the preplanned goals of writing a collective manifesto, planning for the May events, and deciding on a new convenors' committee. Whereas both the PGA and the Encounters brought together organizations and individuals who usually act in a manner more similar to the hammock that Gustavo Esteva (1987) has proposed, the PGA has tried to create a more solid framework.

The strategies for action of the PGA were to realize both local and centralized actions against the WTO during its meeting in May 1998. This meant that actions were held at the site of the WTO meeting in Geneva, but also in other parts of the world. This type of 'global' centralized and decentralized action was something new, though it obviously built upon centralised actions taken at BWI meetings as well as the Amsterdam alternative summit of 1997, the first of a number of demonstrations held in Europe parallel to European Union and Group of Seven (G-7) summits, protesting the policies of these supragovernmental bodies.

The May demonstrations in Geneva were violently suppressed by the Swiss police, several participants were jailed and some internationals were expelled from the country. A few months later, an office used by the alliance, as well as the homes of several organizers, were raided and information and computers were confiscated.[23] This crackdown was an effort by the Swiss government to crush a nascent organization dedicated to non-violent protest against a supranational institution made up of member states supposedly representative of their populations.

Since its formation, the PGA has also included more conservative organizations such as the Worldwide Fund for Nature (WWF) which have more experience in bargaining with intergovernmental organizations.[24] Following the recommendations of Scholte (1998), it is possible to imagine (parts of) the PGA being pulled into a consultative role in the WTO, allowing for NGO input into WTO policy. This would be a repeat of the NGO entrance into World Bank circles since the late 1980s, an entrance whose benefits are, at best, questionable.

The Santiago Summit

Drawing on the examples of the parallel meetings held at the annual BWI conferences, and the 1997 alternative summit in Amsterdam, in April 1998 a Counter-Summit of the Americas was held in Santiago, Chile, parallel to the Summit of the Americas for Heads of State from all the Americas. Some of those at the Counter-Summit in Santiago had also been present at the PGA Conference in Geneva. The event showed an incipient alliance between labour and other social movements, begun at a 1997 meeting in Belo Horizonte, Brazil which had called for the creation of a 'hemispheric social alliance' (Bendaña, 1998).

The Counter-Summit, bringing together indigenous movements, women's groups, environmental organizations and others, was principally sponsored by the American Federation of Labour-Congress of Industrial Organizations (AFL-CIO) and its Latin America affiliates in the Interamerican Regional Workers Organization (ORIT). The presence of the labour organizations at this forum seems to be related to the fact that labour was excluded from the formal talks on the creation of the Free Trade Agreement of the Americas (FTAA),[25] while business had been welcomed (Bendaña, 1998). This shift reflects the increasing weakness of labour organization in relation to capital, and may signal the recognition, from the perspective of organized labour in the US (at least), that it can no longer confide in the corporatist alliances of the past and that if it is to continue to have any strength, it will need to create new alliances that move outside of both national and movement boundaries.

This new tendency in labour organizing is also built upon a history of cross-border and cross-movement efforts in the struggle against the passage of NAFTA during the early 1990s (Gabriel and MacDonald, 1994). Though the movement failed, important connections were made which later played a key role in continued cross-border labour organizing (Brecher and Costello, 1994: 156–7) and in international support for the EZLN after the Chiapas uprising in 1994 (Cleaver, 1998: 627).

Nonetheless, the fact that First World labour organizations have suddenly become aware of their own need to organize with Third World workers, and other movements, should not be accepted without further analysis.[26] The desires of labour as expressed in Santiago are unclear. At the Counter-Summit, labour resisted the more radical positions, and at the other 'labour' counter-summit, held contemporaneously in Santiago, leaders were nearly united in unquestioning fealty to the rule of the market (Bendaña, 1998). Labour's involvement in the Counter-Summit can be seen as a gesture toward other social movements and as a threat for heads of state that had excluded labour from the FTAA talks.

The Counter-Summit also involved many other groups with much more radical agendas, and a split was visible. Though the 'Final Declaration' of the Summit called for 'fair trade, regulated investment, and a conscious consumer strategy which privileges national development projects' (People's Summit, 1998: para. 3), more creative proposals were often voiced by the floor.[27]

Comparisons

The different initiatives described above all show a recognition of the consequences produced by neoliberal global restructuring and are attempts at responding to those problems. These are attempts to create broad networks/coalitions/alliances which address both regional and global entities that continue to gain power relative to national governments. All of these efforts are built upon previously existing networks and maintain network forms of organization, though some elements involved with the PGA, and some of the groups involved in the Santiago summit, are attempting to create more structured organizations.

Strategies
On the level of strategy, the IFG offers local construction of economic alternatives and a 'new protectionism', while the PGA proposes more or less the same with the addition of direct action (civil disobedience) on the local level as well as co-ordinated internationally, to protest corporate power, symbolized by the WTO. The Encounters welcome local construction as well as all forms of local resistance, violent or not, and informal solidarity amongst all groups. The NGO alliances have, up until now, proposed 'alternative development' forms of local construction and heavy lobbying on international decision-makers. The Santiago summit, internally divided, promotes local construction while also calling for inclusion into the FTAA. These strategies offer strengths and weaknesses and reflect the ever-present social movement choices of negotiation, protest or autonomous construction.[28]

The trend described above toward unification of the NGO-led advocacy movements and livelihood movements, as well as the increasingly confrontational postures taken by them, has recently been alluded to by several authors. Zadek and Gatward (1995: 199), equating the anti-WTO protests in India and the Chiapas rebellion, see them as 'model[s] for one form of resistance to what [is] seen as the high handed approach taken by TNGOs' (transnational non-governmental organizations).[29] Though they seem to misplace the causes for grass-roots frustration, placing them on the shoulders of unresponsive TNGOs, their comments show both a criticism toward the large Northern NGOs and a recognition of the limitations of the strategies undertaken by many of them.[30] The increasing frustration with the present state of affairs is also mentioned by Krut (1997: 35) referring to an 'NGO observer' who predicts an increase in ' "uncivil" behaviour from workers and communities directed at TNCs' (transnational corporations). The author points to an increasing awareness among NGOs that their access to UN conferences and multilateral discussions has not provoked any substantive changes in the conclusions brought forward at these meetings (Krut, 1997: 38).

Esteva and Prakesh (1998: 29–31) make a clear distinction between the actions of the Zapatistas and anti-WTO protests in India. In what appears to be a reference to the People's Global Alliance, or similar efforts, they criticize these initiatives, commenting that organizing 'against the GATT or the World Bank, at their headquarters or their jamborees, seems to be useless or counterproductive' (1998: 31) because it serves to 'clothe the emperor', giving legitimacy to power by recognizing it. They correctly point out that the more resistance is focused against international actors, the more bureaucracy is put in place by these actors to try and co-opt/include those in opposition,[31] legitimating themselves in the process.[32] The Zapatistas, according to these authors, while recognizing that the issues which affect them on a local level are global in nature, direct themselves toward the local problem, while also appreciating the importance of international solidarity between organizations in struggle (Esteva and Prakesh, 1998: 35–6).

Epistemological openness and movement goals

In her discussion of the International Forum on Globalization (IFG), Lynch (1998) points out that it pulls together liberal ideas with more 'radical' or 'critical thinking',[33] reflecting a long-term alliance in many parts of the world that has at times been subsumed into the term 'progressive', but which should not be taken for granted. This is true for the various initiatives here under discussion as well, though, as she points out (Lynch, 1998: 166), there is also the reality of the many other interpretations of the world, beginning to be voiced through these different initiatives.

Understanding global restructuring, and so on, as a retreat from the ideals of social justice that modernity has promised, while ostensibly promoting liberal democratic forms of government, makes it possible to understand shifts in old alliances as well as the appearance of new actors. In this context, the openness of labour toward other social movements, as it was in the NAFTA battles and seems to be in the Santiago Counter-Summit, becomes clear. The shift by 'liberal progressives' toward the unusual position that 'corporations [read capital] rule[s] the world'[34] is a recognition that liberal democracy has failed to control capitalism, and explains their new openness to discussions which open onto the economic terrain. These shifts are coupled with increasing grass-roots initiatives which do not share modern interpretations, though their struggles may be similar, or parallel, to more 'modern' movements.

One principal dividing point regarding the goals of the various initiatives discussed above, is whether new global or regional economic structures (WTO, MAI, FTAA, Maastricht) presently in effect or under proposal, are reformable or whether they should be rejected. While all the groups promote increased local political and economic control, there are a plethora of opinions about what type of alternatives can be imagined that move beyond the local. Imagining such structures is especially difficult for those groups which are dependent on the global or regional structures as they stand, and somewhat easier for those who stand on the edges or outside of them.

For this reason, those NGOs (Northern or Southern) which are largely dependent on funding by a state (their own or another) are less likely to promote alternatives which could imply an end to such funding. In the same respect, trade unions will have more difficulty in considering systemic changes that would imply moving away from a consumer society. In differing degrees, both of these groups have positions which are deeply embedded in the existing system. The projects of both of these groups[35] are largely (though not solely) to complete modernity. They propose (or at least accept) the changes to modernity that would be necessary to make it more *inclusive* and more responsible about environmental issues, but a reworking of the system could be threatening economically as well as epistemologically.

The problem of what I term 'epistemological openness' in terms of cross-cultural dialogue, or even international organizing has been discussed by many[36] though what seems to be occurring now is that these discussions are taking place at the level of international organizing among many different types of groups, from grass-roots movements to international NGOs (Lynch, 1998: 166). During most of these interchanges, the epistemological hegemony of modernity still delimits most of the debate, and largely excludes alternative perspectives which may not share the epistemological bases of modernity. This was brought to the fore at the indigenous table of the PGA conference in which several indigenous activists complained about the fact that they were not integrated into the other tables, but were isolated. This implied that their perspective was added to the broader discussions as that of a specific group (as were the women, the students, and so on) and that their input into the 'manifesto', and into the conference as a whole, could not question the modern assumptions which underlined the whole conference. This same procedure seems to have occurred in the Santiago Counter-Summit and was largely the case at both Encounters. As long as women are talking about 'women's issues' and indigenous people are talking about 'indigenous issues', their opinions, and epistemological viewpoints, will remain outside of, or tangential to, the central discussions.

This lack of interchange between modern and non-modern perspectives is negative, both because it effectively eliminates some voices from the discussion and because it reduces the possibilities of creating new visions for the future that don't all emanate from the West, or reinterpretations of the same. Unlike the modern West, most peoples of the world have been *forced* to integrate Western, modern ideas into their own understandings of the world. The West, on the other hand, wielding the epistemological power that it does, has not been forced to take into account any others, and only now is it *beginning* to listen to other voices. If these voices can be heard in the context of protest/construction proposed by the various initiatives discussed in this chapter, the possibilities for more creative forms of resistance, and visions of the future, will be broadened.

Conclusions

The different initiatives presented above represent an increasingly radical challenge to the process of global restructuring as implemented by the international financial institutions and supported by the G-7. All of them focus on combining local forms of resistance with local forms of construction and shy away from hierarchical structures. They share a certain amount of common history and, most probably, contacts. Beyond that, all attempt to bring in widely disparate groups, recognizing the diversity of actors, history, and so on.

Strategies of engagement with capital, the state and with other societal actors, used by the different initiatives, or participants in them, move from armed revolution to civil disobedience and efforts at national and international lobbying. The goals are also quite varied, perhaps as much within each initiative as between them, ranging from

Fordism to local autonomy (and perhaps even some who would call for the dictatorship of the proletariat).

These initiatives go far beyond isolated instances of struggle, or fringe groups with no popular backing. They are reflective of an extremely wide spectrum of interests who all reject neoliberal policies. Their efforts at mobilizing in new forms reflect a frustration with old ones, both on the radical and reformist Left. These initiatives are part of a process and their eventual outcomes are far from defined, but they represent other ways forward. One aspect of their success will be judged by the degree that they can, as a collective body, successfully promote change, while at the same time recognizing as *strengths* the specificities of the groups involved. This involves not only that all groups be *present*, but that their perspectives are listened to and considered. It may be from these perspectives that it will become possible to begin a real questioning of modernity, from without as well as from within.

Notes

* This chapter formed part of the author's Master's Thesis entitled 'Toward "A World in Which Many Worlds Fit": The importance of the Zapatista Army of National Liberation for international organising' presented at the Institute of Social Studies in The Hague in December 1998.

1. I use the term 'livelihood movements' to describe two different, but often related, phenomena: local efforts to resist the expansion of capitalist initiatives or state-sponsored 'development projects' which destroy local forms of economy (Taylor et al., 1993; Ekins, 1992; Guha and Martínez-Alier, 1997: chapter 1); and efforts at construction or reconstruction of local economies, particularly in the wake of economic restructuring which has reduced or eliminated state involvement in the provision of subsidies and services, thus requiring a reorganization of local economies to address this change (Bebbington, 1996; Petras, 1997).

2. The struggle of the Zapatista Army of National Liberation (EZLN) in Mexico has been perhaps the best example of how local struggles have been rapidly made into global issues through the use of email and the internet (Cleaver, 1998; Lins Ribiero, 1998: 344). Another recent example of the effective use of the internet was the NGO campaign against the Multilateral Agreement on Investment (MAI) between late 1997 and mid-1998 in which NGOs mobilized letter writing and call-in campaigns in several of the Organization for Economic Co-operation and Development (OECD) member countries, preventing the approval of the Agreement by the OECD in April of 1998 (Drohan, 1998).

3. The United Nations Development Programme (UNDP) estimated a rate of internet use in 1994 at 1.5 persons per 10000 in 'all developing countries'

compared with 223.2 per 10000 in the 'industrialised countries' (UNDP, 1997: 185).

4. See Friedland (1982: chapter 7).
5. See Albertani (1997), De Angelis (1998), Lane (1997), EZLN (1996), Simoncini (1998), Piazza (1996), Esteva and Prakesh (1998: 173–9) as well as the website at http://www.geocities.com/CapitolHill/3849/ gatherdx.html for more on the Encounters.
6. See Lynch (1998) and Roberts (1998) as well as the website http://www.ifg.org
7. Information on the Santiago Counter-Summit is available at the website http://tripod.com/~redchile/
8. Information on the PGA is available at the website http://www.agp.org/agp/index.html
9. This was the term preferred by the organizers of the event to describe 'Spain'.
10. Some of the initial contact, particularly within Mexico, was built on a women's network 'la reta' (Castells, 1997: 80).
11. For more information on the role of computer networks in the EZLN solidarity campaigns, see Cleaver (1998), Castells (1997: 79–81) and Ronfeldt and Martínez (1997).
12. A respectable decision given the content of many discussions.
13. On a personal level, coming from my own work in the Highlands of Guatemala, I felt familiar with the Highlands of Chiapas and the indigenous communities. The tone and content of the discussions were therefore striking in their limited applicability to the physical environment in which they occurred.
14. The initial proposal by the organizers was to have women's issues subsumed into a subtable that would discuss the 'excluded', prompting a vociferous response from the women present and the creation of an 'unplanned' women's table.
15. This is not a 'universal' form of holding a discussion and effectively eliminates many who are unfamiliar or uncomfortable with it.
16. The slogan refers to the fact that poor Mexican peasants have been making claims on the Mexican government for decades and it was only when they rose up in arms and covered their faces with bandannas that the government made any attempts at listening. The fact that the same situation is more or less repeated at the Encounter is revealing. Though, to be fair, Encounter participants were completely respectful and interested in talking to those Mayans without bandannas as well.
17. In December of 1997, 45 indigenous peasants were killed by paramilitary forces while they prayed in their church in the village of Acteal in Chiapas.
18. See Keck and Sikkink (1998: chapter 4) on environmental networks, Guha and Martínez-Alier (1997) on environmentalisms, Kolk (1996) and Rich (1994: 107–47) on the campaign against the WB in the mid-1980s, and Gale (1996) on the campaign against use of tropical timber.
19. More recently, funding for human rights organizations in Eastern Europe and elsewhere has come from the Soros Foundation, giving a new twist to 'post-Fordism'.
20. There are no published references to the PGA. The following section is based on my personal experiences at the first Conference of the Alliance in February of 1998, on information available at the PGA Website

http://www.agp.org/agp/index.html, and on conversations with other meeting participants and one organizer.

21. These numbers come from a list of participants distributed to those present, and should not be considered to be exact.

22. The attempt at centralization can be seen in the publications produced by the different events. While the First Encounter produced a full book which published the various conclusions of the different subtables (EZLN, 1996) and the Second, a somewhat shorter, similar one (Simoncini, 1998), the PGA Conference produced an 11-page 'manifesto' which attempted to synthesize the analyses and goals of the 300 participants.

23. See http://www.agp.org/agp/unicc.htm and http://www.agp.org/agp/en/index.html for more information on police repression of the PGA in Geneva.

24. The WWF is closely associated to the International Union for the Conservation of Nature (IUCN), one of the most conservative environmental groups, with fifty years of experience in international lobbying (McCormick, 1993). A WWF director has also been a member of the Trilateral Commission (Gill, 1990: 158).

25. This follows the Copenhagen summit of 1995 in which the International Conference of Free Trade Unions (ICFTU) failed to get a special seat for labour with business and state negotiators and was forced to join the parallel NGO Forum (Waterman, 1998: 114).

26. After the support given by the AFL-CIO to US foreign policy during the Cold War, it is hard to imagine that their politics have shifted from corporatism to 'class solidarity'. The AFL-CIO foreign strategy began to change in the late 1980s after internal criticisms about their support for, and collaboration with, US government policies in Central America (Brecher and Costello, 1994: 153; Boswell and Stevis, 1997).

27. The various proposals are available at http://tripod.com/~redchile

28. See Waterman (1998: 212, esp. fig. 7.1b) for more on these choices.

29. These authors reject this form of protest because of the risk of violence against the protesters.

30. This same frustration on the part of grass-roots 'counterpart' organizations was mentioned by a staff member of a Dutch Cofinancing organization who said that many of the groups they work with are appreciative of the material aid that provided, but are also asking for support in providing political solutions to the problems that they face.

31. In the case of the World Bank, this has been borne out (Nelson, 1996), and the case of the WTO, that is at least one of the suggestions being proposed (Scholte, 1998). It should be noted that in the case of the PGA, protest has been responded to, thus far, with repression, rather than offers of 'inclusion' in WTO processes. (Thanks to Micheline Beth Levy for pointing this out.)

32. Krut (1997: 50) points out the following: 'It is ironic that the late twentieth century has seen the unprecedented growth and influence of civil society and unprecedented decline of those national and intergovernmental organisations most open to participation. Having spent five decades lobbying at the gates of the United Nations, non-governmental groups have finally been granted access only to see that real power now lies behind other doors.'

33. I am assuming that much of Marxist thinking would also fall into this category.
34. Witness David Korten's testimony (1995: 1–14).
35. The case of the NGOs is extremely varied, but those which wield most power and funding maintain this goal. This is not to say that there are not many other NGOs, large and small, that recognize and work to support alternative epistemological frameworks. See Verholst (1990) and Lynch (1998: 166–7) regarding openness to other systems of belief.
36. See Esteva (1998), Cox (1992: 41), Waterman (1998: chapter 7). For feminist discussions of solidarity along these lines see Fraser (1989, 1997) and Dean (1997). Cecilia Lynch (1998: 166) has pointed out that 'practice is preceding theory in this domain' in reference to the NGO linkages and unofficial fora at UN conferences in which 'Activists themselves struggle to cope with the resulting confrontation of practices and beliefs.'

References

Albertani, C. (1997) 'Appuntamento a Madrid', *Guerra e Pace* 5 (39/40) Maggio/Junion: 30–2.

Albertani, C. and P. Ranieri (1998) 'Percorsi di liberazione dalla selva Lacandona all'Europa', in A. Simoncini (ed.), *Percorsi di Liberazione Dalla Selva Lacandona all'Europa*, Palermo: Edizioni Della Battaglia, pp. 11–43.

Alvarez, S.E. (1998) 'Latin America feminisms go global', in S.E. Alvarez, E. Dagnino and A. Escobar (eds), *Cultures of Politics, Politics of Culture: Revisioning Latin American Social Movements*, Boulder: Westview Press, pp. 293–324.

Bebbington, A. (1996) 'Movements, modernizations, and markets: indigenous organisations and agrarian strategies in Ecuador', in R. Peet and M. Watts (eds), *Liberation Ecology*, London: Routledge, pp. 86–109.

Bendaña, A. (1998) 'The Santiago People's Summit: A report', http://members.tripod.com/~redchile/areport.htm

Boswell, T. and D. Stevis (1997) 'Globalisation and international labor organizing: a world systems perspective', *Work and Occupations*, 24(3): 288–308.

Brecher, J. and T. Costello (1994) *Global Village or Global Pillage: Economic Reconstruction from the Bottom Up*, Boston, MA: South End Press.

Castells, M. (1997) *The Information Age: Economy, Society and Culture. Volume II: The Power of Identity*, Oxford: Blackwell Publishers.

Castells, M., S. Yazawa and E. Kiselyova (1995–6) 'Insurgents against the global order: a comparative analysis of the Zapatistas in Mexico, the American militia and Japan's AUM Shinrikyo', *Berkeley Journal of Sociology*, 40: 21–61.

Center for Rural Studies (1979) *Planning for International Agriculture: the Trilateral Commission takes on World Hunger*, San Francisco: Earthworks Publications.

Chen, M. Al (1995) 'Engendering world conferences: the international women's movement and the United Nations', *Third World Quarterly*, 16(3): 477–93.

Clarke, T. (n.d.) 'The emergence of corporate rule and what to do about it: a set of working instruments for social movements', http://www.ifg.org/corprule.html

Cleaver, H. (1998) 'The Zapatista effect: the Internet and the rise of an alternative political fabric', *Journal of International Affairs*, 51(2): 621–40.

Cox, R.W. (1992) 'Towards a post-hegemonic conceptualization of world order: reflections on the relevancy of Ibn Khaldun', in J.N. Rosenau and E.-O. Czempiel (eds), *Governance without Government: Order and Change in World Politics*, Cambridge: Cambridge University Press, pp. 132–59.

Danaher, K. (1994) *50 Years is Enough: the Case Against the World Bank and the International Monetary Fund*, Boston: South End Press.

De Angelis, M. (1998) '2nd Encounter for humanity and against neoliberalism. Spain 1997', *Capital and Class*, 65 (Summer): 135–57.

Dean, J. (1997) 'The reflexive solidarity of democratic feminism', in J. Dean (ed.), *Feminism and the New Democracy: Resisting the Political*, London: Sage Publications, pp. 244–63.

Drohan, M. (1998) 'How the Net killed the MAI', *The Globe and Mail*, 29 April.

Ekins, P. (1992) *A New World Order: Grassroots Movements for Social Change*, London. Routledge.

Esteva, G. (1998) 'Lezioni di "Incontrarsi"', in A. Simoncini (ed.), *Percorsi di Liberazione Dalla Selva Lacandona All'Europa*, Palermo: Edizioni Della Battaglia, pp. 45–54.

Esteva, G. (1987) 'Regenerating people's space', *Alternatives*, 10(3): 125–52.

Esteva, G. and M.S. Prakesh (1998) *Grassroots Post-modernism: Remaking the Soil of Cultures*, London: Zed Books.

EZLN (1996) *Cronicas Intergalacticas: Primer Encuentro Intercontinental por la Humanidad y contra el Neoliberalismo*, Mexico.

Fraser, N. (1997) 'Equality, difference and democracy: recent feminist debates in the United States', in J. Dean, *Feminism and the New Democracy: Resiting the Political*, London: Sage Publications, pp. 98–109.

Fraser, N. (1989) 'Towards a discourse theory of solidarity', *Praxis*, 5(4): 425–9.

Friedland, W.H. (1982) *Revolutionary Theory*, New Jersey: Allanheld, Osmun & Co. Publishers Inc.

Gabriel, C. and L. Macdonald (1994) 'NAFTA, women and organising in Canada and Mexico: forging a "Feminist Internationality"', *Millennium*, 23(3): 535–62.

Gale, F.P. (1996) 'The mysterious case of the disappearing environmentalists: the International Tropical Timber Organisation', *Capitalism, Nature, Socialism*, 7(3): 103–17.

Gill, S. (1990) *American Hegemony and the Trilateral Commission*, Cambridge: Cambridge University Press.

Guha, R. and J. Martínez-Alier (1997) *Varieties of Environmentalism*, London: Earthscan.

IFG (International Forum on Globalisation) (n.d.) 'About the IFG', http://www.ifg.org/about.html

Jordan, L. and P. van Tuijl (1998) 'Political responsibility in NGO advocacy: exploring emerging shapes of global democracy', paper presented in the States and Societies Research Seminars, The Hague: Institute of Social Studies, 20 January.

Keck, M.E. and K. Sikkink (1998) *Activists Beyond Borders: Advocacy Networks in International Politics*, Ithaca, NJ: Cornell University Press.

Kolk, A. (1996) *Forests in International Politics: International Organisations, NGOs and the Brazilian Amazon*, Utrecht: International Books.

Korten, D. (1995) *When Corporations Rule the World*, West Hartford: Kumarian Press.

Krut, R. (1997) 'Globalisation and civil society: NGO influence in international decision-making', United Nations Research Institute for Social Development Discussion Paper no 83, Geneva: UNRISD.

Lane, M. (1997) 'Diary of the Second Zapatista Encuentro', *Dollars and Sense*, 214 (Nov.–Dec.): 8–9.

Lins Ribiero, G. (1998) 'Cybercultural politics: political activism at a distance in a transnational world', in S.E. Alvarez, E. Dagnino and A. Escobar (eds), *Cultures of Politics, Politics of Culture: Visioning Latin American Social Movements*, Boulder: Westview Press, pp. 325–52.

Lynch, C. (1998) 'Social movements and the problem of globalisation', *Alternatives*, 23: 149–73.

McCormick, J. (1993) 'International nongovernmental organisations: prospects for a global environmental movement', in S. Kamienicki (ed.), *Environmental Politics in the International Arena: Movements, Parties, Organisations, and Policy*, Albany: State University of New York, pp. 131–44.

Nelson, P. (1996) 'NGO networks and the World Bank's expanding influence', *Millennium: Journal of International Studies*, 25(3): 605–33.

PGA (Peoples' Global Alliance) (1997) 'Peoples' Global Action Manifesto', *PGA Bulletin*, (0) December, http://www.agp.org/agp/enold/bulletin0.html

PGA (1998) 'Peoples' Global Action Manifesto', *PGA Bulletin*, (1) March, http://www.agp.org/agp/enold/bulletin1.html

People's Summit (1998) 'Final Declaration of the Summit: People's Summit of the Americas', http://members.tripod.com/~redchile/denglish.htm

Petras, J. (1997) 'Latin America: the resurgence of the Left', *New Left Review*, 223 (May–June): 17–47.

Piazza, R. (1996) 'Un Incontro in Chiapas', *i Fogli de ORISS*, (6): 9–37.

Rich, B. (1994) *Mortgaging the Earth: the World Bank, Environmental Impoverishment and the Crisis of Development*, Boston: Beacon Press.

Roberts, S.M. (1998) 'Geo-governance in trade and finance and political geographies of dissent', in A. Herod, G.O. Tuathail and S.M. Roberts (eds), *An Unruly World?: Globalisation, Governance and Geography*, London: Routledge, pp. 116–34.

Ronfeldt, D. and A. Martinez (1997) 'A comment on the Zapatista "Netwar"', in J. Arquilla and D. Ronfeldt (eds), *In Athena's Camp: Preparing for Conflict in the Information Age*, Rand, pp. 369–91. http://www.rand.org/publications/MR/MR880/index.html

Scholte, J.A. (1998) 'The WTO and civil society', paper presented at States and Societies Research Seminars, The Hague: Institute of Social Studies.

Simoncini, A. (ed.) (1998) *Percorsi di Liberazione Dalla Selva Lacandona all'Europa: Itinerari documenti testimonianze dal Secondo Incontro Intercontinentale per l'Umanita e contro el Neoliberismo de Madrid*, Palermo: Edizioni Della Battaglia.

Taylor, B., H. Hadsell, L. Lorentzen and R. Scarce (1993) 'Grass-roots resistance: the emergence of popular environmental movements in less affluent countries', in S. Kamienicki (ed.), *Environmental Politics in the International Arena: Movements, Parties, Organisations, and Policy*, Albany: State University of New York Press, pp. 69–89.

UNDP (United Nations Development Program) (1997) *Human Development Report 1997*, Oxford: Oxford University Press.

Verholst, T.G. (1990) *No Life Without Roots: Culture and Development*, London: Zed Books.

Wager, S.J. and D.E. Schulz (1995) 'The Zapatistas' revolt and its implications for civil–military relations and the future of Mexico', *Journal of Interamerican Studies and World Affairs*, 37(1): 1–42.

Waterman, P. (1998) *Globalisation, Solidarity and the New Social Movements*, London: Mansell/Cassell.

Zadek, S. and M. Gatward (1995) 'Transforming the transnational NGOs: social auditing or bust?', in M. Edwards and D. Hulme (eds), *Non-governmental Organizations: Performance and Accountability*, London: Earthscan, pp. 193–205.

9

Collective Movements and Globalization

Antimo Farro and Jean-Guy Vaillancourt

In this chapter we examine the question of the development of social movements in the context of the globalization of the economy and of culture. First we will tackle this question at the theoretical level, in order to characterize these movements and to delineate the oppositions and the alternatives observed at the level of domination and reciprocity in social relationships. We will also analyse this question empirically, in order to explain the evolution of these initiatives by examining the collective action of environmentalists in the various sectors of social life of the Northern and Southern hemispheres of the planet.

The opening section of this chapter will consider the problem of the construction of social movements in relationship to the domination of ruling social actors. Following this, we will analyse the problem of the distinction between these specific actions and other collective phenomena. We will also address the question of the construction of the identity of these actors and of their social movements in the wider context of globalization. Finally, the problem of integrating collective initiatives that are developing, at the local, regional, national, continental or global levels will be looked at through the environmental movement. This will allow us also to discuss the demands that originate simultaneously from the political system and from the systemic level where, ultimately, the control of cultural orientations is determined.

Collective initiatives in the context of global domination

As we enter the twenty-first century, numerous organized collective phenomena unravel. Among other things, this produces social and cultural critiques of the globalization of culture and of the economy resulting from collective initiatives that emerge in industrialized and developing countries. In other words, we target here collective phenomena linked to social actors who are producing critiques of various aspects of social life. These initiatives range from community defence to collective actions. In the case of women and of environmentalists, this collective action intervenes in the issues that pertain to the control of the cultural orientations of social life. The critique of these initiatives is defined in relationship to the domination of social life by ruling actors. This domination includes the globalization of the economy and the planetary diffusion of cultural codes which control the orientation of social life that no longer has industrial production as its centre. Today, the symbols and messages that organize the various sectors of society pertain to individual and collective life. These sectors are made up of health organizations and of educational facilities, as well as of the mass media and the cultural definition of the relationship between social life and the natural environment.

The globalization of the economy and the worldwide diffusion of cultural codes do not simply imply the extension of economic exchanges and the diffusion of messages and of information at the planetary level. They also involve domination by ruling actors who impose their financial strategies and the content of their messages and symbols in the different sectors of social life (Martin and Schumann, 1997). Collective initiatives emerge in order to oppose this domination. In fact, this domination unfurls at the economic level through the activities of ruling actors who, from financial centres like those of New York, Tokyo or London (Sassen, 1991), direct the allocation of resources and the destination of investments for various sectors of social life at the planetary level, and maintain the dominance of developed areas over those that are still underdeveloped. This domination manifests itself also through the treatment of the information that ruling actors use in the definition of the cultural codes which impose parameters on individual and collective life. Since they are constitutive elements in the formation of the highly differentiated social life of today, the codes that are produced and promoted by the ruling actors through the elaboration and the diffusion of information intervene in determining various sectors of society, and therefore affect the capacity of individuals and groups to autonomously construct the meaning of their actions. This is what happens, for example, with the codes indicating the ways to attain a state of equilibrium relative to body and mind. These codes contain within them the major elements necessary for biotechnology applications. Other types of codes include those concerning the type of relationship that must be built up between social life and material forces in order to attain an environmental equilibrium.

Economic investments and the diffusion of codes facilitate the formation of new sectors of social life and the modernization of the others. This brings about important advantages for populations that can enjoy the modernization of certain social sectors, like that of health organizations, for example. Here modernization implies the improvement of the efficiency of medical services. The production and promotion of these specific cultural codes by ruling actors, are also injunctions that intervene simultaneously at the level of contents as well as at the level of criteria. It therefore spells out what individuals and groups must do in order to reach an autonomous construction of meaning, through which they can succeed in becoming a constitutive part of social life. However, because it comes about through an injunction, autonomy (in the sense given to that word by Charles Taylor, 1992) is not a true acquisition by these individuals and groups, but rather an element that defines the relationship of domination between them and the ruling actors.

However, in our opinion, this does not correspond only to a simple refinement of techniques of domination. Those who are submitted to these codes are engaged in a process that is more complex than simple domination by ruling actors over individuals and groups. These cultural codes can bring about, precisely because of this domination, a refusal on the part of those who should simply be the recipients of the messages. What we have then is a refusal to submit to the domination by ruling actors who impose their codes through the cultural globalization superimposed on various sectors of individual and collective life. This domination bears witness to the fact that the globalization of culture, like the globalization of the economy, is characterized by unbalanced and uneven power relationships.

Collective initiatives that resist submission are the first step in the process of the construction of an opposition to social domination. When this refusal takes form, the cultural codes stop being simple instruments of imposition and become references from which the themes of the conflicts in contemporary society are formulated. It follows therefore that when industrial society starts receding, the conflicts switch from the economic to the cultural sphere. This cultural sphere includes personal identity, time and living space, motivation, and the codes of everyday life. The conflicts become manifestations of the logic of domination which affirms itself in highly differentiated systems when ruling actors get involved in the globalization of the economy and of culture.

In sum, collective initiatives develop as a response to domination. They are differentiated from each other by certain aspects of their composition; and there are notable differences between the initiatives undertaken in industrialized countries and those of developing countries. On the one hand, initiatives pertaining to identity (Wieviorka, 1991) are a type of behaviour characterizsed by an auto-referential defence of their members' identity (in the sense put forward by Touraine, 1992, 1993a). This leads in the direction of the closure which they define in relationship to the other actors and components of social life. On the other hand, there are collective initiatives which go in an opposite direction.

Identity-oriented closure

Identity-oriented closure occurs when one refers individually or collectively to myths, or to other extra-social references, in order to defend one's individual or collective specificity. In the context of the globalization of the economy and of culture, this closure allows the development of some coherence in one's life, because individuals and groups do not always succeed in doing so on the basis of their own experience. This closure does not occur indeed when the refusal of domination implies the definition of initiatives on the part of those who try to construct their identity. It does not occur either when these actors are recognized by others as capable of intervening in the production and diffusion of information and of controlling its orientation, as is the case with environmentalists when they try to designate themselves and to be recognized as actors capable of defining alternative models of development. Conversely, we observe this type of closure among those who define themselves in the name of a group whose difference they want to preserve in order to oppose it to the mythical image of the globalization and the internationalization of culture and of the economy, or in order to affirm their superiority over other groups. This is an identitary definition, an hostility expressed towards the other (in the sense used by Taylor, 1993), which aims at diminishing him or refusing him. Linked to this definition, there is also a demeaning of the other person or group.

This phenomenon is found in certain collective initiatives which comprise community closures. They develop in industrial countries in times of crises, like the one involving the destructuring of social life which touches people living in suburbs and other urban zones hit by economic uncertainty and by unemployment. These community closures occur when collective initiatives originating in this context are oriented towards the defence of the identity of the inhabitants of these areas, and of the population of other areas threatened in their interests and in their cultural specificity by immigrants arriving from less developed regions of the planet (Wieviorka, 1991). For example, we can observe such phenomena in certain French cities and in certain areas in the periphery or in the centre of a few Italian cities (Farro, 1995).

In industrialized countries like those of the European Union or of North America, various initiatives of this type are appearing. Certain communities of immigrants coming from outside these countries have established themselves there in specific areas. The members of these communities suffer many difficulties of economic integration, and at the same time they are forced to defend themselves against racist contempt and discrimination. It is precisely because of this problem of integration and of defence that these same immigrants can develop initiatives that go in a direction that is diametrically opposed to that of a communitarian identity and that serve as a fulcrum for the search for a degree of individual economic integration in social life. This also tends to affirm the universal value of the respect of all differences. The initiatives that try to counter the identity closure of the members of these communities usually comes about after many fruitless efforts to integrate economically, and after they have suffered through various racist episodes. These initiatives do not occur on the terrain of democracy nor in the process of trying to gain access to political institutions. They happen on the terrain of the definition of exclusion or of a manifestation of hostility towards the democratic political system from which members of these communities feel excluded.

It is not only in industrialized countries that we find collective initiatives of this type. We can also observe this type of social phenomena in certain developing countries, like in the Muslim areas of Asia and Africa. In Iran for example, initiatives that tend towards identitarian closures and identitarian defence goals have been observed (Khosrokhavar, 1995). Certain kinds of closure can equally end up as religious fundamentalism combined to some form of terrorism. This develops in opposition to a dictatorial local power, since the latter is incapable of guaranteeing socio-economic development or the defence of a mythical identity of the cultural specificity of a people against the cultural impositions originating from the West. This explains in part the situation in Algeria where fundamentalism, on the one hand, finds its origin in the individual and collective revolt which explodes because of the unbearable living conditions and in order to obtain social justice (Addi, 1994: 218–19) and, on the other hand, becomes the context for the formation of a terrorism which develops either against those in power or against all those who, even if they are not linked to this power that they also criticize, are carriers of universalist cultural visions expressed in their professional activities or in the outward manifestations of their way of life.

The initiatives of this first group, which occur both in developing and in industrialized countries, are thus identitarian activities which tend to become totalitarian. They include a refusal to recognize an equality of chances for all, an opposition to the reconnaissance of the equality of all the differences, a rejection of the terrain of political democracy in Western countries, and a struggle for this kind of democracy in the countries that do not have enough of it.

The collective initiatives of a second group, which unfurl in the context of the same industrialized and developing countries where we see the emergence of the identitarian initiatives, develop by moving in a direction that is diametrically opposed to the identitarian activities of the first group.

Autonomy, identity and collective movements

The initiatives of this second group are the conflictual actions of women's and environmental movements that are present in equal strength in the industrialized North and in the developing South. These are movements that originate from a refusal to submit to the domination which does not go in the direction of cultural closure, and which is not drawn up in a mythical fashion. It determines itself either in antagonistic terms in relationship to the dominating cultural visions, or in terms of an opposition and of a search for an alternative to the domination of the ruling actors who control the economic investments and the production and diffusion of information. Those who are involved in such a refusal not only reject the existence of a power disequilibrium. They also testify to the fact that they want to get involved in a process of opposition to domination, and that they want to affirm their individual and collective autonomy in regards to the latter. This is a refusal that is expressed by those who try to affirm their authenticity (Taylor, 1989: 502–5; 1993: 46–7) as individuals and as groups.

They do not accept the cultural impositions of the ruling actors who define the framework for the development of individual and collective existence. These individuals and groups challenge these impositions and are determined to start defining autonomously the construction of the meaning of their action. They are builders of their authenticity, because they know who they really are and because they want to be recognised by others for who they are and for what they do. They thus ask the question of the control of their identity.[1] This must be considered within the context of a relationship which includes the capacity that an actor has of recognizing himself or herself (that is of recognizing the effects of his or her actions as belonging to one's self) and the possibility of being recognized by other actors (Melucci, 1982: 68).

They want to be the builders of their own identity in opposition to the ruling actors who aim at imposing on individuals and groups the codes which should delineate even the content of their autonomy and of their specificity. This identity thus becomes an element of the construction of conflictual collective initiatives. The formation of identity is realized inside these initiatives in two different ways. The first consists of defining it as a confrontation with others, including both partners and adversaries. It consists effectively of a challenge to the imposition of cultural codes, but not through isolated introspection by an individual or by a group. Even if they create their identity, those who construct these initiatives do not do so in isolation. The fact that these individuals discover their identity does not mean that they do it all by themselves; they negotiate it through a dialogue, external as well as internal, with other people. Their identity depends in a crucial manner on the dialogical relationships that they have with others (Taylor, 1992: 34).

The construction of identity which comes about in a dialogical manner thus assumes its particular nature on the conflictual dimension of collective initiatives. Those who construct these initiatives define their identity in opposition to their adversaries, from whom they want to take away the control of certain sectors of social life. The participants in ecological initiatives, for example, define their identity by entering in a dialogue with other actors, like scientists or economists. The latter provide them with the instruments necessary for the definition of a mode of development different from the current one. But they also define this identity in opposition to the actors whom they consider to be their adversaries, because they hold them responsible for a model of development which has brought about pollution and the depletion of resources. Environmentalists want to change this model of development so that it becomes sustainable and compatible with a natural equilibrium. This identity, for sure, is never attained once and for all, and it does not particularly define its social dimension in a definitive manner as in the case of the class identity of actors within the workers' movement. There is therefore another way of constructing the identity of the actors of the collective movements of our time, which is linked to the development of these actions.

This second way of building up an identity consists of defining it solely through the construction of identity and of collective actions. However, the construction of the group and of the individuals who develop these actions does not consist in defining and pursuing an objective that becomes an acquired experience once it is attained. In other words, this identity is not a definitive individual or collective attainment. Individual identity, like group identity, is not the end result of the process, but is tied to the development of action itself. Involvement in the Green movement, for example, does not determine an exclusive or a definitive identity. It is not exclusive because being an environmentalist does not exclude other types of self-definition that can originate from other kinds of involvements. It is not definitive, either, because it can vary through the different redefinitions of individual initiatives as well as through transformations of collective involvement. For this reason, participants in collective initiatives never acquire a definitive collective identity. But this is not the main reason why identity stops being an essential component of these actions. Identity defines the 'we' of the participants who not only distinguish themselves in relationship to other actors, but also intend to propose alternatives to the orientation of social life. These alternatives are in opposition to the ones imposed by the ruling actors.

The conflictual collective initiatives which emerge in both industrialized and developing countries see the combination of this affirmation of identity with other components of action. As a matter of fact, in industrialized countries, there are collective initiatives which intervene in the area of the control of the rationalization of development, of the recognition of the universal value of differences and subjectivities (in the sense that Touraine, 1992, gives to these two words), of the development of democracy and of the respect of human rights. Among these initiatives, some are dedicated to the environment. Those that prevail, in relationship to the activities aimed mostly towards the defence of local communities, are those of the participants who refer to scientific data in order to criticize promoters of a growth model. They accuse these promoters, on the one hand, of polluting and of depleting natural resources (Farro, 1991). In order to define and to search for rational alternatives to this model, they consider it necessary, on the other hand, to implement a sustainable type of development (Prades et al., 1994; Vaillancourt, 1995a and 1995b).

Among these initiatives, we find the actions developed by women who try to orient society in a direction different from the one traced by a male cultural dominance over the rationalization of social life. The women who oppose this dominance, which they accuse of negating the value of their subjectivity, try at the same time and through collective initiatives to affirm themselves. They also want to be recognized by others as actors who are capable themselves of combining emotion and reason at all levels of social life. They can thus succeed both in inserting themselves and in acting in work organizations or in some other organized context of society, in having a political activity and in intervening in the area of the orientations of social life.

In developing countries, we find initiatives that go in the same direction as that which we have just described for industrialized countries. These initiatives include those of the Chiapas Indians who struggle in Southern Mexico to conserve their identity and to defend their interests against the promoters of the extension of neoliberal economics to their region and to the planet as a whole. These initiatives are being developed by actors who are trying, in the second half of the 1990s, to abandon guerrilla warfare in which they were previously involved. In order to place themselves in the arena of political democracy they establish behaviours which, like those of other ethnic groups in Latin America, try to implement actions combining the struggle for the defence of the diversity of the members of these groups with actions in favour of social justice and of the recognition of the universal value of all differences, rather than to try to form communitarian closures (Le Bot, 1995: 458–60).

In another context, in a developing country within the Maghreb, we find the same type of collective initiatives. The women's movement in Tunisia aims, on the one hand, to develop democracy and to oppose the cultural traits of a tradition which condones women's inferiority. On the other hand, these movements fight, by combining the affirmation of feminine subjectivity and certain other traits of the local culture, in order to succeed in imposing themselves and in being recognized as the agents of their liberation. At the same time, the building of a society which can enter modernity by emphasizing their own rational elements in a manner that is different from that of the West can be achieved (Farro, 1995).

The initiatives of this second group also include collective actions which develop in order to affirm the equality of chances, the defence of identity (in the sense of Touraine, 1992), and the autonomy (in the sense of Taylor, 1989: 502–5; 1992: 24–7) of their members in the context of the recognition of the equality of all differences, and which lay in the area of the construction of democracy.

In conclusion, there are, on the one hand, some collective initiatives, those of the first group, that go in the direction of an identitary closure. On the other hand, the second group of actions aim at defining the new fields of social and cultural conflicts. Consequently, it is this second group of initiatives and not the first one, which forms the context for the development of collective movements which construct conflicts in the framework of globalization. Among the initiatives of this second group, it is mostly the collective actions of Green activists that develop a movement which succeeds in building up a conflict, and in pursuing alternatives to globalizing economic and cultural domination.

Globalization issues

Conflictual collective initiatives develop at different levels of social life. Green collective initiatives carry out their activities which focus on sustainable development – that is at the level of the relationship between the economy, society and the biological, chemical and physical forces of the environment (Vaillancourt (1995b) in Mehta and Ouellet (1995)). The activities and demands of Green activists, in the various countries where they operate, are implemented at the level of institutions and at the level which concerns the issues of the model of development that occurs on a planetary scale. There are also initiatives which Green activists carry out when they operate specifically at the local level, as well as at the regional, national, continental or global levels.

At the local level, Green activists put forward demands which aim at protecting certain populations of cities and of the countryside from various forms of pollution and resource depletion. They demand, for example, that industrial enterprises close down their polluting productive installations or stop the irrational exploitation of non-renewable natural resources. Thus they try to improve the living conditions of the populations exposed to the concrete consequences of the materialization of a dominant model of development which refuses to subordinate economic growth to the imperatives of environmental protection and of social equity (Vaillancourt, 1995b).

But Green activists' initiatives are not limited to putting forward these demands. In countries where this is possible – that is, where the political system is more open – they also develop their activities at the institutional level. They try to find various ways of getting access to political institutions: through the election of candidates of Green parties or of other sympathetic political parties, through the pressure that environmental organizations can put at different levels of the political system, through the institutional impact of campaigns for environmental protection in the mass media and so on. Green activists therefore try to find ways to express their interests and their cultural orientations in an institutional context. This often permits them to succeed in securing, at least in countries with an open democratic system, laws and other political decisions which contribute to the defence of their interests and of their cultural orientations. Resource mobilization sociologists (McCarthy and Zald, 1977) as well as political process theorists (Tilly, 1978) have rightly underlined the importance of this institutional access for the development of collective initiatives. Nevertheless, even if this access is important for the development of these initiatives, it does not represent the entire horizon of collective action.

These collective initiatives, in fact, develop activities which do not stop at the institutional level. They rise at a higher level of opposition which Green activists carry out against the ruling actors who define the development strategies. Green activists are in opposition to the actors who manage both the globalization of the economy on the basis of growth, and the globalization of culture through the diffusion of codes produced by the elaboration of information, and they intend to pursue the implementation of sustainable development as an alternative to these globalization trends (Prades et al., 1994).

The international organizations of Green activists are opposed to the power of ruling actors – the latter control the allocation of resources and decide on investments at a planetary level – through the power they exercise on economic centres situated in various zones of the industrialized world. These zones include the financial centres of New York, Tokyo and London (Sassen, 1991), as well as the centres where we find the industrial plants and the organizational networks of scientific and technological research. They oppose this domination which is exercised globally through the control of the direction given to the investments which are made, not so much for the production of goods, as for the production and the diffusion of information concerning the creation of cultural codes capable of defining the specific development and the modernization of sectors of social life like health, mass media, education and the definition of the link which exists between society and nature.

The Green associations do not aim at physically or economically destroying these ruling actors, but they challenge their control of the investment allocations destined to economic growth. They consequently oppose the prevailing definition of the relationship between social life and the natural environment. Associations like the Worldwide Fund for Nature and Greenpeace have had an important organizational expansion in recent years, which corresponds to a broadening and even to a certain reorientation of their activities. When it started in the early 1970s, for example, Greenpeace was only a regional phenomenon limited to the west coast of North America. Since then, it has transformed itself into a real international power which now prefers using persuasion rather than publicity stunts, and which is inclined to tackle the larger, more global, environmental issues rather than those that first attracted its attention, like its ill-conceived campaign in favour of baby seals. Greenpeace has evolved in a more professional direction and now focuses its interest on the large-scale planetary problems which predominate because of the ruling development model, like biodiversity, climate change, toxic pollution and ozone depletion. It does not suggest a return to the antiquated anticapitalist ideologies, but prefers to pursue the implementation of an alternative model of development different from the one imposed by the ruling actors who are not preoccupied with the consequences of economic growth on environmental protection. As a matter of fact, Greenpeace now collaborates with insurance companies worried about the ecological impacts of global warming of the atmosphere, and with industrialists and financiers who want to make profits by selling cars and refrigerators that are less harmful to the environment. It uses market-oriented strategies, like consumer boycotts of certain products, in order to transmit its message on certain specific issues, like the management of oceans and of forests, toxic pollution, energy use, and, especially, nuclear disarmament, which was its first major preoccupation (Vaillancourt, 1996).

Greenpeace and other NGOs like WWF, the Worldwatch Institute, and the World Conservation Union, are associations which collect and diffuse information at the international level, and which always attract the attention of the media. They can monitor the protagonists and the phenomena that transcend national borders, and they do not define themselves in a manner that limits their operations to local and regional scenes. Those they fight or talk with are not only governments, but also multinational corporations and huge international organizations like the World Bank, the International Monetary Fund, the World Commerce Organization, the FAO, UNESCO, and the United Nations Environment Program (UNEP). These environmental NGOs have access to resources that they can rapidly mobilize, and they can effectively mobilize them in order to try to challenge the ruling actors of the world's economy and finance.

These organizations are thus singularly positioned in the unequal relationships of power. They will continue to constitute one of the important components of a collective action which consists of an action by collective actors involved in unequal social relationships concerning the control of the cultural orientations of social life.

The components of collective action

Collective action is not only constructed through a component which develops its initiatives on an international scale, and which acts directly at the level of the globalization of the economy and of culture. In fact, collective action has numerous components which develop within various regional and local contexts.

We briefly mentioned above, in our discussion of the Tunisian experience, that collective initiatives like those of the women's movement assume particular social and cultural characteristics in developing regions of the world like the Maghreb. In fact, the Green initiatives of the Southern regions of the developing world have characteristics, which differentiate them from those in the Northern, developed part of the planet. The Southern Greens are generally more radical and are usually more interested than those of the North in issues of international justice and social equity. Some analyses tend to indicate that the Green movement presents two clearly distinct tendencies, between those groups with a Northern perspective and those with a Southern perspective who are more Third-World-oriented. In her recent book, *Contemporary Movements and Ideologies* Roberta Garner (1996: 361), for example, makes the following remark concerning the new international Green movement:

> One of the most striking characteristics of the movement is the rapid expansion and diversification of its support base between the 1950s and the 1990s from a primarily middle-class movement in the developed nations to a movement which encompasses a varied global array of communities, among them the most marginalized ones.

The sociologist De LaCourt (1992), is of the opinion that a decentralized approach, such as that proposed by E.F. Schumacher in his 1972 book *Small is Beautiful*, could help organizations from the South to liberate themselves from the encroaching Westernization of the Green movement. The Forest People's Alliance, the Rainforest Action Network, the Arctic to Amazonia Alliance, the native Forest Network, the Indigenous People's Union, Chiphko and Appiko are among the organizations which are active in countries like India and Brazil, and at the continental or international level. These organizations are interested in the integration of issues ranging from the local, to the national and global levels. Their strength resides in the fact that they form alliances which transcend their diversity and their differences in order to be able to cope with international social domination (Vaillancourt, 1996).

In their book on globalization, *The Global Trap*, Martin and Schumann (1997: 239 and 242) make the following suggestions:

> Only the replacement of the throwaway economy with one geared to services and solar power, only city planning that centres on human beings and stems the avalanche of cars, will offer any chance of creating for the countries of the South the ecological space they need for their own development . . . A currency tax would also bring in badly needed revenue to support countries in the South unable to keep up in the global markets.

In the Third World, the ecological struggle gravitates around issues of land, water and food. In other words, they are concerned with health, survival and the basic means of subsistence. This struggle is anchored in the fundamental needs of people, and it is tied to the battles for democracy, justice, equal opportunity, individual rights, local control and women's rights. The battle rages between poor people on the one hand, and rich local elites, corrupt governments, and the ruling actors involved in the globalization of the economy and of culture, on the other hand. The Green groups from the South interpret the concept of sustainable development in a radical manner, and they are thus linked to certain radical political ecology groups that emerged in the West during the 1970s. They want development because it assures survival, but they also want that development to be sustainable and equitable.

The local and the global

At the local level, Green initiatives develop in the North as well as in the South in order to deal with specific issues, to defend communities and to formulate demands which aim at protecting local populations from the consequences of pollution on human health, and at bettering the living conditions of local populations preoccupied with pollution and with other aspects of the issue of environmental protection. These local initiatives in the North can be limited to these demands or they can have access to the political system in order to exercise some institutional pressures. But they very rarely come into direct contact with the ruling actors who establish the orientations of economic growth and of the dominant development model to which the various questions of pollution and of environmental protection are linked. At best, they can have indirect contact with those actors through institutionalized forms of public debate linked to impact assessment of development projects. These institutional opportunities, on the other hand, are very rare in the South.

Thus we have a separation which is building up between the collective initiatives of NGOs which, in order to develop their activities, challenge the ruling actors who control the globalization of the economy and of culture on the one hand, and the initiatives that occur at the local level in the Northern part of the world and those that are taking place in developing countries on the other hand. But in spite of this separation, these three different types of Green collective initiatives are all components of a type of action that is unique. In fact, this separation between the different components of action is superseded by the construction of a collective movement which aims at defining alternatives to these dominant cultural values in one or in many sectors of social life, or at challenging their adversaries' control of the cultural orientations of this same social life. It is clear that in the area of the link between social life and the natural environment, the building up of this movement pertains to all levels of action that we have considered. Consequently, the pursuit of alternatives to replace domination is as much the result of the demands developed at the local level as of other initiatives like institutional pressures – both those that are made in developing countries and those that are constructed at the global level by the international environmental NGOs.

These initiatives can only be pursued by the latter organizations when they start challenging the pertinent adversary whom they oppose and who is constituted, as we have seen, by the ruling actors who control the allocation of investments at the planetary level. In fact, even if the local initiatives and those developed in the Third World are the carriers of an opposition to domination and of a definition of alternatives to this control by ruling actors, they cannot oppose these ruling actors if they remain isolated from the initiatives carried out at the global level. These local initiatives cannot challenge these adversaries all by themselves, at the level of the development of their action.

Thus there is a separation between those collective actors who operate at the local and regional levels, and the ruling actors that oppose them. This separation is superseded in action itself by these collective actors, when they link up their activities on the local and regional levels with those of the large international NGOs which tackle the issue of sustainable development at the global level.

Thus, the relationship between the local, regional, national, continental and global components of action, and between the different levels of conflict, is not simply a theoretical issue. The theory only represents what is happening in the collective initiatives and in the conflicts which are defined in the construction of social life. This relationship is verified in fact by the organization of action as well as by the organization of various tools of communication, which the actors use in the development of collective initiatives. This is a relationship which occurs through the direct contact between actors or in an indirect manner. However, in both cases, they occur on the basis of the instruments which the actors use to contact each other right from the beginning of the first stages of the formation of the collective initiative. These actors get together directly, or are linked together through the contacts which are defined between the organizers of their initiatives or by calling upon the mass media.

These actors thus develop circuits of communication which permit them to link together the different levels of conflict inasmuch as they give the same content to the speeches that are delivered, and to the objectives that are pursued by collective action, even if they are involved separately in their conflictual activities at only one of the levels of demands and of political and systemic action. Organizational ties can in fact let the members of an association like WWF, who act at a limited local level by formulating demands addressed to their adversaries, link up with the other members of their organization who are involved in a conflict for the control of the production and the diffusion of information. Similarly, this relationship can be established between the actors of an organization which develops institutional pressures at the local and national levels, and the other actors of this same organization who are active at the global level. This is the case, for example, with the links between the members of an environmental organization who are active at the international level, and those from the local and national groups. The latter consider their demands and the institutional pressures made at the local level, from the point of view of the pursuit of sustainable development and of the construction of a new equilibrium between social life and its environment of material forces and of cultural patrimonies.

These local and national groups cannot in fact deal with the questions of this new equilibrium and of sustainable development through the demands and the institutional pressures that they put forward in relationship with their social adversaries (for example, polluting industries), or their political adversaries (for example local administrations), which they challenge at the local level. They do not have the power to intervene in the area of the control of information or of resources concerning the environment. The organization, however, lets these groups link up with the other environmentalists who are active on the level of systemic conflict, and they thus succeed in participating in activities aiming for the control of the definition of the new equilibrium and of sustainable development, all with the intent of protecting the environment. The large NGOs develop, for example, these organizational relations when they co-ordinate their action among themselves, in certain cases with their local affiliates, as well as with numerous national, regional and local groups.

Linkages through various media are obtained by the rise of means of communication, between the components of collective initiatives which confront adversaries at the level of demands and of institutional actions, and those components that intervene at the systemic level. Such a link is created with various means of communication, between actors trying to act on concrete problems like the closing of a garbage dump or the opposition to an incinerator. In the territorial context, which depends on municipal institutions, these same actors want to obtain certain political interventions, like measures for the protection of natural resources inside that zone, while other actors act at the systemic level with initiatives like those dedicated to the elimination of products which they consider to be responsible for the extension of the hole in the ozone layer.

Organizational tools and means of communication permit the linking up of conflictual initiatives developed by actors at the organizational and at the political level with the actions taken up at the systemic level; they thus facilitate the recomposition of the action developed at the various levels of social life by collective actors who challenge the ruling actors about the control of investments, and about the production and diffusion of information concerning the globalization of culture and of the economy.

Conclusion

Collective initiatives develop in opposition to the domination of the ruling actors who manage the globalization of the economy and of culture. These initiatives which take place in developed and in developing countries, are of two types. The first comprises actions of groups and communities that are reacting to cultural and economic domination through identitary means. The actions which go in this direction include the refusal of differences, of equality of chances and of democracy. These collective initiatives react against globalization through an identitary kind of closure and recoil.

The second type of action concerns the conflictual initiatives which are built up at the local, regional, national, continental or global levels, in order to do two things. On the one hand, they oppose the domination of ruling actors, and on the other hand, they struggle against the latter in order to take away from them the control of the allocation of investments and the control of the production and the diffusion of the cultural codes which define the orientations of the globalization of the economy and of culture. These initiatives take place at various levels of social life, through the development of demands, through a limited access to the political system, through cultural activities which carry antagonistic visions in opposition to the dominant ones, or through system-wide conflict with the ruling actors. These initiatives are divided at the level of the planet and at the level of the numerous sectors of social life. They also succeed, as the Green associations have shown, in connecting up with each other and in being the carriers of a collective movement which develops in the context of the globalization of the economy and of culture.

Note

1. A discussion of the sociological debate on identity can be found in Sciolla, 1983; see also Calhoun, 1994.

References

Addi, L. (1994) *L'Algérie et la démocratie. Pouvoir et crise du politique dans l'Algérie contemporaine*, Paris: La Découverte.
Auclair, S. and J.-G. Vaillancourt (1992) 'Le développement durable: du concept

à l'application', in J. Prades, R. Tessier and J.-G. Vaillancourt (eds), *Gestion de l'environnement, éthique et société*, Montreal: Fides, pp. 251–81.

Calhoun, C. (1994) *Social Theory and the Politics of Identity*, Cambridge, MA: Blackwell.

Cornéliau, L. (1997) 'Les Assises nationales du développement durable: une première', *Ecodécision*, 24 (Spring): 11.

De La Court, Thijs (1992) *Different Worlds: Development Cooperation Beyond the Nineties*, Utrecht: International Books.

Della Porta (1996) *Movimenti collettivi e sistema politico in Italia. 1960–1995*, Roma and Bari: Laterza.

Diani, M. (1988) *Isole dell'arcipelago . . . Il movimento ecologista in Italia*, Bologna: Il Mulino.

Diani, M. (1995) *Green Networks: a Structural Analysis of the Italian Environmental Movement*, Edinburgh: Edinburgh University Press.

Dubet, F. and Wieviorka, M. (eds) (1995) *Penser le sujet, Autour d'Alain Touraine*, Paris: Fayard.

Eisenstein, H. (1991) *Gender Shock: Practicing Feminism on Two Continents*, Boston, MA: Beacon Press.

Farro, A.L. (1986) *Conflitti sociali e città, Napoli 1970–1980*, Milan: Franco Angeli.

Farro, A.L. (1991) *La lente verde. Cultura politica e azione collettiva ambientaliste*, Milano: Franco Angeli.

Farro, A.L. (1995) 'Ristrutturazione metropolitana e processi migratori', in *Sociologia urbana e rurale*, 47: 69–81.

Farro, A.L. (1998) *I movimenti sociali. Diversità, azione collettiva e globalizzazione*, Milan: Franco Angeli.

Hamel, P. (1995) 'Collective action and the paradigm of individualism', in L. Maheu (ed.), *Social Movements and Social Classes: the Future of Collective Action*, London: Sage, pp. 236–57.

Garner, R. (1996) *Contemporary Movements and Ideologies*, New York: McGraw Hill.

Giugni, M. (1995) *Entre stratégie et opportunité. Les nouveaux mouvements sociaux en Suisse*, Zurich: Seismo.

Göle, N. (1993) *Musulmanes et modernes. Voile et civilisation en Turquie*, Paris: La Découverte.

Goodland, R. (1995) 'The concept of sustainability', *Ecodécision*, 15 (Winter): 30–32.

Jenkins, J. (1983) 'Resource mobilization theory and the study of social movements', *Annual Review of Sociology*, vol. 9, pp. 527–53.

Kriesi, H. (1989) 'New social movements and the new class in the Netherlands', *American Journal of Sociology*, 94: 1078–116.

Khosrokhavar, F. (1995) 'Le quasi-individu: de la néo-communauté à la nécro-communauté', in F. Dubet and M. Wieviorka (eds), *Penser le sujet, Autour d'Alain Touraine*, Paris: Fayard, pp. 235–55.

Le Bot, Y. (1995) 'Ethnicité, mouvement social et modernité. A propos des mouvements communautaires à caractère ethnique en Amérique latine', in F. Dubet et M. Wievorka (eds) *Penser le sujet*, pp. 451–60.

Lustiger-Thaler, H. and L. Maheu (1995) 'Social movements and the challenge of urban politics', in L. Maheu (ed.), *Social Movements and Social Classes: the Future of Collective Action*, London: Sage, pp. 151–68.

Maheu, L. (ed.) (1995) *Social Movements and Social Classes: the Future of Collective Action*, London: Sage.

Martin, H.-P. and H. Schumann (1997) *The Global Trap: Globalisation and the Assault on Democracy and Prosperity*, Montreal: Black Rose Books.

McAdam, D. (1982) *Political Process and the Development of Black Insurgency 1930–1970*, Chicago: University of Chicago Press.

McCarthy, J.D. and M.N. Zald (1977) 'Resource mobilization and social movements: a partial theory', *American Journal of Sociology*, 82(6) (May): 1212–41.

Mehta, M. and D.E. Ouellet (eds) (1995) *Environmental Sociology: Theory and Practice*, North York: Captus Press.

Melucci, A. (1982) *L'invenzione del presente. Movimenti, identità, bisogni individuali*, Bologna: II Mulino.

Melucci, A. (ed.) (1984) *Altri codici. Aree di movimento nella metropoli*, Bologna: II Mulino.

Melucci, A. (1989) *Nomads of the Present: Social Movements and Individual Needs in Contemporary Society*, London: Hutchinson Radius.

Obershall, A. (1973) *Social Conflict and Social Movements*, Englewood Cliffs, NJ: Prentice Hall.

Petrella, R. (1977) *Écueils de la mondialisation, Urgence d'un nouveau contrat social*, Montreal: Fides.

Prades, A., Tessier, R. and J.-G. Vaillancourt (eds) (1994) *Instituer le développement durable. Ethique de l'écodécision et sociologie de l'environnement*, Montreal: Fides.

Princen, T. and M. Finger (1994) *Environmental NGOs in World Politics: Linking the Local and the Global*, London: Routledge.

Sachs, I. (1997) 'Sur un ciel d'hiver, quelques hirondelles . . .', *Ecodécision*, 24 (Spring): 20–2.

Sachs, W. (1993) *Global Ecology: a New Arena for Political Conflicts*, London: Zed Books.

Sassen, S. (1991) *The Global City: New York, London, Tokyo*, Princeton, NJ: Princeton University Press.

Sciolla, L. (ed.) (1983) *Identità. Percorsi di analisi in sociologia*, Turin: Rosenberg and Sellier.

Tarrow, S. (1994) *Power in Movement: Social Movements, Collective Action and Politics*, Cambridge: Cambridge University Press.

Taylor, B.R. (1995) *Ecological Resistance Movements: the Global Emergence of Radical and Popular Environmentalism*, Albany, NY: SUNY Press.

Taylor, C. (1989) *Sources of the Self: the Making of the Modern Identity*, Cambridge, MA: Harvard University Press.

Taylor, C. (1992) *Multiculturalism and 'The Politics of Recognition'* (With commentary by Amy Gutmann, edited by Steven C. Rockefeller, Michael Walzer, Susan Wolf), Princeton, NY: Princeton University Press.

Tilly, C. (1978) *From Mobilization to Revolution*, New York: Random House.

Tilly, C. (1986) *The Contentious French*, Cambridge, MA: Harvard University Press.

Touraine, A. (1992) *Critique de la modernité*, Paris: Fayard.

Touraine, A. (1993a) *La voix et le regard. Sociologie des mouvements sociaux*, Paris: Seuil (1st edition 1978).

Touraine, A. (1993b) *Production de la société*, revised edition, Paris: Seuil (1st edition in 1973).

Touraine, A. (1997) *Pourrons-nous vivre ensemble? Egaux et différents*, Paris: Fayard.

Vaillancourt, J.-G. (1981) 'Évolution, diversité et spécificité des associations écologiques québécoises: de la contre-culture et du conservationisme à l'environnementalisme et à l'écosocialisme', in J.-G. Vaillancourt (ed.), 'Écologie sociale et mouvements écologiques', Special issue of *Sociologie et sociétés*, XIII(1): 81–98.

Vaillancourt, J.-G. (1982) *Mouvement écologiste, énergie et environnement. Essais d'écosociologie*, Montreal: Éditions St-Martin.

Vaillancourt, J.-G. (ed.) (1995a) *Réaliser le développement durable (Implementing Sustainable Development)*, special issue of *Ecodécision*, 15 (Winter).

Vaillancourt, J.-G. (1995b) 'Sustainable development: a sociologist's view of the definition, origins and implications of the concept', in M. Mehta and D.E. Ouellet (eds) *Environmental Sociology: Theory and Practice*, North York, Ontario: Captus Press, pp. 219–30.

Vaillancourt, J.-G. (1996) 'L'internationalisation du mouvement vert', *Ecodécision*, 22, Autumn: 21–5.

Wieviorka, M. (1988) *Société et terrorisme*, Paris: Fayard.

Wieviorka, M. (1991) *L'espace du racisme*, Paris: Seuil.

Wieviorka, M. (ed.) (1996a), *Une société fragmentée? Le multiculturalisme en débat*, Paris: La Découverte.

Wieviorka, M. (1996b) *Culture, société et démocratie*, in M. Wieviorka (ed.), *Une société fragmentée? Le multiculturalisme en débat*, Paris: La Découverte, pp. 11–60.

World Commission on Environment and Development (1987) *Our Common Future*, Oxford: Oxford University Press.

10
Environmental Movements in the Global South: Outline of a Critique of the 'Livelihood' Approach

Ranjit Dwivedi[1]

Introduction

The burgeoning of environmental movements has been a major political development in the global South in the closing decades of the twentieth century. Their politics and practices have increasingly impacted upon the policy and political agendas of states and governments. Their rise to prominence has heralded a new consciousness around environmental issues, hitherto deemed insignificant, if not downright irrelevant in mainstream policy-making. More significantly, the growth of these movements has taken place at a time of unprecedented changes in power equations among states, markets and civil societies. With policy agendas of Southern states and governments structurally redefined in the processes of liberalization, privatization and globalization, collective actions around environmental issues gain additional significance as mechanisms of challenge and negotiation taking roots in the civil society.

Parallel to the political prominence of environmental movements is their marked pluriformity in practices. Contemporary environmental movements are characterized by diverse actions, actors and issues. The different political and institutional contexts in which they operate and their varied political orientations augment their diverse practices. The situation is complicated further when actions deemed to be environmental cross-cut parallel forms of collective actions in the field of ethnicity, gender, regional autonomy, labour and human rights.

In environmental thought, just a cursory look at popular concepts – eco-socialism, eco-feminism, political ecology, deep ecology, sustainable development, alternative development, and so on – reveals the diverse ideologies, analytics and approaches to environmental crises, conflicts and actions. Each approach in turn serves normative, strategic and/or empirical purposes causing subtle changes to the conceptions and meanings of environmental collective actions.

In conceptual terms, 'environment movement' is best understood as an 'envelope', because it encompases a variety of socially and discursively constructed ideologies and actions, theories and practices. This paper 'unpacks the envelope' to outline a broad critique of the livelihood approach to environmental struggles in the global South. In the process, it specifically attempts to assess the emerging trends therein that seem to have been somewhat neglected in the relevant literature. To that end this chapter draws upon political ecology/political economy of resource use literature and a parallel body of analytics in social movement literature and development studies.

Approaching environment movements: North and South

The term 'environment' implies anything from 'microbic action of organisms to world population' (Humphrey and Buttel, 1982: 2). Environment is a fluid concept that is socially contested and contingent and has been represented in multiple ways ranging from the scientific-rational to the religious-mystic. Contemporary discussions on environment emphasize several critical areas: quality of atmosphere, water quality, loss of soil productivity, loss of genetic diversity, deforestation, toxic contamination, hazardous material, depletion of indigenous and dependence on imported resources (Sklair, 1994: 207). Humphrey and Buttel (1982: 3) include air and water quality, food supply, fuel and forest reserves and the availability of other scarce natural resources. To them, environment is 'the physical and material bases of all life, including land, air, water as well as the vital material and energy resources in the surroundings of a society'. Collective actions around the environment signal conflicts and crises in the material and physical bases of life. They may be defined as public, political actions of protest, resistance and reconstruction concerned with the issues of environmental alteration, degradation and destruction.

The literature on the emergence of environmental movements is extensive. In the North, particularly in Europe, studies dwell on the structural conditions in the 1970s that generated environmental mobilization. The economic affluence in the post-war North had by and large resolved the quantitative aspects of distribution. It was the qualitative aspects exemplified in environmental conditions and quality of life that caused concerns for pollution, industrial waste and urban decay, the 'effluents of affluence' (Guha and Martínez-Alier, 1997: 31). They became new sites of politics while wilderness areas and clean air became new symbols of healthy society and living (Nash, 1982). Environmental mobilization thus came to be conceptualized as a form of 'post-material' politics distinct from the materialist politics of the 'Left-red' labour and trade union platforms. Studies in Europe (and elsewhere) have shown that the core members in the mobilization belong mostly to the middle class living in material conditions that facilitate their relative neglect of material, economic and redistributive demands (Offe, 1985; Eder, 1995). At stake are issues beyond class and structures of privilege, cultural values and other symbolic aspects. The emergence of this post-material politics has led some scholars to characterize environmentalism as a 'full stomach' phenomenon and Green politics as the ultimate luxury of consumer society (Moore, 1989).

In Europe, the environmental movement became the exemplar of the 'new social movement' (NSM) analytic (Cohen, 1985). The 'newness' was in direct contrast to the 'old' class-based politics of the labour movement. NSMs were new responses to new grievances. The emergence of new societal cleavages and conflicts around issues of identity, values and solidarity could no longer be encapsulated within the overarching political economic conflicts in the production process. In fact, not only were new social movements different from the old, they were endowed with the necessary agency to fuel macro-level societal transformation replacing class as historical actors (Touraine, 1985; Offe, 1985). As markers of their times of post/high/late/advanced modernity, new social movements symbolized shifting objectives from those centred predominantly on economic interests to that based on cultural identities and orientations (Melucci, 1989). In the NSM analytic, environmental movements emerge from the caustic chaos of industrial society in which nature and environment undergo radical and often unintended but permanent transformation having far-reaching socio-ecological consequences (Giddens, 1990; Beck, 1995). As new political forces they express a generalized desire for community, self-realization and personal satisfaction and propagate alternative cultural codes, in particular lifestyles, while resisting and potentially altering the representation of nature as resources for economic exploitation and progress.

On the other side of the Atlantic, a movement's organizational dimensions rather than its transformation potential has been regarded as its dominant analytic. The focus shifts from the structural preconditions that foster new movements to the problems of mobilization, organiza-

tion and strategic decision-making. Movement analysis is rife with terminologies such as social movement *organization*, social movement
sector and social movement *industry*, an indication of the interest in the
resource mobilization aspects of social movements. The latter has a
more expressed focus on the movement's politics based as it is on the
premise that while social discontent can be universal, collective action
is not. Thus whereas the NSM analytic stresses on *why* (new) social actors
emerge, the resource mobilization theory stresses on *how* they mobilize.
Applied to environmental mobilization, the resource mobilisation
approach conceptualizes it as a conglomerate of rationally organized
sets of practices. It is a useful analytic to analyse micro-level operations
of environmental organizations and bureaucratic networks such as
UNEP, Greenpeace, Sierra Club, IUCN, WWF, and Friends of the Earth,
the mobilization of resources at different levels, issues of leadership and
decision-making, strategic interests and protest events, competition
between them for resources. Environment movement in this perspective is how organizations and networks do what they do.

Contemporary scholarship on environmental movements has highlighted several limitations in these analytics and has advanced theory
building in several interesting directions. For instance, the grand theory
orientation of the NSM approach has been criticized for assuming collective actions to follow from new forms of structural domination; it
also tends to valorize their transformation potential. Likewise, the
resource mobilization approach reduces environment mobilization to
an aggregate of people organizing resources to fight for their interests.
Perhaps most importantly, contemporary scholarship has drawn attention to a genre of environmental collective actions emerging in the
Third World that is qualitatively different from the causes and concerns
expressed in First World movements (Bryant, 1992; Peet and Watts,
1996; Friedmann and Rangan, 1993).

Scholarship on environmental movements in the Third World has
viewed it as essentially actions by the marginalized poor to protect their
environmental means of livelihood and sustenance. Environmental
resources such as land, water and forests constitute the material bases
of the production and reproduction of the economic poor. Actions in
defence of such resources amidst growing encroachment and degradation by the richer and better-off sections of the society is what distinguishes Third World environmentalism from that in the First World. In
the South, approaches to environmental movements share the disen-
chantment with their European counterparts regarding the veracity
of 'Left–Right conflict' as *the* central analytic and class politics as the
appropriate and ultimate public action. Although environmental

movements are seen as emerging outside the purview of class politics, environmental conflict is theorized in class terms between the rich and the poor.

The differences in the movements across North and South has been highlighted recently by a number of scholars. According to Redclift (1987: 159):

> The two principal components of environmental movements in the South are of marginal importance to most movements in the developed countries. They are that those who constitute the movement are engaged in a livelihood struggle and secondly that they recognise that this livelihood struggle can be successful only if the environment is managed in a sustainable way.

Redclift's formulation finds an echo in subsequent works. From what is predominantly a political economy approach to resource struggles, scholars attribute the rise and growth of environmental movements in the South to the predatory exploitation of natural resources that feeds the process of development in postcolonial societies, the non-local (that is, national and global) production relations governing natural resource use and transformation and the inequality in resource distribution (Shiva and Bandyopadhyay, 1989). To them, environmental struggles for the most part are between those who have benefited from economic development and those who bear its costs. Shiva (1991: 19) locates the Indian environment movement as a response to the resource- and energy-intensive 'development project' of the country's economic elite:

> The resource demand of development has led to the narrowing of the natural resource base for the survival of the economically poor and powerless either by direct transfer of resources away from basic needs or by destruction of the essential ecological process that ensure the renewability of the life-supporting natural resources. In the light of this background ecology movements emerged as the people's response to this new threat to their survival and as a demand for the ecological conservation of vital life-supporting systems.

The main sites of environmental conflicts and movements in the South are energy- and resource-intensive activities and projects such as big dams, commercial forestry, mining, energy-intensive agriculture and mechanized fisheries, projects and activities that threaten and erode the resource base of peasants and other artisanal groups. The material as opposed to the symbolic form of expression of southern movements is rooted in the political economy of the South distinctly different from the 'post-industrial' North. Here political expressions of different orientations including environmental ones are (still) conditioned by industry-peasant conflicts. As Gadgil and Guha (1994) remark, in the developing world, 'environmentalism has its origins in conflicts between competing groups – typically peasants and industry – over productive resources . . . [as] the intensification of resource use undermines existing but subsistence oriented economic activities . . . [Here] environmental conflict is for the most part, only another form of economic conflict'.

Unlike the North, the conflicts are not so much over how the environment should be used but over who should use and benefit from it (Gadgil and Guha, 1994). As Martínez-Alier has noted, in the southern environmental movements the epithet 'environmental' is relevant 'insofar as they express objectives in terms of ecological requirements for life' (cited in Peet and Watts, 1996: 3). Thus one can argue that it is not so much lifestyles as life chances that constitute the battleground of environmental politics in the South.

The distinctiveness in approach between the South and the North veers around the preference for a political economy approach to resource distribution and use in the former as opposed to either an organizational or new social movement approach in the North. In the case of the Southern movements, equity issues feature as importantly as sustainability and efficiency for the agenda of democratic renewal and an ecologically responsible society. The stated difference in approaches nonetheless does not obliterate an observable commonality. Like their European counterparts, Southern environmental movements have been subjected to a predominantly systemic analysis. Environmental movements in both the North and the South tend to be considered as responses to systemic contradictions. Whether pursuing post-material values or material requirements of life, they are endowed with a generalized radicalism that is directed at the system as a whole. The explanatory domain seems to focus overarchingly on macro-level structural contradictions and crises. While movements emanate from systemic contradiction, the latter does not automatically produce organized resistance. It would therefore be pertinent to argue that in structural approaches whereas conflict is theorized, the responses are not. Thus they remain appropriate to analyse conflicts rather than movements. In the specific context of the Third World, the mediation between structural contradictions, deprivations and various forms of sociopolitical actions is crucial in order to gain a fuller understanding of the politics and practices of environmental movements (Peet and Watts, 1996).

Environmental movements in the South: actors, practices and issues

As has been indicated earlier, one needs to be careful in attributing causal connections between socio-economic factors that are deemed to generate environmental movements and their practices. Rather than celebrating a generalized transformation potential of environmental movements the task at hand is to account for the diversity and contextual specificity of environmental movements. To us a way forward is to map the range of issues, actors and practices that constitute the diversity in these movements. In recognizing first the diversity in forms and practices such mapping could better anticipate emerging trends in them.

The mapping attempted below is in two stages. Its overall purpose is limited to highlighting issues, actors and actions in movements broadly deemed environmental in the Third World context.

Stage one (illustrated in Table 10.1) plots some well-known cross-continental empirical cases of popular 'environmental' mobilizations in the South to show a variety of issues and actions that have featured in the politics of these movements. Stage two (illustrated in Table 10.2) offers a more complex mapping that attempts to capture the various dimensions in environmental mobilization and attempts to match the diversity in themes and stakes with actors and practices.

The seven cases mentioned above (in Table 10.1) are popular environmental movements and between them cover issues such as deforestation, water quality, depletion of indigenous resources, human resettlement and threat to public health, toxic contamination and atmospheric pollution. Whether threatened by development projects and activities or by measures of environmental protection as in the case of the Zapatista rebellion, these mobilizations denote struggles for protecting environmental conditions of livelihoods and sustenance of directly affected local communities. Yet as the mapping above indicates, environmental mobilization involves actors other than local communities and actions other than those geared towards defensive pursuits of livelihood. Instead of limiting Third World environmental mobilization into one centred around livelihood issues one needs to perceive environmental movements in their multidimensionality, inclusive of a broader corpus of actors, themes, stakes and practices. Table 10.2

Table 10.1 Environmental movements in the South: popular cases

Movements	Issues	Actions	Actors	Ideals
Chipko Movement (India)	Deforestation and commercial logging in the Himalayan foothills; Local people's rights to resources	Hugging of trees; Satyagraha; Eco-restoration; Local projects for resource harvesting; National and international lobbying	Local communities; women; local activists and organizations	Gandhian; Marxist; Local resource control and management
Chico dam movement (Philippines)	Eviction due to the construction of the dam; Right to ancestral domain and cultural integrity; Self-government	Militant and armed resistance followed by a phase of peaceful protest	Local Igorot people; Catholic Church; New people's army; National environmental groups	Marxist; Cultural and political rights
Rubber-tappers' Movement (Brazil)	Evictions due to land speculation from ranchers; Demands for extractive reserves	Peaceful protest through *empates* (stand-offs); Alliance building	Rubber-tappers' union; North American environmental groups; local Indian peasants; Brazilian Workers' Party	Local resource management

Movement	Issues	Action	Actors	Goals
Zapatista Rebellion (Mexico)	Displacement due to proposed 'bio-reserve'; forest conservation; Abolition of legal rights of Indian settlers	Violent uprising followed by extensive national and international campaign	Local population in Chiapas and Oaxaca; International action groups and networks	Political reforms; Indian rights to resources
Ogoni Movement (Nigeria)	Oil operations by MNCs such as Shell and Chevron; threats to livelihoods through pollution and contamination of land and water	From peaceful demonstrations to a separatist movement	Ogoni people's organizations and action groups; Greenpeace and other international NGOs	Resist oil exploration; Better environment management; sharing of benefits
Green Belt Movement (Kenya)	Desertification; Local needs of women; Denotification of 'green-belts'; Democratization and governance	Planting trees; Protest actions and advocacy work; Networking with other environmental groups in Africa	National Council for Women; UNDP; Novib; Danish Children project	Human rights; Women's rights
Narmada Movement (India)	Displacement; Environmental impact; Right to information and participation of local communities	Peaceful protests at the local and national levels; Public litigation; Extensive lobbying and campaign at the international level	Affected people; Local, national and international NGOs, human rights groups, environmentalists and engineers	Sustainable and equitable development; Local resource harvesting and management

Sources: Guha (1989); Hilhorst (1997); Osaghae (1995); Hecht and Cockburn (1989); Ndegwa (1996); Castells (1997); Dwivedi (1998).

Table 10.2 Diversity in environmental movements: multiple dimensions

Dimensions	Themes	Stakes	Actors	Practices
Reactive (defensive)	Political status of interest	Gains and losses in resource alteration and distribution	Local affected communities and groups	Resistance against eviction and displacement; Negotiations of compensation and liabilities
Redefinition of property rights and usufruct	Individual and common property resources; Intellectual property rights; Local control and management of resources	Loss of livelihoods; Local rights to resource use and benefits	Local communities and groups such as artisans, peasants, forest and fisher folks, pastoral groups; Local action and support groups.	Protest actions and resistance; Restorative and co-operative practices for more sustainable and equitable management.
Redefinition of impact	Risks, uncertainties and hazards; Benefit claims.	Information; Knowledge claims; Public health; Socio-environmental impact of trade and investment, reforms, adjustment and globalization.	Affected groups and communities, Knowledge and professional class; National and global networks	Mobilization of counter-claims in knowledge; Science-based risk politics around environment and social impact of projects, pollution and biodiversity losses, toxic dumping; Demands for protective clauses, restorative policies

Reformation of institutions	Transparency and accountability in decision-making procedures and processes; norms and rules	Duties and responsibilities of state and inter-state agencies and TNCs; Citizens' rights; 'Political closure' and democratization of institutions.	NGOs and action groups; Knowledge class.	Public domain politics: Public campaigns, lobbying and litigation; Building civil-society networks; Demands for participation and accountability
Radical (revivalistic and revolutionary)	Control of political economy; Cultural and civilizational identity.	Political power and autonomy; Right to autonomous and self-development; Cultural values and lifestyles.	Political action groups; Indigenous people's movements; Utopian groups.	Actions for decentralization and regional autonomy; Ethnic, religious and identity based actions for preservation of cultural and natural diversity; Actions against consumer culture.

Source: Own research; influenced by social movement classification in Touraine (1985) and adaptations and insights provided in Castells (1997).

attempts to project some possible dimensions in Third World environmental movements.

Notwithstanding the limited purpose and base of the mapping in Table 10.1, it hints at the themes and actors in the movements, the diverse ideals and degrees of radicalism and the politics of transcending localities to form national and transnational links. The mapping offered in Table 10.2 expands on these aspects. It classifies multiple dimensions, themes and actions that feature or are emerging in environmental movements (particularly though not exclusively in the South). These dimensions and their respective themes are not to be viewed hierarchically although the classification does imply varying degrees of environmental consciousness in different aspects of movements. Neither are the dimensions to be seen as mutually exclusive types of movements. In empirical terms, a particular movement at a given point in time can compositely reflect multidimensionality and hence a cluster of themes, practices and actors either fully or partially.

Viewed as a heuristic devise, the mapping in Table 10.2 is helpful to identify and deliberate on aspects that fall outside the net of the 'livelihood' approaches to environmental movement in the South. Before we identify these aspects, we summarize four 'tendencies' discernible in existing studies on environmental movements. First, such studies tend to view environmental movements as local manifestations of nationally and globally generated resource conflicts. Second, they consider locally situated victims of environmental degradation and destruction to be the main actors in these movements. Third, is their 'anti-science' characterization of such movements, since science is characterized as Western, homogenizing, alienating and the centralizing force underlying modernization and development (Shiva, 1991). Fourth, they tend to associate with the ideals of these movements, 'new visions of development' based on new productive rationalities, environmental sensibility and cultural pluralism.

Set against the mapping in Table 10.2, these tendencies give limited and partial account of environmental movements. As the mapping suggests, movements address a more complex bundle of issues than local resource conflicts. The struggles are played out over interests, knowledge, values and meanings in local as well as national and global arenas. In a similar vein, movement actors comprise not just 'affected poor' and their support groups but a variety of action groups spread from the local to the global and engaged in diverse practices and networks. The involvement and participation of different class of actors suggest that environmental movements in the South (as in the North) straddle class

borders rather than polarizing around them. The reliance on professionals, experts and the knowledge class in general also signifies
their 'science-base' (Buttel and Taylor, 1994; Castells, 1997). And finally,
actions deemed environmental exude varied degrees of radicalism and
consciousness. On one end of the spectrum, we have 'reactive' responses
seeking political status of interests. Attributing a priori an environmental awareness to such mobilizations is untenable as being affected
by one problem does not automatically engender a willingness to take
collective action with respect to a range of issues. On the other end, we
have a 'radical' set of responses where environmental concerns either
feature as part of a larger set of political and cultural stakes or (less
frequently) constitute alternative imaginaries as in 'deep-ecology'
politics.

In our view, the multidimensionality accounted for in Table 10.2 contains two interrelated aspects that may be said to fall outside the net of
livelihood approaches: (i) the local–global nexus; and (ii) the epistemic
dimension of struggles. While each of these aspects require specific focus
and understanding, they signal budding trends in collective actions
around the environment. In other words, they are aspects potentially
contributing to the future agenda of environmental movements in the
south.

The local–global nexus

In the analysis of environmental actions, locality is considered to be a
significant cultural and environmental condition that is affected by
larger political economic processes. Collective actions around environment are seen to unfold within the particularities of the local. We have
argued earlier that this is a partial view of environmental movements
that overlooks actions beyond the grassroots. A related concern is the
conversion of the locality from a condition of action to an 'actor' and
to an 'ideology' of resistance and reconstruction. Meegan speaks of
locality as actor *if* interests and identities are locally defined and *if* they
act on the basis of locally situated organizations (cited in Friedmann
and Rangan, 1993: 4). Such a formulation, with all its caveats, explains
only the local dimension of environmental struggles. The interconnections at the national and global levels, with 'non-local' actors, structures
and discourses are left unaddressed. The simultaneous conversion of
locality into ideology causes it to reincarnate as localism. In much of
the scholarly work on environmental movements, localism has served
as a powerful ideal that propounds 'delinking' as a political strategy of

actions directed against 'non-local' agents be it the state or the forces of globalization. To Castells (1997: 124),

> even in the most defensive expressions . . . to assert the priority of local struggles over the use of a given space by 'outside interest', such as companies dumping toxics or airports extending their runways, bears the profound meaning of denying abstract priorities of technical and economic interests over actual experiences of actual uses by actual people.

While abstract priorities cajoled in terms such as 'national good', 'public interest' or for that matter 'economic development' are implied environmental battlegrounds, the organization and production of their denial are more often than not an outcome of actors who transcend their locality. In other words, the local asserts itself when it is effectively *linked* with national, regional and global arenas. In so far as localism as a theory and ideology ignores this dimension of environmental struggles, it devoids the multi-level and multidimensional expressions of environmental issues including locally-based livelihood struggles; its strategic agenda of 'delinking' remains at best an ambiguous political assertion of the local and at worst a narrowly conceived celebration of it.

Two arguments may be advanced in support of what is called the local–global nexus. The first is derived from social movement theory. The state-of-the-art literature on movements views them not as actors but as networks, action-systems and cognitive space (Diani and Eyerman, 1992; Melucci, 1992; Eyerman and Jamison, 1991). Each of these modes of conceptualization incorporates the multidimensionality actors and issues in social movements. Their application in the specific context of environmental movements underscores connection across issues and actors. Thus, for example, the Narmada movement in India is at the same time a local response to displacement, a broader struggle over environmental and economic impact, a national struggle for resettlement policies and part of a global struggle against 'mega-dam' projects. In spatial terms, it spans the local and the global, geographically and cognitively. While the local is indeed a significant link in the chain of networks, it is shaped by (and shapes) discourses and practices outside it. Rather than viewing such movements through the lens of localism, it appears more appropriate to view their local–global nexus with regards to stakes and practices.

A related argument is derived from critical globalism perspectives that have drawn attention to the profound impact of globalization in reshaping the local and the national (Giddens, 1990). Moving beyond the goals of local empowerment and national welfarism, these perspectives stress global reforms through collective actions and the strengthening of global civics to counter, tame or reverse the adverse impact of economic globalization. Not surprisingly, it is the globalized practices of social movements, including those around environment, that lend credence to these perspectives. Partly because environmental risks and hazards increasingly have assumed global dimensions where boundaries matter little. Partly because the local or for that matter, the national realms are increasingly getting exposed to global dynamics. A Chipko or a Narmada can be celebrated for their 'profound meaning' of the local people asserting and empowering themselves. The more important aspect is whether the profundity is enhanced when issues such as commercial logging or development-induced displacement are challenged at multiple levels.

The critical gains of environmental movements towards combating, regulating or minimizing environmental risks and hazards reinforce the local–global nexus. Southern environmental movements have one foot in local-level mobilizations and the other in struggles over the politics of environmental and social clauses in multilateral trade and investment bodies, such as the World Trade Organization or the Multilateral Environment Agreements (MEAs). The latter struggle is as profound in its meaning, if not more, compared to the defensive and reactive responses at the local level. In any case, the issues contested in the global struggles have local implications and concern local lives and livelihoods, be it trade practices, operations of TNCs or toxic dumping. Considering the sharpening divisions between northern and southern movements on these and related issues such as labour standards, fair trade, biotechnology and intellectual property rights, one gets to acknowledge the rather contradictory nature of the local–global connections. On the one hand, southern environmental movements are increasingly globalizing their protest in social movement and NGO networks so as to be more effective in preventing national and global interests from encroaching the local. Yet, at the same time they confront these very global 'allies' in setting the agenda for global environmental reforms. Much to their chagrin, their struggle against northern states, TNCs and NGOs in trade and investment politics brings them closer to their respective (southern) states against whom they contest with regards to other environmental issues. Critical globalism points to both the potential for and challenges in global regulation of environmental risks and hazards. However, as an analytic it needs to be engaged rather than celebrated, very much like localism.

The epistemic dimension of environmental struggles

As stated earlier, one of the fundamental characteristics of southern movements has been their material basis. The materiality of environmental struggles does not discount its epistemic dimension, nor does it define it. Southern environmental mobilizations struggle as much over meanings and knowledge as over material resources. Only a few scholars reflect on this aspect (Guha, 1989; Moore, 1993). Those others who recognize this aspect commit themselves to a form of cultural determinism where the epistemic struggles get reduced to one between indigenous/local/traditional knowledge and Eurocentric/modern/scientific knowledge. The strong flavour of localism in such formulations aside, they make environmentalism in the South essentially anti-science in orientation.

Yet this to us is only a part of the story. To elevate a movement rhetoric to the status of an analytic has its limitations, two of which are mentioned here. First, pertains to the knowledge endowments and entitlements of local community groups. It is true that the knowledge of local communities has often been sidelined and eroded in so-called scientific discourses and practices be it concerning management of commons and forest resources, water harvesting and farming, fishing and pastoral practices. The realization today, thanks to bureaucratic failures and popular protests, has resulted in a reverse discourse exemplified in common slogans such as 'learning from the farmer' and 'putting people first'. But consider the following. What kind of knowledge is it when affected communities facing displacement in a dam walk with their own sets of dumpy-levels along with the government surveyors to cross-check the marking of elevation and submergence levels? Local? Indigenous? What kind of a knowledge is it when sympathetic engineers join local communities to initiate drought prevention projects? Setting a binary duel between indigenous and scientific knowledge lands us in a discursive cul de sac. Clearly the questions above point to the syncretic knowledge and idioms in protest and restorative actions of local communities. The way forward then is to take cognizance of knowledge claims and knowledge interests in environmental action beyond the purview of locality and materiality.

This brings us to a second limitation in binary and exclusionist projections of knowledge struggles which is more striking. It concerns the role of the professional, 'knowledge' class in environmental movements. The multifaceted role of this class of actors constitutes an important dimension of contemporary environmentalism in the South. Given that *impacts* of and *risks* in development projects and economic activities are major contested sites, the expertise of the knowledge class becomes an important resource for movements, at times more crucial than mass support at the local level (Dwivedi, 1998). Buttel and Taylor (1994: 223) underscore this aspect in their observation:

> Modern environmentalism, where the rubber meets the road, is increasingly an arena characterised by the deployment of scientific and technical knowledge, often in combat with rival data and knowledge claims that are set forth by their industrial, governmental and quasi-governmental adversaries in an attempt to deconstruct and delegitimate claims.

The overarching significance of this aspect has led Giddens (1990), Castells (1997) and Beck (1995) to characterize environmentalism as a science-based movement. In a more nuanced reading of this aspect, we characterize it as *risk politics* of environmental movements (Dwivedi, 1998). Through risk politics, environmental movements question the trustworthiness of agencies and institutions that handle uncertainties, attach probabilities and calculate risks and liabilities. Risk politics exposes the fact that probabilistic assumptions often tend to become political assertions. To Giddens (1990) it is often the case that, to muster public acceptance of proposed interventions, official experts tend to fudge or conceal the true nature of risks or even the fact that there are risks at all. He considers the circumstance more harmful 'where the full extent of a particular set of dangers and the risks associated with them is not realised by the experts. For in this case what is in question is not only the limits of, or gaps in, expert knowledge but an inadequacy which compromises the very idea of expertise' (1990: 131). Through the deployment of experts and professionals environmental movements claim to unravel hidden and unknown dangers, uncertainties and risks and their distributional implications.

Whether in conflicts around dams, terminator genes or nuclear technology, impact and risk assessments manifest as a major dimension in contemporary environmental movements. Thus whereas environmental movement rhetoric (in its hard form) can convey a populist language that is anti-science and anti-technology in tenor, their cognitive practices appear to be very much within a scientized domain. Recognizing this dimension of knowledge struggle and the scientific basis of it takes us beyond its popular conception as 'indigenous' or 'civilizational'. This 'discourse-against' (and its flip side, the preservation of indigenous culture) surely highlights the semiotic and value incompatibility aspects in southern environmental movements but exudes a strong oriental flavour that can be neutralized by approaching movements in terms of their multiple cognitive practices.

Assessing prospects

The implications of the two aspects considered above for a fuller understanding of environmental movements in the South appear substantive. In the first instance, the two themes take us beyond the 'livelihood' discourse that has so far constituted Third World environmentalism. Rather than restricting the meaning and agency of environmental action to struggles over livelihood and survival, the plea here is to adopt a more inclusive approach to Third World environmentalism that recognizes multiple agencies and practices. Second, these aspects suggest that southern environmental movements need not be conceptualized as formations that envision 'alternative development' at the local level, whatever the contour of the latter may be. Rather, both the local–global nexus and power–knowledge nexus are pointers to an attempt at democratic renewal at different levels for seeking an ecologically responsible society. The politics of environmental risks and hazards that environmental movements currently engage do not pertain simply to risks to livelihoods but in fact cover a wider spectrum of uncertainties and risks. In that context demands of transparency, information-sharing and participation in decision-making have become critical axes of environmental politics. Accountability rather than alternatives seem to be the defining feature of environmental movements. To that extent, the increasing globalization of environmental protest can be seen as an effective response to counter the current global hegemonies of the TNC–World Bank–IMF–WTO complex and to make these institutions accountable for their deeds and misdeeds.

In our assessment of the prospects of southern environmental movements we consider the local–global nexus and the knowledge–power nexus as key elements that will influence practices and thinking in environmental politics in the coming decades. Considering these as trends in environment movement politics, we anticipate three likely developments on the basis of supportive evidence.

First, a sharpening of resource struggles and conflicts at local level as a result of increasing market and state-led drives for resource 'development'. This will result largely from the resource demands and impact of economic globalization in large parts of the global south. While not all struggle sites are expected to generate local environmental movements, the intensification of resource conflicts around issues of land and forest rights and access to water and shelter will make them central to the environmental movements' agenda.

Second, the increasing proclivity of market and policy actors to negotiate and accommodate environmental concerns. The pressures on these actors to accommodate environmental concerns could result in better institutions for risk and impact assessments, mitigation and compensation. Along with institutionalization, a certain degree of professionalization of environmental issues and concerns is to be expected. Here we note the growing significance of the professional, knowledge class in the global South in influencing both environment politics and policies. Already, the all-round presence of the knowledge class can be seen in grassroots activism, local community organizations, policy-level lobbying and global networks. It is through the mediation of this class that environmental concerns of a wider citizenry (than those at risk of livelihood losses) over such issues as air, water and noise pollution, public goods supply, health issues and provisions and rights to information and participation could get articulated. Together with rural livelihood issues, they could constitute the basis of environmental activism in the coming decades.

Third, the enmeshing of environmental groups with other civil-society actors and movements in the sphere of human rights, gender, ethnicity and cultures. While there has been noticeable cross-cutting in these areas as far as 'grass-roots' activism is concerned, the future trend is likely to be one where similarities in practices and politics will blur differences in approaches. Already the cross-cutting has yielded platforms like the environmental justice movement which combine environmental concerns from a human rights perspective. The political–economic–ecological diversities in the different regions of the global South will obviously result in different recombinations. Yet, the recombination holds promise for a democratic renewal in the global South to make the development experience therein sustainable, participatory and, above all, accountable.

Note

1. This is a substantially revised version of a paper presented at the 14th World Sociology Congress held at Montreal in 1998. The author would like to thank

ISS state–society staff group for generous support to participate in the congress and to Jan Nederveen Pieterse, P.K. Vijayan, Karen Gabriel and Sharada Srinivasan for comments on the paper.

References

Beck, U. (1995) *Ecological Politics in an Age of Risk*, Ilford: Frank Cass.

Bryant, R. (1992) 'Political ecology: an emerging research agenda in Third-World studies', *Political Geography*, 11(1): 12–36.

Buttel, F. and P. Taylor (1994) 'Environmental sociology and global environmental change: a critical assessment', in M. Redclift and T. Benton (eds), *Social Theory and the Global Environment*, London and New York: Routledge, pp. 228–55.

Castells, M. (1997) 'The power of identity', *The Information Age: Economy, Society and Culture*, vol. II, Oxford: Blackwell.

Cohen, J.L. (1985) 'Strategy and identity: new theoretical paradigms and contemporary social movements', *Social Research*, 52(4): 663–716.

Diani, M. and R. Eyerman (eds) (1992) *Studying Collective Action*, London: Sage.

Dwivedi, R. (1998) 'Resisting dams and "development": contemporary significance of the campaign against the Narmada Projects in India', *European Journal of Development Research*, 10(2): 135–83.

Eder, C. (1995) 'Does social class matter in the study of social movements?: a theory of middle-class radicalism', in L. Maheu (ed.), *Social Movements and Social Classes: the Future of Collective Action*, London: Sage Studies in International Sociology, pp. 21–54.

Eyerman, R. and A. Jamison (1991) *Social Movements: a Cognitive Approach*, Cambridge: Polity Press.

Friedmann, J. and H. Rangan (eds) (1993) *In Defence of Livelihood: Comparative Studies on Environmental Action*, West Hartford: Kumarian Press.

Gadgil, M. and R. Guha (1994) 'Ecological conflicts and environmental movements in India', *Development and Change*, 25: 109–48.

Gadgil, M. and R. Guha (1995) *Ecology and Equity: the Use and Abuse of Nature in Contemporary India*, London and New York: Routledge.

Giddens, A. (1990) *The Consequences of Modernity*, Cambridge: Polity Press.

Guha, R. (1989) *The Unquiet Woods: Ecological Changes and Peasant Resistance in the Himalaya*, New Delhi: Oxford University Press.

Guha, R. and J. Martínez-Alier (1997) *Varieties of Environmentalism: Essays North and South*, London: Earthscan.

Hecht, S.B. and A. Cockburn (1989) *The Fate of the Forest: Developers, Defenders and Destroyers of the Amazon*, London: Verso.

Hilhorst, D. (1997) 'Discourse formation in social movements: issues of collective action', in H. de Haan and N. Long (eds), *Images and Realities of Rural Life: Wageningen Perspectives on Rural Transformations*, Assen: Van Gorum, pp. 121–52.

Humphrey, C.R. and F.H. Buttel (1982) 'Exploring environmental sociology', excerpted in M. Redclift and G. Woodgate (eds) (1995) *The Sociology of the Environment*, vol. III. Aldershot: Edgar Elgar, pp. 189–215.

Melucci, A. (1989) *Nomads of the Present: Social Movements and Individual Needs in Contemporary Society*, edited by J. Keane and P. Mier, London: Radius.

Melucci, A. (1992) 'Frontier Land: Collective Action Between Action and Systems', in M. Diani and R. Eyerman (eds), *Studying Collective Action*, London: Sage, pp. 238–58.

Moore, C. (1989) 'Foreword', in P. Marsden-Smedly (ed.), *Britiain in the Eighties: The Spectator View of the Thatcher Decade*, London: Grafton.

Moore, D.S. (1993) 'Contesting Terrain in Zimbabwe's Eastern Higlands: Political, Ecology, Ethnography and Peasant Resource Struggles', *Economic Geography*, 69(4): 380–401.

Nash, R. (1982) *Wilderness and the American Mind*, New Haven: Yale University Press.

Ndegwa, S.N. (1996) *The Two Faces of Civil Society: NGOs and Politics in Africa*, West Hartford, CT: Kumarian Press.

Offe, C. (1985) 'New Social Movements: Challenging the Boundaries of Institutional Politics', *Social Research*, 52(4): 817–68.

Osaghae, E.E. (1995) 'The Ogoni Uprising: Oil Politics, Minority Agitation and the Future of the Nigerian State', *African Affairs*, 94: 325–44.

Peet, R. and M. Watts (eds) (1996) *Liberation Ecologies: Environment, Development, Social Movements*, London and New York: Routledge.

Redclift, M. (1987) *Sustainable Development: Exploring the Contradictions*, London: Methuen.

Shiva, V. (1991) *Ecology and the Politics of Survival*, New Delhi: United Nations University and Sage.

Shiva, V. and J. Bandyopadhyay (1989) 'Political economy of ecology movements', *IFDA Dossier*, 71: 37–60.

Sklair, L. (1994) 'Global Sociology and Global Environmental Change', in M. Redclift and T. Benton (eds), *Social Theory and the Global Environment*, London and New York: Routledge, pp. 228–55.

Touraine, A. (1985) 'An introduction to the study of social movements', *Social Research*, 52(4): 749–88.

Index

Torness actions, 95
Totalitarianism, 211
Touraine, Alain, 51, 140, 215
Trade Traps and Gender Gaps: Women Unveiling the Market, 127
Transnational corporations (TNCs), 241
Transnational feminist networks, 111–39
  Association of Women of the Mediterranean Region (AWMR), 131–3
  Development Alternatives with Women for a New Era (DAWN), 121–3
  future of, 133–6
  social theory, 112–13
  Women in Development Europe (WIDE), 123–7
  women and gender, 113–17
  Women Living Under Muslim Laws (WLUML), 127–31
Transnational non-governmental organizations (TNGOs), 195
  see also Non-governmental organizations (NGOs)
Transnationalism, 114
Triad zone, 5, 35
Triadization, 3, 31
Trident submarines, 102
Trilateral Commission, 190
Truncated globalization, 3
Tunisia, women's movement in, 214, 218
Turkey, attitude to homosexuality, 176

UNEP *see* United Nations Environment Program
UNESCO, 217
Unidimensional modernity, 12
Union of Palestinian Working Women Committees, 129
United Nations Commission on the Status of Women, 118
United Nations Conferences on Women, 121, 191
United Nations Environment Program (UNEP), 217, 230

United Nations Environmental Programme, 71
United Nations Working Group on Contemporary Forms of Slavery, 154
United States, participation in arms race, 91
Universalism, 72–4
Urbanization, and rise of non-traditional relationships, 171
Utopianism, 68

Velvet revolution, 26
Vermont Yankee Power Station, 93
Vietnam War, 94

Walker, R.B.J., 71, 73
Wallerstein, Immanuel, 170
WAPHA *see* Women's Alliance for Peace and Human Rights in Afghanistan
Warsaw Pact, 91
Washington consensus, 11
WEDO *see* Women's Environment and Development Organization
Welfare state
  aims, 173–4
  establishment of, 173
  and rise of non-traditional relationships, 171
Welfare Warriors, 149
Western bias in reporting of collective action, 111
WHISPER *see* Women Hurt in Systems of Prostitution Engaged in Revolt
WIDE *see* Network Women in Development Europe
WLUML *see* Women Living Under Muslim Laws
Women
  anti-militarism of, 93
  conferences on, 115
  constraints faced by, 113
  non-governmental organizations, 115
Women Against Fundamentalism, 155, 157
Women against Pit Closure, 102